MAXIMUM COACHING

Getting the Most Out of Yourself and Your Athletes

Zack Ohlin

To order, please visit www.HachetteLearning.com or contact Customer Service at education@hachette.co.uk / +44 (0)1235 827827.

ISBN: 978 1 0360 0413 2

First published in 2025 by
Hachette Learning,
An Hachette UK Company
Carmelite House
50 Victoria Embankment
London EC4Y 0DZ

www.HachetteLearning.com

The authorised representative in the EEA is Hachette Ireland,
8 Castlecourt Centre, Dublin 15, D15 XTP3, Ireland (email: info@hbgi.ie)

Impression number 10 9 8 7 6 5 4 3 2 1

Year 2029 2028 2027 2026 2025

Cover photo TK

Illustrations by DC Graphic Design Limited, Hextable, Kent.

Typeset in the UK.

Printed in the UK.

A catalogue record for this title is available from the British Library.

To my parents

Contents

About the Author

Zack Ohlin is an award-winning professional tennis coach and coach developer. His coaching has taken him from the grassroots to the Grand Slams and over 25 countries on the professional tour. He has coached numerous national and international junior champions who have reached as high as top 20 in the world, as well as professional athletes who have represented their country at Davis Cup and Billie Jean King Cup.

As a coach educator, Zack has trained and presented to coaches in both Canada and Sweden. He holds a master of education in high performance coaching and technical leadership from the University of British Columbia, an advanced coaching diploma from the Canadian Sport Institute, and a Coach 3 certification from Tennis Canada. He lives in Montreal, Canada, where he coaches at the National Tennis Centre.

Foreword

A few years ago, I watched a renowned coach in his first session with the national team of a top-tier nation in a highly competitive international sport. He had just taken over as head coach, and the world championships were about a year away. The team was in the doldrums—a run of poor results, an aging group of core players, a fraying culture riven with factions, a sense that they might no longer be able to compete. But of course, the coach knew that. He had been hired to come in and fix those things.

The players had been invited to a three-day mini-camp, and the first thing on the agenda that morning was a meeting in which the coach introduced himself and his plan to the players. The meeting was very good, from my perspective. It was well run and organized; he was the kind of coach who thought a lot about where players should sit, for example. That morning, chairs had been set up in a semi-circle so that everyone could see everyone else when they spoke, and the coach shuffled the players around as soon as they came in so they weren't sitting next to the guys they knew best. His message, meanwhile, was clear and compelling. He had a plan and it was smart. He believed in them but would hold them to high standards. He was both funny and serious. Players spoke and shared insights during the meeting, which showed that while the coach was in charge, he thought it was their team too. He mentioned details that showed he knew the players as individuals. Every minute was used well, which suggested that he had taken his own preparation seriously. Each of the assistant coaches had clearly been expected to prepare and practice what they would say, and so the meeting was crisp and energetic. It ended exactly on time.

This is all to say that it was a very good meeting, but I don't think it accomplished much. I don't say that to denigrate the things the coach did well that morning, because I've seen a *lot* of meetings that were not nearly as well run as that one, even at the most elite levels. But the players were, at best, cautious. I watched them walk out of the room, alone or in twos and threes, their body language reserved and anxious.

There wasn't much eye contact. They'd seen their share of meetings, and one meeting—even a good one—couldn't answer The Question.

The Question hangs unspoken over every coach and every team. The players had given a large part of their lives to the game—it was a profession to them now; it was their identity—and their hope was that they could become the best version of themselves individually and as a team. Could the coach help them do that? Could he make them better? Was he capable of helping them achieve what they dreamed of? That was The Question. That *is* The Question for any coach at the elite level, where sport is more than just play: *Can you help us get closer to doing what we dream of doing, of being who we dream of being?* No single meeting was going to convince anyone, but in an hour's time on the field they would start proving themselves to the new boss and he would start proving himself to them.

Training started at 10am. By 10.01, the players were going full gas. By 10.05, there were shouts of encouragement and celebration among the players. At 10.10, the coach brought them in, panting, and broke down the subtleties of their defending and simple fixes they should focus on. By 10.20, the defense was better, and just as importantly, the players themselves saw the difference and could explain it. They could remind each other: "A little tighter there—stay connected!" They were starting to believe. You could see the transformation not just in the way they spoke to one another, but in the glances they gave each other during their moments of downtime. *Holy crap. It's happening.* By 10.30, every player had begun to believe that the answer to The Question was "yes." By 11am, some exclamation points had been added to the answer: "Yes!!"

That session was a triumph of planning and teaching and culture. I've rarely seen a group of players leave training so differently than when they walked into it—heads held high, arms over shoulders, lingering in groups to talk tactics, work on skills, or just bond a little. Everyone wanted to be a part of it, to stand in the glow of optimism and belief for a little longer; nobody wanted to hit the showers.

Interestingly, what happened in that 90 minutes was in some ways not that different from what happened in the meeting. The message—here is how we are going to play—was clear and compelling. The coach showed, over and over again, that he believed in them but would hold them to high standards. He was both funny and serious. Every minute was used well. But now the players were transformed.

Had they been in sessions with coaches who knew the game before? Yes, hundreds of them. But coaching, as Zack Ohlin writes in this book, is a performance profession, "and in performance professions, execution counts. Knowledge without execution is wasted."

Somehow there is magic in great execution by a coach: in being able to bring players together on the court or the field or the ice and show them the path. To make their goals feel achievable, close enough to touch. A good meeting is a nice thing, but a great session that is artfully crafted and intentionally implemented can make players *feel* something transformational. Call it belief in the process of getting better.

"Every coach loves the sport he or she coaches, but only some coaches love *teaching* the sport," I scribbled in my notebook later that day. I had been struck by his joy during the session: the pleasure he took in designing exercises the players would love and learn from, the seriousness with which he attended to what the players were actually doing and whether they were progressing, his ability to make every player feel seen, the change that came about from his tiny pieces of feedback.

A coach, Zack Ohlin tells us, is like an athlete, in that their success comes down to their ability to make a certain inexplicable magic happen time and again in both the physical world of ball and goal and court, and in the psychological realm of players' minds. The coach that day had walked out on the field and proved this to everyone. He threw five touchdown passes. He won in straight sets. He scored a hat trick and added two assists for good measure. He brought the process to life and made people believers. And by the end of the mini-camp, every player believed a new era had arrived, that greatness was possible, that they wanted to be a part of it and could contribute to it.

As I read this book, I could not stop thinking about that coach. Not just his pleasure and pride in the craft of teaching, but in his systems of improving his own coaching—the relentless reading, the observers he asked to come in and give him feedback, the daily habit of reflecting and discussing what could be better tomorrow.

“High performance” is a term that is used loosely and widely in the world of sport. A friend of mine who works as a sports scientist with elite professional clubs in half a dozen sports opines that if “high performance” is measured by the quality of the development environment and not the athletes when they arrive, the term is often a misnomer: there are precious few programs obsessed with marginal gains and committed to the follow-through on each tiny lever of improvement. A lot of teams might steal the idea of circling staff up to discuss how they performed that day and how they could be better tomorrow, but very few would diligently put the key observations into practice. Fewer still would be using the idea six months later.

Put another way, almost everyone in the coaching profession would agree that a certain set of premises are true about athletes and their development. For example, almost everyone would likely agree that every athlete needs to practice to achieve excellence, and that some athletes practice better than others; their mindsets cause them to get better a little faster than, say, the teammate standing right next to them. They are more reflective. Or their preparation is better: they walk out onto the court thinking about getting better, not just getting through practice. They relish feedback and use it to improve, rather than just nod in agreement and persist in doing things the same way they have always done. They study the game on their own. Almost everyone would agree that some players have a mindset that helps them get more out of the people around them. They can check their ego and balance that with pride in their own performance.

Every coach would agree that those things are true about athletes. But fewer would recognize that they are also true about themselves as coaches—their own willingness to practice and reflect, and their own mindsets about improving their performance can cause them to improve faster than the person next to them. For those who are inclined to believe in this premise, who want to put in the work to achieve marginal gains in their own craft and who want a road map to get there, this book will be invaluable.

It begins with the premise that coaches have much in common with the athletes they coach, and that their path to development requires a similar degree of careful attention. It outlines key skills on which to focus and the steps that can yield improvement. Perhaps most importantly, it grounds those discussions in cognitive science, translated for ease of application by a coach who has himself spent years on just such a journey.

I can attest to this last part myself. I've known Zack Ohlin for more than five years, since he wrote me one day to ask if I would watch a video of his training sessions with elite tennis players and critique his coaching. How could he get better at making them better? He shared the video uncut. He didn't want me to see his best moments; he wanted me to see everything. We chatted again after he had tried some of the things I suggested. What had helped and, just as importantly, what hadn't? He was reflective and self-critical and obsessed with *why*. Why did A work and B didn't? We discussed what he did on and off the court—I still remember the booklets he made to help players learn how better to read the body language of opponents before they struck the ball. His journey, I can attest, is one of not just knowledge and study in the abstract, but practice and constant self-reflection and humility. If coaches are like athletes, Zack is the guy who always reflects a little more, who thinks about each bit of feedback, whose mindset means he spends the drive home thinking about what it will take to improve. What he's learned in doing that, which he shares in this book, will be gold for people who also seek to be elite at the craft of coaching.

Doug Lemov

Part 1
The Coach Is an Athlete

Working with young people is a sacred trust.

—Nick Saviano

This book will be divided into three parts. In Part 1, we'll discuss what it means to be a coach, and, more importantly, what it means to get better as a coach. In Part 2, we'll look at how exactly we should go about improving ourselves. And in Part 3, we'll talk about the fundamental skills that underlie successful coaching.

But why should we strive to get better? Why do we have to put ourselves under such pressure? The answer, of course, revolves around the most important people in coaching: our athletes.

The Imbalance of Importance

In the media we often hear thoughts much like the one quoted above, reminding us that teaching is a noble profession, that as coaches we have the opportunity to change lives, that children are easily influenced and need role models. And this is all true. But in our profession—that is, high-performance coaching—there is something even more critical to consider. It's what I call the *imbalance of importance.*

Throughout the course of your career, how many athletes will consider you their coach? A dozen? Two dozen? Fifty? A hundred? The answer will vary depending on your sport, but for most of us, the answer is at least five. Now answer this: How many careers does each player get?

One.

That's it. One shot. One career. One chance to achieve what for most of them has been a lifelong dream. In some cases, it will pay for their education. In others, it will pay for their kids' education. And it may fundamentally change who they are as a person—their identity, their beliefs, their values, and their skills. But they'll only get one athletic career.

There is a massive imbalance of importance in the coach–player relationship. We will all coach multiple athletes. They will all get only one career. My coaching mistakes may not significantly change the trajectory of my life—I'll work with other players, and as we know, it's the players who make the coach. One good win and my career is better off. One struggling player, and I can sweep that under the rug.

But for them? A failure of mine can be immensely impactful—changing the way they see themselves or their sport. It could lessen their enjoyment, create more pressure, or reduce their participation.

This is not to say that every coaching interaction we have will be laden with this immense burden, each conversation carrying with it the pressure of a life-or-death outcome. In fact, most actions we take as coaches will sit in the gray zone, having neither a large positive nor negative outcome. But in the aggregate, our behavior as leaders is significantly more impactful to the athletes we coach than it is to ourselves.

The Extraordinary Goal

As a coach, how do you know if you're doing a good job? Is it the number of titles won? Number of medals? Highest rankings? Or is your success measured by the impact you have on your athletes' lives?

I'd suggest that both play a role. It goes without saying that the role of a coach is a personal one—we coach people, not sports. Our players are people first, athletes second. And just like many of you, my primary goal is to make a positive difference in the lives of my pupils.

But we can't deny the fact that high-performance sport is a results-oriented business. If you want your athletes to win major trophies, you've got to make sure they get better than the others. If you want your teams to win more games, you've got to make sure that you teach them what it takes before the opposition does. And if you want to ensure you keep collecting a paycheck, you've got to make sure that your coaching improves player performance faster than no coaching at all.

Regardless of whether we take the personal lens or the athletic lens, success as a performance coach comes down to one thing: beating the curve.

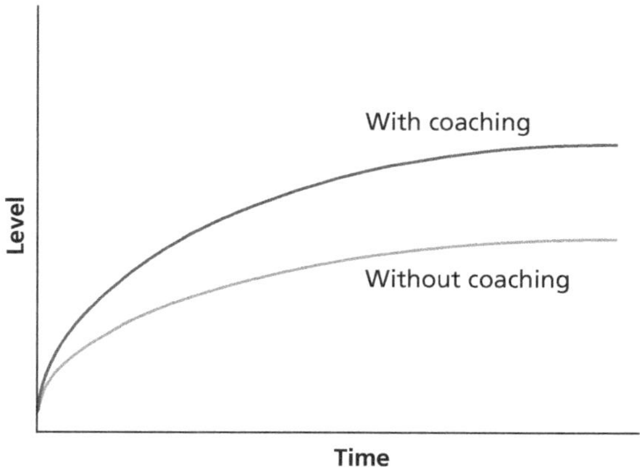

Figure 1. Your coaching must accelerate the improvement curve.

At the developmental levels, your job is to make sure that your coaching accelerates improvement. The key word here is *accelerates*. The vast majority of people, especially at the developmental levels, will improve only with practice. Think about it: take ten 9-year-olds, give them a few soccer balls, and put them on a pitch for two hours a week for a year. Will they improve? Absolutely. Would they improve more with your coaching? That's the question you need to ask yourself.

Even at higher, more competitive levels, players still have a lot of room for growth, and they can easily improve on their own, without intervention. Especially for athletes who are still growing, and perhaps going through puberty, the physical changes alone can lead to greater results without any coaching.

Our first job as coaches, then, is to ensure that our influence, however that may present itself, is leading to improvements *greater* than those that would be achieved on their own. In other words, we need to beat the curve.

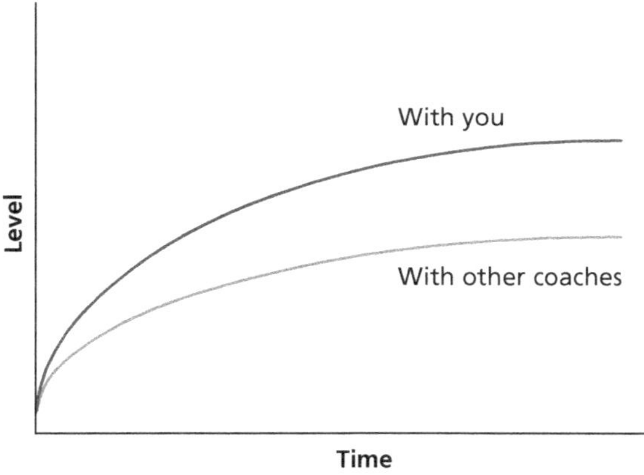

Figure 2. Your goal is to improve player performance faster than other coaches.

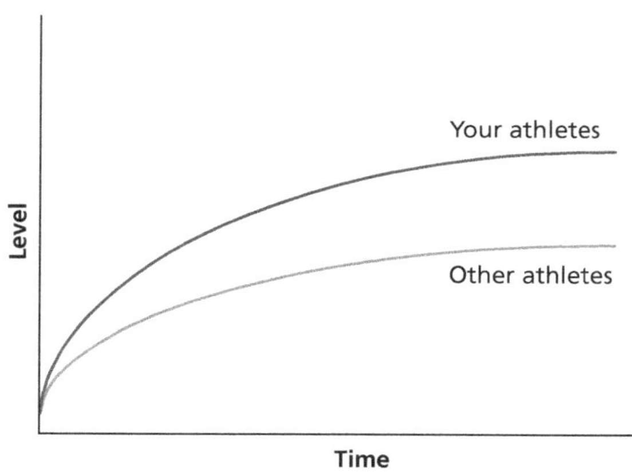

Figure 3. Your goal is for your players to improve faster than their competitors.

At the performance level, the concept of beating the curve applies not to the improvements that players would make without coaching, but rather to the improvements they would make with another person's coaching.

Consider Jessica Pegula, an American professional tennis player and at the time of writing, the world's number 3 ranked tennis player. She began the first year of her full-time professional career in 2011 ranked 861 and finished in 2012 ranked 151. This was a very respectable jump for the promising then-18-year-old (not only was Pegula a highly ranked junior, but her father is a billionaire; there would be no shortage of resources for the young talent). But in the next five years, her ranking plateaued, hovering between 123 and 250. In 2017, she hired a new coach, and by the end of 2019 she was ranked 76, inside the top 100 for the first time in her career. In 2019, she hired yet another coach, David Witt, and the two remain together at the time of writing. What has Witt's influence been? Two singles titles and three finals, and seven doubles titles and three finals, including at the French Open. Also, quarterfinal appearances at three of the four Grand Slams, and, of course, a steady rate of improvement that has seen her climb to number 3 in the world in singles and number 2 in doubles at the age of 29, making her the fifth-oldest player in the top 20.

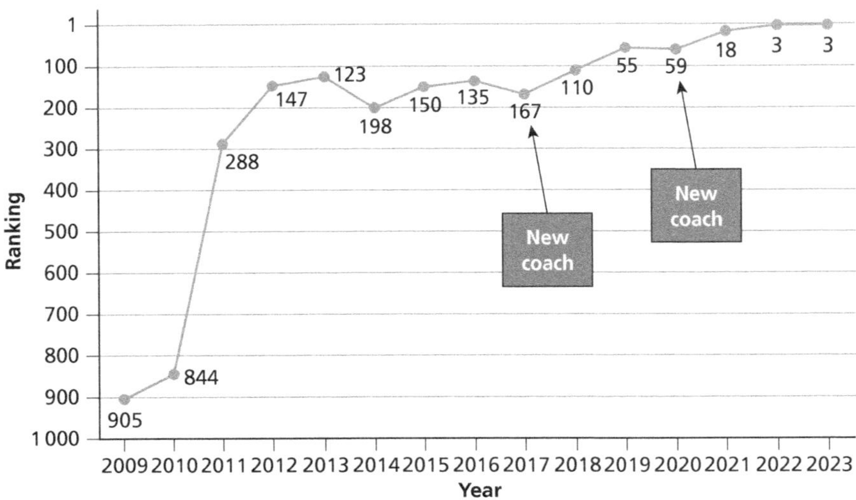

Figure 4. Jessica Pegula's professional ranking progression.

This is a remarkable turn of events. Pegula spent years grinding on the secondary tours before all of a sudden, seemingly out of nowhere, rising not just to the Grand Slam level but into the top five in the world. What caused this change?

Of course, it's impossible to know for sure. Any number of factors could have led to such a development: a change in diet, a jump in confidence, a new fitness program. But in the absence of such changes, it's not unreasonable to imagine that it could be, at least partially, the result of Witt's coaching.

This is what we are aiming for: to make a noticeable difference, especially compared to other coaches or athletes. Now, not everyone can be number 1 in the world. But performance sport is about competition, and we owe it to our athletes to be just as competitive about our coaching as they are about their playing.

I'm not saying that this is a coach-versus-coach battle. I'm not saying that there should be coach rankings, or a coach leaderboard, or for that matter that we should celebrate our players' or team's wins as our own. In all of this, we should retain the sense of duty central to our profession:

we are doing this for them. And in so doing, we should do it to the highest level possible and strive to do it better day after day.

Coaching is often compared to teaching. After all, both professions involve instructing pupils who are generally minors. As coaches, we have a lot to learn from those teachers who excel, but there is one important distinction between teachers and coaches: how we define success.

The mandate of a teacher is, in its simplest form, to bring all students up to a required level of proficiency. This is why we have minimum passing grades and state-run exams. Think about it: the entire education system is designed with the goal of ensuring that students, whether at the primary, secondary, or university level, reach a minimum level of competency in their required subjects. After all, this is how we determine whether or not someone passes a class, advances from one grade to another, or ultimately receives their degree. Of course, teachers do much more than just that—from inspiring young children to running extracurricular activities and helping star students get scholarships to their dream schools. But at its base, teaching is about helping a large number of pupils achieve an average level of competency.

Performance coaching, on the other hand, exists at the other end of the spectrum, wherein we help a small number of players achieve an incredibly high level of competency—often in the top 1%. As Marlene Nobrega, former long-time Tennis Canada physiotherapist, once said to me, "The average teenager does not have a physiotherapist." In other words, there is nothing normal about high-performance sport. Not mentally, and certainly not physically. But as they say, to achieve the extraordinary, you can't just do the ordinary. If our goal is to develop players who will be in the top 1%, then shouldn't our own training reflect that? If we want our results to be extraordinary, shouldn't our own professional development go above and beyond?

High-performance sport plays an outsize role in the lives of many athletes. Not only is it emotionally meaningful, it takes up a significant amount of time during what are often our athletes' formative years. They have goals—extraordinary ones—and we owe it to them to take our own development just as seriously as they take theirs.

In the coming chapters, we'll discuss in more detail *how* to get better at coaching. What makes coaching so unique? Are you born a good coach, or can you get better at coaching? Does experience equate to skill? And if not, what should you be doing to develop yourself?

If you're looking for the answers to these questions, keep reading.

Chapter 1
Coaching Is a Performance Profession

Coaching Is Performing

In February of 2015, I walked through the doors of the SK8ON Hockey School in Toronto, Canada. By that point in time, I had already been exposed to a host of different tennis environments, including public and private clubs and federations and academies on three different continents. But this was distinctly different—and not just because of how cold it was.

While tennis is, at its core, a so-called gentlemanly sport, hockey might well be its polar opposite. I walked in cautiously, eyeing the kids covered in gear and the parents pulling huge equipment bags behind them. Everyone seemed to be moving about on a different path, like ants, and I stood in the middle, well outside of my comfort zone.

I was there to shadow Jari Byrski, the legendary hockey skills coach. Over the last thirty years, Jari has developed the skills of NHL all-stars like Jason Spezza, Steven Stamkos, Alex Pietrangelo, and others, as well as consulted for various NHL teams. I was a young coach—19 at the time—and eager to learn from anyone who had achieved any level of international coaching success, no matter the sport or the domain. What I didn't realize, as I sat down on the bench rink-side, was that I had just been given a front-row seat to the performance of a lifetime.

As the clock struck 4.00pm, fifteen players skated onto the ice and placed their water bottles on the ledge. Within a minute or two, they were doing skating exercises, weaving and bobbing, sometimes on one foot, sometimes on two, Jari leading the group with his booming Polish-accented voice. As soon as one round of exercises was done, one coach led a small-space stick-handling exercise while the others set up stations. Once the stations were set up, the players went to their assigned locations and began practicing. Each coach clearly knew their responsibility, providing feedback only to the athletes at their station. The players rotated quickly, and each time new stations had to be set up, one coach would gather them off to the side to run another stick-handling drill. The practice, only an hour long, felt faster than I could take notes, teaching and learning occurring at every minute. At 5.00pm, the buzzer sounded, and the athletes skated off, their water bottles untouched.

That practice, I came to realize, was not so much a practice as it was a symphony—orchestrated by Jari and performed by himself and his assistant coaches. Each and every one of them knew exactly what to do and when to do it, and they executed it flawlessly.

This was my first exposure to the idea that coaches, just like athletes, can be performers. After all, there are a number of similarities between coaching and performing. For one, *coaching occurs in real time*—practice starts at 4.00pm and ends at 5.00pm, and you've got to be "on" for every minute of that hour. A lawyer drafting an argument can step out of their office to take a break or pause mid-sentence to consider their phrasing. For coaches, there is no pause button—only "play"—and coaches can't change channels, either. An accountant might choose to work on one client's financials before switching to another. But coaches? We have to deal with whatever comes our way, when it comes our way. We can't decide what to say to a player until we see what they need to hear, and we can't pick and choose when an athlete will be low on confidence or start missing their shots. Coaching occurs in real time—there is no pausing, and we have limited control over what happens (we'll discuss this more in Chapter 2).

Not only that, but *coaches only get one shot*. An artist recording a song in a studio is performing live, in real time—but they'll get as many takes as they need (or can afford). On the other hand, have you ever been given the chance to "redo" a practice? Didn't think so. From the sidelines, watching a coach at work is like watching a musician. You're watching a performance! You get one shot—no pausing, no slowing down, no do-overs. Just as a musician has an expectant audience, we have our players. And as mentioned in the introduction, we have a responsibility to them! From the first buzzer to the last, we have to be ready.

Unlike a concert, however, in coaching *every performance is different.* Although I know a few coaches who have given the same lesson twice (or more than twice), for most of us no two sessions are identical. No two people are the same, and two players working on the same skill at the same level will still require different feedback. They evolve at different rates and in different ways. They respond differently to stress, to fatigue, to challenge. In dealing with different ages, genders, skills, times of year, surfaces, and conditions, we adapt and adjust. In fact, that might be *why* you coach. A carpenter building a desk doesn't encounter this sort of variability—at least not to the same extent. But coaches, along with teachers, doctors, psychologists, and others, interact so deeply with people that every day is not just different, it poses a new challenge.

There is one last aspect of coaching which makes us performers: *we operate under pressure*. An obvious example of this is in competition. It's Game 7 of the Eastern Conference Finals, and you're on the bench. The opposing team scores in the final minutes, and you head into overtime. Score, and you're headed to the Stanley Cup Finals. Allow a goal, and your season ends in an instant. Are you feeling the pressure? Numerous successful Olympic coaches have admitted to feeling nervous during important games. Legendary UCLA basketball coach John Wooden spent every game anxiously rubbing a small metal cross in his pocket. In these moments, with the crowd watching and the game on the line, what play do you call? Who do you substitute? It's time to perform under pressure.

But beyond the highlight reel moments, is there not also pressure in our daily training environment? I'd argue there is. We've all had the experience of a parent or boss watching practice from the sideline. Regardless of whether or not they were invited, there's a certain amount of pressure. But setting aside unwelcome visitors, consider the pressure, beneficial or not, that we can put on ourselves, as illustrated by the story of the 2008 Great Britain Cycling Team.

In 2002, Sir Dave Brailsford became the head of British Cycling. He was a former professional cyclist with an MBA, and he assumed his position at a time when British cycling was nothing to shout about: in 76 years, Britain had won just a single gold medal. What he did, however, revolutionized the sport for the country. Using the theory of marginal gains, he hypothesized that if he and his team could identify all the factors leading to cycling success, and then improve each one by just 1%, they would see outsized results. James Clear describes Brailsford's approach:

> *Brailsford and his coaches began by making small adjustments you might expect from a professional cycling team. They redesigned the bike seats to make them more comfortable and rubbed alcohol on the tires for a better grip. They asked riders to wear electrically heated overshorts to maintain ideal muscle temperature while riding and used biofeedback sensors to monitor how each athlete responded to a particular workout. The team tested various fabrics in a wind tunnel and had their outdoor riders switch to indoor racing suits, which proved to be lighter and more aerodynamic.*
>
> *But they didn't stop there. Brailsford and his team continued to find 1 percent improvements in overlooked and unexpected areas. They tested different types of massage gels to see which one led to the fastest muscle recovery. They hired a surgeon to teach each rider the best way to wash their hands to reduce the chances of catching a cold. They determined the type of pillow and mattress that led to the best night's sleep for each rider. They even painted the inside of the team truck white, which helped them spot little bits of dust that would normally slip by unnoticed but could degrade the performance of the finely tuned bikes. (Clear, 2018)*

Five years later, at the Beijing Olympics, his team won seven out of a maximum ten possible gold medals in track cycling, and did the same four years later in London. Over the next ten years, British cyclists won five Tour de France titles and countless world championships and gold medals—more than any other nation.

Brailsford and his team were *obsessed* with the small details. While not everyone can influence the microscopic factors that Brailsford did, many of us are equally obsessed with perfecting every last detail in our own coaching contexts. Does this not create some pressure? I'd certainly argue it does. Brailsford even alluded to it, saying in an interview, "One caveat is that the whole marginal gains approach doesn't work if only half the team buy in. In that case, the search for small improvements will cause resentment" (Harrell, 2015).

But nobody's perfect! It's unreasonable to expect yourself to maximize every single aspect of your coaching. That's why I remind myself of the apocryphal autopilot story. A gentleman is riding in the cockpit on a flight to Hawaii and notices what the pilot tells him is the "inertial guidance system." The system's goal is to get the plane to within 1000 yards of the runway within five minutes of the arrival time. The autopilot begins by setting a course from point A to point B. However, after some time, when it realizes its original alignment is slightly off, it adjusts. This process repeats, as the autopilot continues to make adjustments to its slightly flawed calculations, until the plane is close enough to land. When asked, the pilot says, "I arrive at my destination 100% of the time, despite being off course 90% of the time."

Figure 1.1. The Autopilot Analogy.

Performance coaching at the highest level exists at the intersection of these two philosophies: striving to maximize every single detail while recognizing the unpredictability of the environment and aiming to respond as best as possible. And this approach, combined with the duty we have to our players, makes for pressure.

Let's review. Coaches are performers. They have to perform in real time, without being able to pause or slow down. They only get one chance—if they screw up they will have to live with the consequences. Every performance is different, with different goals and outcomes. And every performance comes with some level of pressure, whether that be in practice or in competition.

This is not to suggest that coaching is somehow more difficult or noble than other professions. Coaching is also not the only performance profession. There are plenty—teaching, nursing, counseling, and tutoring, just to name a few. The goal of this chapter is simply to illustrate how clear and important this distinction is, because the difference between performance and non-performance professions is large, and the implications of this are even larger.

Coaching Is about Execution, Not Knowledge

To coach is to perform—but how does this affect us?

Steph Curry is widely regarded as the greatest shooter in NBA history. In college, he set career-scoring records for the Davidson Wildcats and set the single-season NCAA record for most three-pointers made. He has set the NBA record for number of three-pointers made in a season three times and holds the record for most career three-pointers.

Because of this, his advice on shooting is often sought out, and there's one tip he has given repeatedly: hold the ball in your fingertips, not your palms. It's not hard to find clips from interviews or online courses in which he repeats this advice. In one video, he states: "You don't want the ball sitting on your palm." In another, "The first thing I say is to keep the ball off your palm" (Scot Shot Basketball, 2018). This advice is echoed by other greats, such as Reggie Miller: "Most shooters like to have the fingertips all on the basketball. [...] You shoot the basketball with your fingertips and your wrist" (Scot Shot Basketball, 2018).

There's some logic to this argument, as when the ball is released, it indeed leaves the palm and rolls off the fingertips. And shooting the ball like one does in shot put, pushing forward with the palm, would be inefficient. But the fact of the matter is that nearly every NBA player brings the ball up on their palm. And even more fascinating is that Curry does too!

How can this happen? How is it that Steph Curry, the greatest shooter of all time, doesn't know exactly what he's doing when he's shooting the ball? Does this make him any less of a professional? Of course not. In fact, you might argue that it's his ability to forget what he is doing that allows him to perform so well. Above all, he is successful not because of his knowledge, but because of his skill.[1] He doesn't get paid to tell people how he shoots—he gets paid to shoot, and he does it extremely well.

There are coaches—I'm sure you know them—who do good work without knowing why or how it works. That's not to say that they can't tell you which drill is for which purpose, or what the drill accomplishes—it just means that they don't necessarily understand the underlying mechanisms. And yet they get results, year after year.

There are even more coaches with the opposite problem—coaches whose knowledge far outweighs their skill. I was one such coach. At 21, I knew a ton—not just about tennis, but about coaching too. I had a clear philosophy, I understood both the tactical and technical parts of the game, and I could talk all day about skill development, practice structure, and sports psychology. But it would take years before I would start to really see results. I knew more than I could do.

Coaching is a performance profession, and in performance professions, execution counts. Knowledge without execution is wasted. On the other hand, skill without understanding can still get the job done.

You might be able to identify a flaw in someone's running mechanics, but can you help them *feel* it? And more importantly, can you help them fix it? You might recognize that in certain situations, you need a more empathetic tone of voice. But have you mastered that voice? Does it come naturally to you?

The population of people who *know* how to hit a home run is significantly larger than the population of people who *can* hit a home run. The importance of these two qualities is not lost on us when discussing athletes—execution matters. Why should it be any different for coaches?

1 Skill acquisition experts often refer to the distinction between "knowledge about" and "knowledge of." "Knowledge about" is information that someone can recite verbally, whereas "knowledge of" is information showcased through someone's behavior (or in our case, performance). As an example, it is the difference between knowing a recipe and actually being able to cook the dish. For simplicity, we'll use the terms "knowledge" and "skill" throughout this book.

The majority of coaching advice is incredibly simple and repeated ad nauseam. Show them you care. Pay attention to the details. Push people outside of their comfort zone. Communicate clearly. But if it were truly that simple, we'd all be winning Olympic medals. It's not just about what you know. It's about what you can do.

This is not to say that knowledge-building is of no use to us sports coaches. If that were the case, I wouldn't be writing this book. Expanding your knowledge base, whether that be knowledge of your sport, of psychology, of learning, or of any other subject, is a valuable and worthwhile pursuit. In fact, it's essential. In a study of fourteen "serial winning coaches" (coaches who had won Olympic gold or world championship medals over an extended period of time with multiple different athletes or teams), researchers found that they all engaged in an "obsessive pursuit of knowledge" (Mallett et al., 2016).

However, equally if not more important is the quest to be able to apply that knowledge—to observe the technique you understand, to enact the psychological principle you learned, or to challenge your athletes the way you planned. This is what drives player development. Not knowledge, but skill. As Mallett et al. write, high-performance coaches can improve through carefully designed "learning tasks that require the application of a recently acquired knowledge base to a specific and real situation the coach is trying to resolve" (2016, p. 316). In other words, coaches need to be able to apply what they have learned in order to get better.

Can We Get Better at Coaching?

We've established that coaching is a performance profession. And to perform well, we can't just *know* about our field, we have to be able to *execute*. To understand how that affects our own development as coaches, however, we'll need to take a brief detour.

The Bob Dylan album *Blood on the Tracks* is considered by many to be about the dissolution of Dylan's marriage to Sara Lownds.[2] Because of this, people tend to paint the writing and recording of the album

2 Dylan denies that the album is in any way autobiographical.

as an enlightened, inspired, almost magical affair—a work of genius. Ellen Bernstein, his then-girlfriend and a Columbia Records employee, said "He knew as soon as he heard something whether or not it was what he was going for. It never took him more than one time to know. ... He worked so instinctively." Historian Clinton Heylin describes the recording sessions:

> *Including that first take of "If You See Her, Say Hello," he recorded 6 songs over 10 takes solo before being joined in the studio by Eric Weissberg's band Deliverance, with whom he tackled 4 songs in 13 takes. There was little in terms of rehearsal ... In all there was less than half the takes of the previous day, but the session was no less productive. Five songs intended for the album were attempted over 13 takes, plus one warm-up cover. (Heylin, 2019)*

This depiction of Dylan's as the heartbroken genius who walks into the studio and brings music to life is attractive, no doubt. However, it neglects a few important details. In terms of the lyrics, what was seen by many as a spontaneous outpouring of emotion was actually the result of three notebooks of lyrics, filled from cover to cover, with lines crossed out and rewritten, worked on until they were perfect. And the recording process? It may have gone quickly once he was in the studio, but Dylan had already performed the songs multiple times for friends as well as for Mike Bloomfield, with whom he had discussed the potential of a backing group.

Dylan began working on the record in the spring of 1974 and finished recording in December—all told, recording took at least six months. Was it fast by music industry standards? Yes. But it was not a stroke of genius, inspiration that flowed out of his heart and onto the strings of the guitar. It was a process, worked at for months on end, until the final result was something that people would listen to and appreciate, without seeing or thinking about what went on behind the scenes.

Much like Dylan, some coaches will do things that impress us. They will have a keen eye, be a great communicator, or have a knack for knowing how hard to push. When asked, many observers will ascribe this level of skill to experience. "She's been doing this for years," "This isn't his first rodeo." The fact of the matter is, however, that these expert coaches, with years of experience, are easily outnumbered by the coaches with the same level of experience but not the same level of skill.

What would you tell an athlete looking for advice? Is it enough simply to play the game until you master it? Or is there more to the equation? I'd suggest there are more variables—things like practice, mindset, reflection, and mentorship, to name just a few.

Just like Dylan, expert coaches don't get good through genius or inspiration. Their skill is the result of a never-ending process of improvement. Consider what Dean Lockwood had to say about Pat Summitt, a record-setting women's basketball coach with multiple NCAA champion wins:

> *It impressed me how much of a student she was, what a learner. Here she is, someone in such command of her world, her team and her program, and I'm twenty-six years old, and yet she's looking at my stuff saying, "What can I glean from this, what can I get out of this guy that can help us?" I would see her in Stokely standing at one end of the arena, leaning against a wall, watching us for twenty or thirty or forty minutes. (Summitt, 2013, p. 250)*

Or this description of John Wooden, considered by some to be the greatest coach of all time:

> *Whenever Wooden's machine encountered big problems, his instinct was to delve into the smallest details. If the pyramid defines the modern-day image of the man, the more indelible picture in the minds of the men who played for him is that of the three-by-five index card. Every morning before practice, Wooden spent two to three hours drafting his practice plan and then transferring it onto those cards. When practice was over, Wooden filed the cards away for safekeeping. His outline on those cards was precise. His penmanship, exquisite. (Davis, 2014, p. 176)*

Or, this quote, from a study of Vince Lombardi's life and career:

> *Lombardi was forty-five years old when he finally received [the opportunity to be head coach of the Green Bay Packers]. ... It should also be noted ... that he spent twenty years within the function of coaching and building the expertise of his craft. He did not leapfrog from one career to another in search of a larger pay check. He remained focused on his goals and pursued his coaching vocation. (Petit, 2016)*

These coaches are not so much obsessed with their sport as they are obsessed with their *coaching*. Across numerous interviews, biographies, and studies of some of the best coaches who have ever lived, one thing stands in common: they are looking for every possible avenue for improvement. For each of them, their journey to the top was just that—a journey. In most cases, it was long, and in all cases, it was a work in progress. Expert coaches feel an almost obsessive need to get better, to master their craft.

Sometimes, this desire leads them to seek out new information, to learn more about the game, about themselves, or about coaching. Other times, they end up working on their skills, practicing, and observing other coaches. And very frequently, they are reflecting, brainstorming, and finding solutions. This book delves into all of these approaches—showing you how you can embark upon the same journey, working diligently to improve the *skill* of coaching.

Coaching Better in the Moment

I started this chapter by comparing coaches to elite performers—musicians, dancers, athletes. To finish, I'd like to return to that comparison and ask you to think of your own players or team members. How much of your work is helping them improve, and how much is helping them perform—at the game, match, meet, or competition? Giving a pre-game pep talk? You're helping them perform. Running a practice? You're helping them improve. Ensuring they sleep well the night before? You're helping them perform. You get the idea.

Depending on your sport and your circumstances, the distribution of time and effort spent on each will differ. But almost all of us, at some point or another, engage in both of these endeavors. Maximizing outcomes in sports (or any other performance profession) relies on a balance between improving skills and maximizing performance. And it should come as no surprise that this balance exists for coaches, too. I've already outlined how the best coaches take an eager, almost aggressive approach to their own development. But it's just as important to take steps to ensure your optimal performance. An excellent coach who is burned out, distracted, or simply exhausted isn't an excellent coach.

In recent years, more attention has been devoted to coach wellbeing and wellness. Shows like the popular *Ted Lasso* shine a spotlight on the stress some leaders experience, and a recent scoping review found that over one third of all studies of coach burnout were conducted in the last ten years (Olusoga et al., 2019). Sport governing bodies and private individuals have started offering resources and services aimed to support worn-down coaches. Not only do these efforts ensure that coaches stay in the profession longer, they also increase the quality of said coaches' performances. It's difficult to be empathetic and athlete-centered if you are feeling burned out or depressed. But this is only one factor influencing coach performance. Later, we'll discuss the others, namely: focus (you can't coach well if you are distracted), physical health (you can't give 100% of your energy if your body lets you down), and preparation. Ultimately, it's important to remind ourselves that coaching better is not just about developing our skills. It's also about giving ourselves the best chance to be present and high-performing in the moment.

For now, though, remember these key points:

1. Coaching is a performance profession. Rather than bankers or plumbers, who are valued primarily for their knowledge, we are like athletes—our value is in our skill.
2. The best coaches in history have been obsessed with improving their coaching, and they have done so in a variety of different ways.
3. Not only do we have to work on our coaching "game," we also have to make sure that, just like athletes, we are physically and mentally fit for our own performance—that is, whenever we are coaching.

Chapter 2
Coaching Is an Open Skill

In 1963, Barbara Knapp suggested that all sports lie on a continuum from open to closed (Knapp, 1963). Open skills are more externally paced and dependent on their environment, whereas closed skills are more predictable. Take, for example, an ice hockey player carrying the puck into the offensive zone, observing and reacting to the defenders' best efforts, compared to someone throwing a dart at their own pace, undisturbed by their opponent.

Open skills generally follow a cycle: perception, decision, execution, and feedback. In the case of our hockey player, they must first perceive the defenders, recognizing their positioning, their orientation, and their movements. Then, they must decide what to do: pass, shoot, or retain possession. Once they execute, they receive feedback on their performance, both internally (from kinesthetic sensations) and externally (through the actions of the opponents or a response from a coach). Contrast this with closed skills, which only consist of execution and feedback, and do not include perception or decision-making. Consider a gymnast who is preparing to perform a routine at a competition. They know exactly what moves they will perform and when; there is no decision to be made, and as such, no perceiving to do.[3] They go out, execute the movement, and then receive feedback from themselves, their coaches, and the judges.

3 It's worth noting that this is not entirely accurate, as gymnasts may have to make small adjustments mid-routine depending on their performance. However, on the spectrum of open to closed, gymnastics is much closer to closed than it is to open. The amount of perception and decision-making is far less than, say, basketball, given that the gymnast decides the pace of execution and does not respond to their opponent in the moment.

As with most scales, very few activities lie completely on one end of the spectrum. Nothing is completely closed, nor is anything entirely open, but the distinction is important. Imagine you are working with an athlete to develop a specific skill. You practice it, make corrections, and get them to repeat it until it looks great. When tested, the athlete executes it perfectly. Come competition, however, the player's execution breaks down, and they revert to old habits, using skills or techniques you wanted to change or get rid of. They know what they want to do, and they may even tell you that they are trying to do it! But in the heat of the moment, they struggle.

Barring any choking or performance anxiety, what's happening here is most likely the result of a learning environment that doesn't take into account the open skill nature of the sport. In the world of skill acquisition, motor patterns are developed through perception–action couplings. In other words, the brain associates a particular movement with the relevant information (in this case, the perceptual cues and the tactical intention). If a skill is acquired in a closed context, without any perceptual or tactical information, then it will not transfer to a competitive environment in which the athlete must recognize what's going on and make decisions as to how to react.

In Chapter 9, we'll discuss in more detail how this affects the work we do with our players. But for now, simply note that, for open skills to transfer to the performance environment, they must be practiced in a context that includes elements of perception and decision-making.

With that in mind, let's consider how this affects our *own* development.

Coaching as an Open Skill

We've established that open skills are ones whose execution is dependent on the performer's perception and decision-making. Take 60 seconds to come up with anything you may have to *perceive* when coaching, including any information you may have to gather, whether in training, in competition, or in between. Then take another 60 seconds to think about the *decisions* you might have to make. When the time is up, take a look at the lists below.

Here are a few examples that I came up with of things you might *perceive* when coaching:

- a player's mood
- the movement of a player's forearm during their swing
- the tactics being used
- the positioning of the opponents
- the spin of the ball
- the direction of the wind
- how successfully a player is executing a specific skill
- an athlete's energy level

Here are some examples of *decisions* you might have to make:

- what tone to use
- what feedback to give in practice
- what game plan to go with ahead of a match
- which player to take out/put in
- whether to make a task easier or harder
- whether to push an athlete or let them rest

As coaches, we are constantly observing and deciding, whether we know it or not. In training, we watch our athletes perform, evaluating them and choosing how to respond, what drills to use, and how to adapt training activities. In competition, we monitor performance, choosing what to say, which players to substitute, and what strategies to implement. In between, we are building relationships with players; noticing their energy levels, their mood, and their facial expressions; and deciding what role to play in their lives, or what style of leadership suits them best. The fact that a lot of this is happening subconsciously doesn't matter. What's important is that we are *always* perceiving and deciding. Coaching is an open skill.

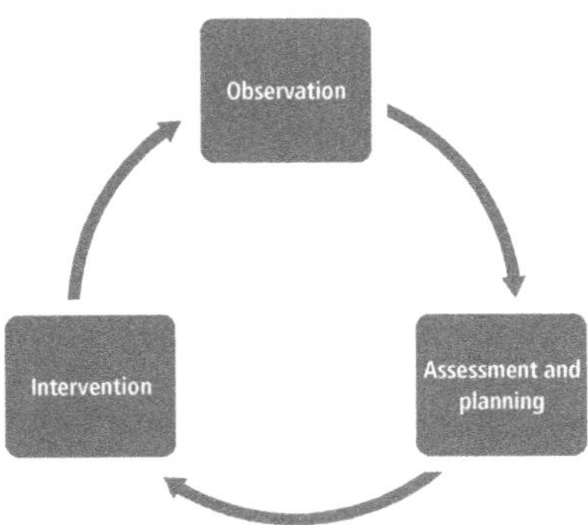

Figure 2.1. The Coaching Cycle.

But why does this matter? And how does knowing this help us become better?

Developing Open Skills

Consider the story of legendary tennis coach Vic Braden, told in Malcolm Gladwell's *Blink* (2007). In tennis, players are given two chances to serve the ball into the service box. If they miss both serves, this is called a *double fault*, and they lose the point. Professional players double fault, on average, once every 20 points. As the story goes, Braden started noticing that he could predict double faults before the server had even begun their motion. At one tournament, he brought along a few friends, and every time he sensed a mistake coming, he signaled them. Over the course of a few hours, he predicted 20 out of 20 double faults.

Regardless of whether the story has been embellished or Braden was simply lucky, I'm sure we can all think of a coach who just *sees* things better than us. The coach who can walk into the locker room or onto the field and identify exactly what's happening and what needs to be done. Or the coach who doesn't seem phased by conflict, who always knows what to say, who handles difficult encounters and challenging situations with ease. The common belief held by most coaches, whether they realize it or not, is that these are gifts—qualities that were granted to these coaches at birth or instilled in them at an early age. Of course, it's true that some people are born with the gift of gab, and others aren't.

And some coaches may have spent time working under a legendary coach who helped them develop their eye. But this doesn't change the fact that these are skills, not traits, and they can be improved, just like breaststroke technique or core strength. As we discussed in Chapter 1, what appears masterful from the outside is most often the result of deliberate practice, rather than genius or innate talent.

There are many examples of people using open skill training to develop themselves in unorthodox ways. For example, take the story of Maggie (EconTalk, 2013). Maggie was a reading teacher who was struggling to respond to wrong answers during class discussions. She wanted to make clear that the student's answer was incorrect, but did not know how to do so without shutting down the discussion or discouraging her students. She knew that this was a problem, but in the heat of the moment, while running the discussion, she couldn't figure out what to do. Her principal recommended she get together with another teacher who was good at managing discussions, and they practiced three times per week, with one of them posing questions and the other responding with unexpected incorrect answers. They would practice handling student responses and then reflect on what they did well and what they could have done better. After a few weeks, Maggie was so at ease responding to unexpected wrong answers that she could do it automatically, correcting the student but keeping the discussion flowing, all without thinking about it.

Maggie's story is a perfect example of an open skill approach to coaching, or in this case teaching. She knew what she wanted to get better at, but teaching is a performance profession too, and she couldn't just "flick a switch" to improve. She needed to practice. Not just any practice, but open skill practice. When her colleague rehearsed with her, they provided genuine unexpected answers. This meant that she had to *perceive* (Why is this answer wrong?) and *decide* (How do I want to respond?). Thanks to an open skill approach, she could transfer her newly acquired abilities back into the classroom.

We'll discuss other techniques and strategies for coaching skills practice later, in Chapter 5. But before we get there, let's look at how we can improve our perception and decision-making skills.

Improving Perception

Observe Your Observation

Before we consider *what* you're looking for, let's think about *how* you're looking for it.

First, it's important to understand a few things about how our eyes work. When both eyes focus on a point, this is called *fixation*. Our ability to fixate and see in fine detail is remarkably limited—to about a 3-degree radius. To get a sense of how small that is, extend your arm so that it is straight in front of you and point your thumb at the sky. The focus of your visual field is roughly the width of your thumb in this position.

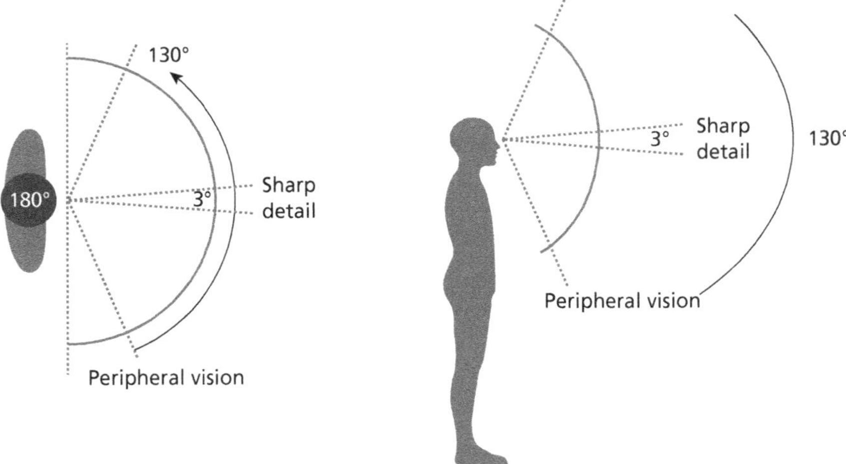

Figure 2.2. Illustration of the human visual field. (Adapted from Kushalnagar, et al. (2011). Multi-view platform: An accessible live classroom viewing approach for low vision students.)

Not only can our eyes only focus on a very limited arc, but they cannot track objects that move too quickly across our field of vision. To track an object as it moves and keep it in focus the entire time, it must be moving no faster than 70 degrees per second, roughly the speed of a person walking left to right 6 feet in front of you. In comparison, tracking the trajectory of a spiked volleyball requires visual angular velocities greater than 500 degrees per second.

So, what happens when we "watch the ball"? We use saccadic eye movements, meaning that our eyes predict the trajectory of the ball by moving from point to point, focusing at each instant but essentially turning off in between. This temporary blindness is called *saccadic suppression*.

With these two concepts—the size of our visual field and saccadic suppression—in mind, there are two takeaways for coaches. First is the importance of using peripheral vision. To quote Knudson and Kluka, authors of the article "The impact of vision and vision training on sport performance":

> *Because the focus of the visual field is so small, peripheral vision becomes very important, particularly in sport. Peripheral visual information is processed quickly to facilitate the detection of motion so that visual focus can be directed to other events. Peripheral vision is stressed in basketball because awareness of motion to the side or above allows the eyes and the athlete to react to more game events. (Knudson and Kluka, 1997, p. 17)*

When you are observing technique, think about where you are directing your gaze. Focusing too intently on something small may narrow your field of vision and cause you to miss out on other cues, hence the term "tunnel vision." Similarly, it may be beneficial to focus on a midpoint, a point in the middle of the action you are watching, which will allow you to collect most of your information through your peripheral vision. For example, if I'm observing a tennis player's shoulder turn, I may choose to focus on their chest, allowing my peripheral vision to gather information about not just their shoulder, but also their hips, which allow the shoulders to turn, and their head, whose positioning may affect balance when rotating. Were I to focus only on the right shoulder, for example, I might not be able to observe the rotation of the hips.

Figure 2.3. Illustration of how focusing on a midpoint can help you collect information through your peripheral vision.

Another takeaway applies when we observe fast gestures or movements close to us. Again, quoting Knudson and Kluka:

> *Teachers who observe human movement need to remember that they usually cannot maintain visual focus on objects that are moving fast or close to them because of the high eye angular velocities required. In observing a gymnastic routine the teacher must observe one or two critical features of the movement rather than trying to track the entire routine. (Knudson and Kluka, 1997, p. 18)*

In other words, rather than trying to track the entire movement and missing out on information due to saccadic suppression, it may be beneficial to pick a few checkpoints—points in an athlete's movements that you know what you want to see—and simply observe those. If I am watching a player serve and intend to observe the returner's movement, I'll need to shift my focus to the returner just before the server makes contact. Our job is not to collect all the information, just all the relevant information. Knowing what to discard and collect, and when, is crucial.

If you've been following along, you may have already thought to yourself: "If my ability to track movement is based on angular velocities, can't I just back up?" And the answer is yes! Remember the example Knudson and Kluka gave: we can track the equivalent of a person walking 6 feet in front of us. But what if they're farther away? Think of when you're sitting in a car, looking out of the window. The bushes right next to you fly by, while the houses in the distance pass by more slowly. Of course, what we gain in tracking ability we lose in acuity (the accuracy of our vision). But it's worth experimenting with. Consider what you are looking for, and in how much detail you need to see it, and play around with your distance from the action to determine the best distance for your observation.

We can't discuss observation without mentioning angles. Here, peripheral vision is once again of paramount importance. Let's imagine that I'm watching a tennis match. For me to do my job correctly, I need to be able to analyze what is going on and evaluate my player's decision-making, as well as the outcomes and the other options available to them. If I watch from the long side of the court, how does that affect what I see? Unless I'm very far away from the court, I'll have to swivel my head left and right to follow the progress of the point. Each time I do so, one of the two players will be outside of my field of vision. If the ball is on one side of the court, and the player on the other side adjusts their positioning, I won't be able to notice. Compare this to if I watch from the back of the court (the short side). In this scenario, I can keep both players in my field of vision, allowing me to pick up information through my peripheral vision at all times. Note that this also applies in practice, when I choose the best angle to observe everything at once. This provides me with far more information and allows me to give more and better feedback.

Of course, there is one problem: watching from the back of the court makes it slightly more difficult to observe the depth or trajectory of the ball, particularly on the far side of the court. If I were especially interested in observing these things, I might choose to watch from the long side of the court and sacrifice the other information I gain from watching from the back. There is no right angle,[4] just different angles for different purposes.

This also applies when you are observing technique. You may not be able to see certain body parts or movements from certain angles. In those cases, you may need to adjust your positioning or make use of an assistant or video technology. Note, however, that it is best to stay

4 Insert your own geometry joke here.

consistent in the angle you observe from. This will allow you to more accurately measure change, rather than having to ask yourself if what you're seeing looks different because it actually *is* different or simply because you've changed angles.

Lastly, at times we may be required to jump into a game or act as a training partner. In tennis, this might involve rallying or feeding a ball. In baseball, this might mean hitting fungoes, or in soccer making a pass. In these moments, consider what information you might be missing out on. In all cases, however, we may be tempted to direct our eyes to the ball, puck, or object we're manipulating at the critical instant (when we hit or release it). While this is beneficial to *our* performance and is likely what we were trained to do, it in fact impedes our ability to observe our athletes. At this critical instant, our players will be reacting, and there's information to gather, no matter the sport. In tennis, I might be interested in which of their feet lands first, or where they're looking. In baseball, I might want to watch how they prepare their hands. If you're willing to disregard that information because it isn't relevant to your objective, that's fine. But to be the best observers we can be, we must be aware of what we're missing.

Watch Video

Good observational technique is only one piece of the puzzle, however. Two people can be standing in the same spot, looking at the same person, and see vastly different things. Knowing *what* to look for is just as important as knowing *how* to look for it, and there are a couple of ways to get better at it.

Search YouTube for slow-motion footage of any athlete's technique, and you'll find hundreds of thousands of videos. Similarly, a quick App Store search for "video analysis" returns dozens of apps. This intersection of sports and technology is not just beneficial to our athletes—it can also be helpful for us coaches in developing our eye. Imagine you want to get better at observing a basketball player's foot position when they are taking a jump shot. One technique you might use is Watch-Write-Watch:

1. Collect a few videos of players taking jump shots. They can be of your athletes or strangers.
2. For each jump shot, watch the video, stop it, and write down what you saw.

3. Once you're done, watch it again in slow motion.
4. Were your observations accurate?

Note: the writing part is critical. Otherwise, it's too easy for us to fool ourselves into thinking that we saw something in real time when in fact we only noticed it in slow motion. Writing your observations down holds you accountable.

This method doesn't just apply to technical observations. It can also be used to improve your ability to observe behavior in a practice or decision-making in a game. Particularly when what you are observing occurs at a fast pace, the Watch-Write-Watch technique can be incredibly valuable. It will help you to realize just how much you're missing!

Watching video can also help you notice any "clues" that a particular movement is occurring. For example, in rewatching the video, you may notice that when the basketball player points his foot a certain way, it reveals the logo on the side of his shorts. The logo, or more specifically, the angle of his hips, is not specifically what you are looking for, but it may be a more easily observable action than the angle of his foot.

Note that I used the word *clue*. Be careful with these sorts of observations, as they will not always correlate perfectly to the targeted action. The idea is that you can look for the clues, and if they are there, narrow your observation and consider the possibility that the event is occurring. They are not meant to replace the original event.

At the same time, however, the benefit of clues is that you can then use them as cues with your athletes. For example, you can say "Show me the logo!" to get someone to point their foot.

Passenger Coaching

Another way to develop your observational skills is to co-observe with an expert coach, someone whose skills you trust, and take note of either the actions they are taking (or not taking), or the feedback they are giving (or not giving). When doing so, it's important to make sure you are not just passively watching the session. Instead, you should be "passenger coaching": observing the athlete, forming your own conclusions based on what you saw, and then taking note of what the expert coach does as feedback for yourself.

The effect of passenger coaching is enhanced when you are given the chance to ask the coach what it is that they are seeing. You might consider asking them what clues they are looking for, where they direct their gaze, or if there are auditory or other hints that can help you observe.

Keep in mind that there are many acclaimed coaches with poor observation skills. Don't be afraid to double-check with video or to stick to your guns if you believe you are seeing something.

Have a Structure

Our goal is to be able observe automatically—to be able to rapidly perceive the necessary details without thought or hesitation, so that we can respond appropriately. You may find that you can already do this in certain situations. You may observe other coaches who, as mentioned, can seemingly see the invisible. But no matter how good you or they are, at some point or another, you'll find yourself in a situation where you just can't seem to "see it."

In these moments, it's crucial to have a structure to fall back on—an all-encompassing list that you can run through. Note my use of the word *structure*, rather than *checklist*. A structure is comprehensive—it doesn't leave room for oversight. A checklist is sometimes just what's most frequently done or observed or what's at the front of our mind.

Kovacs and Ellenbecker's 8-Stage Model of the Serve	
Phases	**Stages**
Preparation	Start
	Release
	Loading
	Cocking
Acceleration	Acceleration
	Contact
Follow-through	Deceleration
	Finish

FeelTennis 7-Step Serve Checklist
Steps
1. Stance
2. Grip
3. The hitting part
4. Backswing and toss
5. Serve in two parts
6. The power move
7. Putting it all together

Sources: Kovacs and Ellenbecker, 2011; Mencinger, n.d.

Consider the difference between the above structure (on the left) and checklist (on the right). Going through the checklist, it's easy to imagine a perfect serve: get the right stance and grip, toss the ball and take a backswing, then put it all together and hit! However, the structure by Kovacs and Ellenbecker (2011) is more comprehensive and doesn't leave room for oversight. Consider something like the loading of the legs or the landing position, neither of which appear in the checklist. The structure, however, starts with fundamental principles—preparation, acceleration, and follow-through—ensuring that nothing is missed.

Creating a structure is often a useful developmental exercise in and of itself. In making one, you may come to realize that you have certain blind spots: areas that are relevant, but which you never intentionally observe. Not only will this help your perception skills, but it may also influence the type of feedback you give—after all, you won't give feedback on something you're not seeing.

Lastly, recall that structures can be used not only for technical observations, but also for tactical, mental, and physical ones as well. For example, here is a structure I developed to help my own observation of players' tactical skills.

Tactical Skills in Tennis	
Pre-match	Can identify opponent's strengths and weaknesses (if given the chance to scout) and formulate a game plan based on the six main tactics.
During match	Can make changes to game plan based on progress of match.
	Can recognize momentum and exert influence over it.
During point	Can make appropriate decisions given the game plan and a) the athlete's position, b) the opponent's position, c) the ball they're receiving, and d) the ball they just sent.
Post-match	Can identify both key points and overall tendencies of the match.

Improving Decision-Making

Decision Mapping

One of the most useful tools at our disposal is decision mapping. A decision map helps you anticipate difficult situations and plan your response. Making one is simple:

1. Predict potential decision points—moments of a practice or a game in which you will be called upon to make a decision.
2. List the potential responses available to you.
3. List any factors that could influence your decision.
4. Evaluate your options, listing their pros and cons.
5. Make a choice as to how you will proceed.

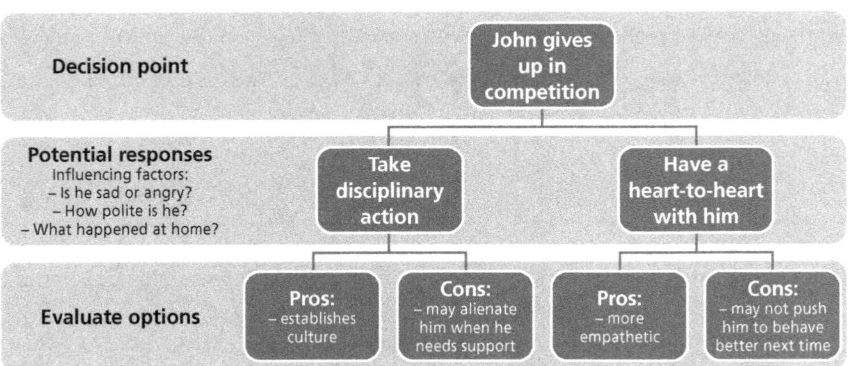

Figure 2.4. Decision map for coaching John after he shows poor effort.

This may seem like a simple planning exercise, and in a sense it is. As we all know, "failing to plan is planning to fail." How can you make confident, well-thought-out decisions if you haven't considered them fully in advance?

But what makes decision mapping especially beneficial is that it is also a practice activity designed to improve your skills. It does this in two ways. First, as you perform the exercise more and more, your ability to identify potential decision points, options, and influencing factors becomes better, allowing you to operate faster and with more precision. While you will at first make your decision map on paper, you may find over time that you can make it a mental exercise without sacrificing quality.

Second, it brings decision-making to the forefront of your mind. You may find that you don't struggle with decision-making. This could be because you are particularly good at it, but it could also be because you are always making the same decisions. For example, someone who always orders takeout from the same restaurant doesn't have to decide what to cook. Of course, having clear principles and sticking to them is important. But no two people are the same, and in the complex environment of high-performance sport, every situation is worth considering carefully. As the saying goes: "To the man with a hammer, everything's a nail." Experienced decision-makers stick to their principles, but they recognize when different situations call for different approaches. The habit of decision mapping forces you to step back and consider all the possibilities as well as your basis for making decisions. You may find that most of the time, your gut was right and the path forward was clear. But there will be moments when you realize that you've overlooked something, or that you've formed a habit that isn't productive. It's in these moments that decision mapping is beneficial. It ensures that we are acting based on well-reasoned responses to the information available.

Ghost Coaching

There is an abundance of coaching videos online. Watch one with the sound off. Observe the athlete and consider what feedback you would give or what intervention you would make. As the video progresses, notice if the athlete's performance improves. If it does, is it because they did what you would have suggested? Or did they find another solution? Based on what you observe, come up with the next task or progression you would implement.

Once done, rewatch the video with the sound on, paying attention to the coach's feedback and behavior. Did their interventions align with yours? If not, did the player respond to the coach's intervention, and did it benefit them? Having heard the coach's feedback, do you feel differently about the decisions you made earlier?

This sort of decision-making practice can be conducted in person as well. As part of my coaching, I am very often abroad at international tennis tournaments, and given the nature of the sport, I spend a lot of time hanging around the tournament site waiting for a match to start. As a result, I am often able to watch other coaches hard at work. While it's tempting to simply sit back and watch, I often push myself to engage in the exercise I just described. I watch a few repetitions and decide on an intervention I would take. I observe or listen to the coach (if they're within earshot) and watch the player to notice any changes in process or outcome. If they improve, is it because they're doing what I would have suggested? If this is so, great. But if not, I've just discovered another possible route to the solution I was aiming for. That doesn't mean that my intervention wasn't right—just that it wasn't the *only* right one. If, on the other hand, the player doesn't improve, were they attempting what I would have suggested? If they were, and it wasn't working, why not? What would I adjust?

This sort of exercise is beneficial because it is very close to real-time practice coaching, like Maggie, the reading teacher from earlier, did. Think about it: I'm watching a real player, in a real practice environment. I have to perceive and make decisions in real time, and I get feedback instantaneously. Contrast this with the other approaches many of us take to improve our skills: watching a webinar, reading a book, or listening to a podcast. These are great habits, but would we recommend them to our athletes as their primary method of development? Of course not. Ghost coaching is *practice*, and not only that, it's *open skill* practice.

Lastly, a note about coaching content on social media is warranted. Every day, more coaching content gets posted, and I think most would agree that the quality is rather hit-or-miss. It can be easy to dismiss or even critique much of what we see online, and while that approach can be harmless, I would suggest an alternative response that can improve our coaching skills. Upon encountering a coaching practice you disagree with, ask yourself the following questions:

1. Why do I think this is wrong, bad, inefficient, or ineffective?

   Be specific. What exactly don't you like about it? Why don't you like it? Do you have a good reason, or is it just personal preference? Do you have sources to back up your claims?

   As coaches, we have a duty to our athletes to adopt evidence-based practices. What if your player came to you with this video and asked you why you weren't coaching this way? Would you be able to articulate your point of view clearly? Furthermore, what if you were training a team of coaches? How would you persuade them?

2. What would I do differently?

   It's no use pointing out the flaws in something if you don't have a solution. Not only is it generally unpleasant, but it ultimately does not help you in your coaching. Ask yourself: Is it *what* the coach is doing or the *way* they're doing it that's ineffective?

3. What external factors would change my mind?

   Lastly, play devil's advocate. If you think what you're seeing is inefficient, ask yourself: In what situations *would* this be the right approach? There are a few benefits to this line of questioning. First, it builds empathy and increases your open-mindedness to new ideas. Second, it makes you a more complete coach. If your blanket response to something is, "That's not how I do things," then you close yourself off to the possibility of doing something new when the situation demands it. The curse of social media is that it removes all context; it's our job to add it back in.

Conclusion

As discussed, our priority as coaches must be to perform at our best when it counts—not at home when we are planning our sessions, but when we are face-to-face with our athletes in practice or in competition. There is no use being a perfect coach on paper if we cannot execute in the moment. That's why it's important not just to develop our skills, but also our ability to perceive and make decisions, so that we can instantly identify *how* and *when* to use our skills under pressure. This is just one more way in which coaches are athletes who must perform and practice, rather than simple sources of information.

In reading this book, you've demonstrated a clear desire to get better. And as we discussed in Chapter 1, getting better at coaching is not just about learning more, it's about improving our ability to execute in the moment. In other words, what we *do* is more important than what we *know*.

However, coaches are not street performers doing the same routine every 15 minutes and passing a hat around for tips. At least, the good coaches aren't. The good coaches know that coaching is all about adaptability. No two players are the same, no two practices are the same, and no two games are the same. Coaching is about problem-solving, and sometimes, you can't plan for whatever problems you'll encounter. However, you can prepare for them through practice.

Just like a skilled wide receiver can run, fight off the defense, and track a football before catching it in midair, the best coaches are the ones who are able to identify what is happening in front of them and quickly decide how to respond. Coaching is a dance—fall out of step with your partner, and the success of your session or game is in jeopardy.

We've all been there: We plan a practice session perfectly. We know exactly what we'll do, how long it will take, and how the athlete will respond. Until we don't. The athlete just isn't "getting it." The team's energy level is low. The players finished the drills quicker than anticipated. We stop and try to figure out what we should do, but our athletes are right in front of us, expectant. In the end, we walk off the court or field feeling like we could have done better.

Not anymore. With regular open-skill practice in perception and decision-making, we can improve our ability to handle these situations, identifying what's going on, anticipating potential problems, and adjusting instantaneously.

Hopefully it's becoming clearer: coaches are, in fact, athletes. We have to perform in the moment, under pressure. And we have to react and respond to unexpected events. But if we want to be elite—to reach the highest levels of the game and of our profession—then we'll need to do a bit more.

Chapter 3
Effective Professional Development for Coaches

At the age of 80, legendary cellist and composer Pablo Casals was asked why he still practiced four to five hours a day. He responded, "Because I think I'm making progress."

In 1997, Steve Jobs returned to Apple, then on the verge of bankruptcy, and began problem-solving, looking to right the ship by identifying issues within the company. One of those issues, he noticed, was that while Apple was working on a lot of projects, none of them were aligned, each one taking the company in a different direction. One day, he stood at a whiteboard and drew the following:

	Consumer	Professional
Desktop		
Portable		

Figure 3.1. Steve Jobs's product strategy structure.

The goal, he announced, was to deliver a world-class product in each of the four quadrants. This structure, which provided a clear vision and focus for the team, is part of the reason the iPhone, iPad, and Mac are now household names.

While they'll never do the job for you, structures such as these are critical for success in any high-performance endeavor, be it business or sport. Following Jobs's decree, anyone pitching a project at Apple would have to demonstrate where it fit into the matrix, or if there was a justification for a new category. Anyone working on an existing product would have to constantly remember where it sat within the structure as part of the larger vision. That's the beauty of organized structures: they ensure that no detail is missed while constantly keeping the bigger picture in sight. Whether it's the strategic planning of a Fortune 500 company or the player development model of a championship football club, structures are ever-present in successful organizations, and that's why we should make use of one when evaluating, planning, and implementing our own professional development as coaches. Throughout this book, I'll fall back on the structure depicted in Figure 3.2 (page 42) to guide our developmental journey. This will offer us the following benefits:

1. It will help us determine what we need to get better at.

   You don't know what you're seeing if you don't know what to look for. While an art critic and I could look at the same painting, our descriptions of it would differ greatly. We both have a set of eyes and are looking at the same painting, in the same conditions. But the art critic will have more to look for—perhaps things that I haven't even considered. Despite being presented with the same information, one of us is able to extract so much more from it due largely to the presence of a structure.

   If we can analyze our coaching through a clear and comprehensive framework, it will help us identify our weak spots and our strengths, and prevent us from relying on gut intuition, emotion, or circumstance alone.

2. It will help us become complete coaches.

   Similarly, a painter who is only taught Cubism will not be as versatile as one who is taught a multitude of styles. And a Cubist who is only familiar with Cezanian Cubism will not have as complete a structure of knowledge as one who also studies Analytical and Synthetic Cubisms. Having a complete structure helps us ensure that we have no blind spots—that we can coach any athlete in any situation.

3. It will help us discuss coaching with colleagues and mentors.

   Continuing with the example of the art world, the conversations that I and the art critic have will be severely limited by one thing: my vocabulary. I may be able to appreciate a certain technique used by the artist, but without knowing what it's called, I'll be forced to describe it in my layman's vocabulary. At best this will be slow, and at worst I'll fail to get my point across. A structure gives us the vocabulary to discuss the elements of our coaching and our coaching development with other coaches.

4. It will keep us on task.

   Lastly, putting labels on the elements of our professional development will help us see when we are on task and when we are deviating from our original goals. If I'm working simply on "people skills," then I'm at risk of drifting from topic to topic whenever I am faced with a new challenge. If, however, I identify "having a warm but demanding tone when pushing athletes' limits" as my goal, then I am more likely to stay focused and therefore achieve it.

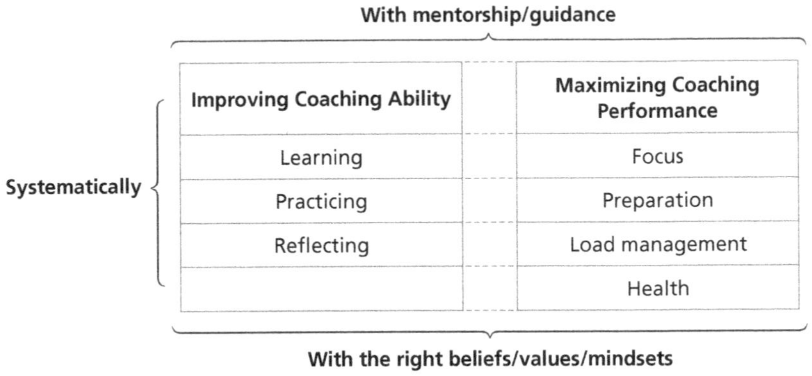

With mentorship/guidance

	Improving Coaching Ability	Maximizing Coaching Performance
Systematically	Learning	Focus
	Practicing	Preparation
	Reflecting	Load management
		Health

With the right beliefs/values/mindsets

Figure 3.2. Professional development for coaches.

This structure identifies, piece by piece, the core components of professional development for sports coaches.

Improving Coaching Ability

Working from the inside out, we'll start with the actions that are the mark of an excellent coach:

1. Learning
2. Practicing
3. Reflecting

Knowledge gathering is what we would traditionally consider "learning"—taking in new information and encoding it into long-term memory. Coaches can learn in various ways, whether through podcasts, books, blogs, articles, interviews, conferences, courses, workshops, or informal discussions. Coaches can also learn about a variety of topics, the most obvious being their sport (and the technical, tactical, physical, and psychological aspects of it). But coach education can and should go much further than this. Good coaches educate themselves not only on their sport, but also on teaching methods, educational psychology, sports psychology, coaching philosophies, leadership, and more.

The best coaches are not just students of the game, they are students of the art of coaching.

Practice is an attempt to repeatedly apply said information to a real or simulated coaching context such that it becomes effective and automatic. In the world of coaching and coach development, practice is simultaneously less common and yet possibly more important than knowledge gathering. Practice is what allows us to apply our knowledge and enact change in our athletes. As discussed in Chapter 1, coaching is a skill, and just like any other skill, coaching can be improved with practice. In Chapter 2, I gave some examples of practice to improve perception and decision-making.

Lastly, we have the hallmark of many a great coach: reflection. From Mourinho to Wooden, every great coach, at one point or another, describes a process of tinkering, adjusting, problem-solving, and reviewing. Reflection, whether it be on what has worked or what hasn't, is central to learning, and in an environment as complex as coaching it is crucial to forward progress.

Later, in Chapter 5, we'll go into more detail on how best to learn, practice, and reflect.

Systematic Development

The abovementioned behaviors may or may not strike you as new or unusual. After all, most of us are passionate about our sport and eager to learn more about it. And most of us have probably been made to practice and reflect throughout various courses, licenses, or certifications.

Where coaches can go wrong is in *how* they engage in these behaviors—for example, educating themselves haphazardly without thinking about when or why they should learn something. For maximum improvement, coaches must develop their skills in a *systematic* fashion. What does this mean? Consider the Ebbinghaus Forgetting Curve:

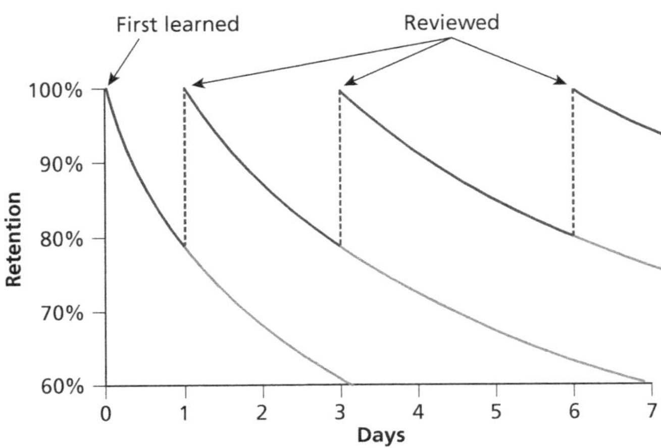

Figure 3.3. The Ebbinghaus Forgetting Curve.

The Forgetting Curve, developed by German psychologist Hermann Ebbinghaus, shows us that most information we learn is not remembered or retained in the long term (Ebbinghaus, 1913). However, our recall can be restored through regular review, each time strengthening the memory and delaying the forgetting of new learning. Anyone who has learned a language with cue cards or a mobile app has, knowingly or not, used a technique known as "spaced repetition," which aims to counteract the forgetting curve.

Learners using spaced repetition have a box of cue cards they review every day. Each wrong answer stays in the once-a-day pile. With each correct answer, the cue card is moved to the next box, which begins with a review once every three days and progresses to once every six months. When reviewing every three days, the correct answers get moved to the once-a-week box, while the wrong ones get moved back to the once-every-three-days box, and so on. Through this process, the brain is forced to recall the knowledge with decreasing frequency until it is effectively "mastered" (Smolen et al., 2016).

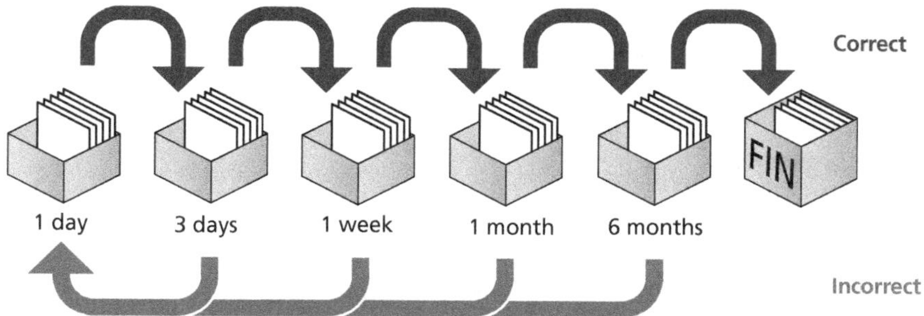

Figure 3.4. Spaced repetition.

We can also refer to "supercompensation," a key ingredient in physical training. In supercompensation, the body is subjected to a load through training, and as a result performance temporarily drops while the body is fatigued. With time and rest, however, the body recovers and becomes slightly stronger than before (overcompensating for the fatigue), and the process can be restarted (Gambetta, 2007).

However, if the rest period is too long, or the workout too easy, the gains the body makes are not retained. Conversely, if the rest period is too short, or the load too high, the body becomes increasingly fatigued and is never given the chance to compensate. When the combination of rest and load are just right, however, remarkable progress is possible.

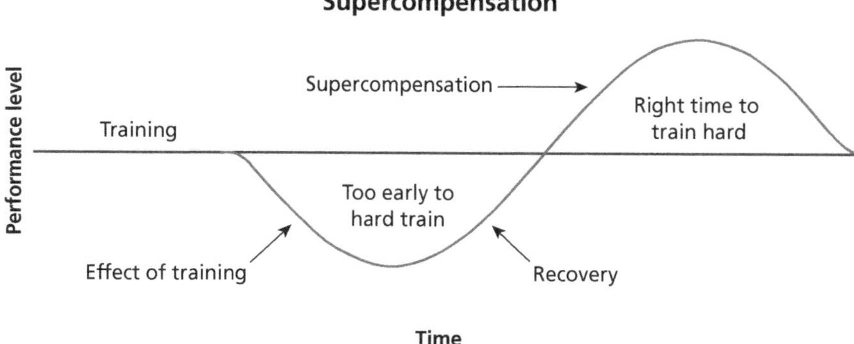

Figure 3.5. Supercompensation.

Both spaced repetition and supercompensation highlight the importance of a systematic approach to development. In the former, we see that if someone neglects to study or practice what they have recently learned, then progress is lost. In the latter, we see the importance of timing—practice must be frequent enough to make progress and infrequent enough to allow for rest and recovery. In both models, we see the value of an appropriate difficulty level—finding the ideal challenge point for optimal growth.

A systematic approach can and should be applied to the development of coaching skills. Let's imagine a fictitious coach named Adam. Adam has chosen to improve how he starts his sessions. He wants to begin with a high level of positive energy and wants to get his team working on an engaging activity right from the start.

After his first day coaching with these objectives in mind, Adam recognizes that he needs to work on some things. First, his energy was great, but his positivity was interpreted as an invitation to be social. His players started chatting with him and thus began the session late. Second, in an attempt to start the first drill quickly, he cut his instructions short, and the team ended up confused and disorganized.

At this point, Adam has a choice: between the distracted approach and the focused approach. The distracted approach is what happens to most of us. Adam reflects on the weak points of the session and identifies some ways to address them. But on the second day of coaching, he has a meeting with a parent and forgets to plan the starting activity. On day 3, he reads a blog post about the latest research on physical warm-ups and ends up focusing on that, rather than the start of the practice. By day 4, he still remembers his objectives but has forgotten the exact details of what happened on the first day and is forced to start from square one.

This can happen to all of us. We are eager to improve and get results. On top of that, we operate in an environment that is unpredictable and constantly changing, requiring us to shift our focus and priorities from day to day. However, the distracted approach will not lead to sustained coaching improvements, for the reasons outlined above. As the saying goes, "He who chases two rabbits ends up catching none." That's why we have the focused approach.

In the focused approach, Adam reflects after day 1 and writes down one or two actions he'll take the next day. He plans the day ahead of him and, recognizing the parent meeting, sets time aside in the morning to plan his session as well as the meeting. That way, he's able to implement the action points from the previous day. He reflects on how it went and writes down his new action items and makes a plan for day 3. On day 3, he reads the blog post about physical warm-ups but files it away for next week, focusing instead on his existing goals. By day 4, he's made a lot of progress. He's finding the balance between positive and casual communication and figuring out which types of activities work best to start the practice. With another week or two of practice, these skills will have become automatic, and he can begin to focus on other areas of improvement.

At this point, it's important to mention that not all work is the same. In fact, some things are *not* "better than nothing." Doing five push-ups once a week will not make you fitter. It's simply too low of a load and too low of a frequency.[5] Some processes are not simple, linear functions, where what you put in is what you get out. Some things, like learning or getting fitter, depend on timing, volume, and intensity—not just for maximum gain, but for *any* gain.

What does this mean? It means that reading the odd blog post, watching the occasional documentary, or listening to the hottest new podcast will not by themselves make you a better coach. At least, none of these will improve your coaching *skill*. You may learn something that you didn't know before, and that knowledge may help you in your job. But as discussed in Chapter 1, coaching is about so much more than knowledge. Skill is what counts, and skill cannot be developed without a systematic approach. In other words, when working on our coaching, we need to consider:

a) what we're working on
b) how we're working on it
c) when we're working on it.

We'll discuss this in more detail in Chapter 5.

5 You could argue that it will encourage you to lead a healthier lifestyle, to identify as someone who works out, to "get the ball rolling." But in terms of directly contributing to a physiological change, it will have no effect.

ACTIVITY: Check the box next to each statement that applies to you:

- ○ I sometimes get distracted from my goals, focusing on too many different things at once (trying to catch two rabbits).
- ○ I sometimes forget to work on my goals and lose the progress I've made.
- ○ I sometimes burn myself out.
- ○ I sometimes get the balance just right and see improvements in my coaching.

Observing and Decision-Making

As I alluded to in Chapter 1, our coaching level is not just about what we *can* do, it's about what we *do* do. It is a reflection of how good we are at bringing our best selves to the court, track, field, or gym, day in and day out. The sports history books are full of talented athletes who ran circles around their teammates in practices but underperformed on game day—or, conversely, players who weren't no. 1 on the team, but gave a solid performance every game, rain or shine. Your level as a performer is not just about what you are capable of; it's also about what you can be counted on to deliver.

One of the attributes athletes look for in a coach is emotional constancy. No one wants a coach who is cheerful one day and angry the next. Athletes want predictable responses. That's not to say that coaches must be robots, just that they should be consistent with their past self, so that athletes know what to expect—what rules to play by. It sounds simple, but with the personal and professional stresses many of us face, it's not easy. A long day or a stressful game can easily lead to an emotional reaction or an unenthusiastic response. Managing our emotions is just as important as teaching a forehand or planning a full-court press.

Emotional constancy isn't the only way in which we must perform, however. Of equal importance is our mental acuity. In an hour of practice, how many actions are you observing? You're observing the simple stuff, of course, such as passes, goals, shot attempts, etc. Then, you're observing a few layers deeper: movement patterns, team communication, body language. Then, even deeper: shin angle, stride timing, and so on. In one hour, I'd suggest you observe at least one thousand actions, if not more. That's not to say that you have to act on all of them, or even remember them all. Some of them will not be particularly unusual or exceptional, and you'll discard them. But some will be memorable or noteworthy and require a response. In an hour, how many decisions do you have to make? Important examples include whether to respond calmly or intensely, whether to give more rest time or less, or whether to give feedback or let your players figure it out. Like observations, you make hundreds if not thousands of small decisions every hour.

How many observations or decisions do you allow yourself to miss or get wrong? How many would you want your athletes to miss? To be the best coaches we can be, we need to strive for perfection, even if it's not attainable. Any piece of information I miss because I'm distracted, tired, or frustrated might be crucial. Any incorrect decision *could* affect the way my player progresses.

Emotional and mental consistency are invaluable to us as coaches. And yet, our environment is seemingly set up to impede our performance.

In 2008, a team of researchers manipulated the order of choices that customers were given when buying a new car from a dealership (Levav et al., 2008). Some clients were first presented with the decisions with the most options. In other words, they started their experience by picking out the precise interior from a palette of 56 colors, or the exact engine configuration from one of 25 options. Other clients began with simpler decisions that gradually became more complex.

What the researchers found was that by manipulating the order of the decisions, they could get customers to spend up to $2,000 more on their cars. Buyers whose encounter started with more difficult decisions gradually grew tired of having to consider the various options and eventually settled for the default. This is known as "decision fatigue," the idea that the more decisions you make throughout the day, the worse your decision-making ability becomes. You get tired, and it becomes increasingly tempting to stick with the status quo.

In some cases, this can have alarming effects. A well-publicized study of prisoners coming up for parole found that inmates who had their cases heard right before lunch, when the board was tired after a morning of adjudication, were far less likely to be granted parole than those who had their cases heard right after lunch, when the board was refreshed (Danziger et al., 2011).[6] While our decision fatigue will not affect anyone's freedom, it could affect the quality of our coaching. Each session and each drill involves decisions that must be made and things that must be focused on. Leaders like Mark Zuckerberg and Steve Jobs have been known to wear the same outfit every day as a way of eliminating the need to make decisions. For coaches, there are things we can do to reduce our decision fatigue, things like planning and rehearsing.

It shouldn't surprise you to learn that, just like decision-making, focusing ability can vary considerably depending on the circumstances. Studies have repeatedly shown the impact of nutrition, sleep, stress, and lifestyle on concentration (Gibson and Green, 2002; Killgore, 2010; Pérez-Olmos and Ibáñez-Pinilla, 2014).

We don't expect our athletes to be perfect, and we shouldn't expect ourselves to be either. But we do ask our athletes to bring their maximum effort and focus when it's time, and we should be doing the same. The list of factors influencing our performance is long, from work-life balance to team selection decisions. Some we have control over, some we don't. In all cases, however, we can develop techniques and strategies to remain fully present in the moment and give our best to our athletes. We'll discuss coaching performance in more detail in Chapter 6.

ACTIVITY: How often would you say you are performing at your best when coaching? Draw a point on the scale.

Never 50% of the time Always

---

6 In some cases, the chance of being granted parole varied by as much as 60 percentage points. However, critics of the study have suggested that the effect may be due to scheduling. Judges may schedule cases that they know to be "simpler" before a break, while scheduling more complicated cases earlier in the session, when they have time. (Weinshall-Margel et al., 2011)

Beliefs, Values, and Mindsets

At the bottom of our structure, supporting everything we do, are our beliefs, values, and mindsets. The definitions of these terms can vary greatly from context to context, so for clarity's sake, we will use the following definitions throughout this book.

Belief: an idea accepted as true without rigorous evidence

Beliefs, which are often formed through lived experience or from influential figures or societal norms, are always affecting the way we act, in ways both large and small. Consider the following examples of beliefs and the influence they might have:

Belief: "Kids these days don't know how to work hard."

Influence: A coach with this belief, when faced with an athlete who seemingly quits or gives up, may assume it's because all kids these days are like that, as opposed to inquiring whether or not there are other factors at play.

Belief: "Our team is clutch."

Influence: A coach with this belief may feel relaxed in pressure situations, may demonstrate confidence to their athletes, and may approach tense moments with enthusiasm.

Belief: "Sport teaches life lessons."

Influence: A coach with this belief may spend more time getting to know their athletes as people rather than focusing only on their relationship to the sport. A coach with this belief may also spend more time addressing topics outside of sport.

From these examples, you can see that a coach's beliefs will inevitably influence the way they coach, whether it is in big or small ways. That's not to say that any particular beliefs are inherently helpful or harmful, just that we must recognize our core beliefs and work to benefit from them while minimizing harmful effects.

Value: a principle considered to be of great importance

Values are principles, usually single words, which we hold in great stead and therefore prioritize, whether in our personal or professional lives.

Where beliefs are more overarching, values can be context specific. Rather than dictate what we do or don't do, they often determine the extent to which we do the things we do. Again, consider some examples, like effort, respect, or loyalty. Few coaches would claim that effort, respect, or loyalty are unimportant. But a coach who *values* effort will prioritize it in their work—whether in the feedback they give, the drills they plan, or the athletes they recruit. A coach who values respect may give precedence to athletes supporting each other and being good teammates, whereas a coach who values competitiveness may allow trash-talking during scrimmages. That's not to say that a coach can't value both, just to show that our values influence how we evaluate things. Values are what allow us to determine what is good and what is bad.

Whereas beliefs often shape what we do, values often determine where we put our emphasis.

> *Mindset: a collection of beliefs, values, and other constructs that leads to specific behaviors*

Lastly, a mindset is comprised of values and beliefs and it informs someone's thinking and behavior. The most well-known examples are the fixed and growth mindsets, summarized in Table 3.1.

Table 3.1. Fixed vs. growth mindset

	Growth Mindset	Fixed Mindset
Beliefs	Intelligence/skill can be developed. Feedback is a learning opportunity. Challenges help me grow.	Intelligence/skill is static and unchangeable. Feedback is criticism. When others succeed, I fail. If I have to work hard, it means I'm not good.
Values	Effort, Adversity, Learning, Feedback	Intelligence, Skill, Winning, Praise

However, there are many other mindsets, such as the following:

- Victim mindset
- Positive mindset
- Negative mindset

- Abundance mindset
- Scarcity mindset

As mindsets are comprised of beliefs and values, they can also influence our behavior. Take, for example, the abundance mindset. People with an abundance mindset believe that there is enough out there for everyone—that the universe contains enough time and resources for all. A scarcity mindset, on the other hand, holds that resources are limited. When someone else gets something, that means there's less out there in the world for them.

A coach with a scarcity mindset, upon seeing a good result from a competing coach's team, might feel frustrated—if another team is winning, that means that my team is losing. A coach with an abundance mindset, on the other hand, might see this as a positive—a competing team doing better gives us a greater challenge and a chance to get better. Plus, it might give me something to learn, not to mention that the other team winning doesn't actually hurt us unless we're playing against them.

Our beliefs, values, and mindsets can propel us to new heights, boosting our confidence, strengthening our relationships, and fueling our passion; or they can hold us back, fostering doubt, weakening trust, and putting us down. Great coaches have certain beliefs, values, and mindsets in common, and I'll discuss those as well as ways to develop them in yourself in Chapter 4.

Guidance and Mentorship

Several years ago, I took up golf. Since the mechanics are not too dissimilar from tennis, I was able to reach a respectable level within a year or so. When the Covid-19 pandemic arrived and opportunities for athletic pursuits dwindled, my friend Andrew decided that he too would begin golfing. In his youth he was a decent tennis and basketball player, but he never got past a regional level and still plays with stiff, slightly unconventional strokes. I was excited to have a friend to golf with but didn't think he would be particularly well-suited to a game of grace and fluidity.

That being said, those of us who have golfed know that experience does not always equate to skill. Courses around the world are littered with veterans of the game with faulty swings, unpredictable chips, and irregular putting strokes. This was what I expected from Andrew: that he would find a swing that worked for him, arhythmic and uncoordinated as it might be, and stick with it.

But Andrew didn't just hit buckets at the range, like I did. He found a qualified pro, took lessons, wrote down key points on his phone, and dedicated time to practice in between sessions. Within 6 months, he was beating me consistently. Rather than do what so many do (rely on tips from friends or YouTube videos) or what I had done (practice without instruction), he had engaged a coach, someone who knew how to help him get better, and he was rewarded for it.

Presumably, if you are reading this, then you believe in the value a coach can bring to a player's development. But coaches aren't just for athletes.

In 2011, surgeon Atul Gawande felt that he needed to change something. He had been operating for eight years, and for the first few he had gotten better and better, as measured by his rates of complications. As he explained in a *New Yorker* article (Gawande, 2011), every operation comes with its own set of judgments and decisions. In the case of an appendectomy, for example, the surgeon will have to choose the method (whether to make a small incision and insert a laparoscope, or to make a larger one and proceed by hand), the tools (whether to use a hook, a pair of scissors, or a dissector), and any other significant details, such as the height and orientation of the operating table. If all goes well, the appendix is extracted, and the patient is sewn back up. But there can be complications: an infection, a loss of blood, a wrong diagnosis. Being able to handle these complications as efficiently and effectively as possible is the mark of a good surgeon.

Over the years, Gawande had been comparing his results to the national norms. For the first 5 years or so, his rates of complications had declined, until he was beating the average. But sometime around 2009, he began to plateau, and in 2011, worried that his results would falter, he called up the surgeon he trained under during his residency, Robert Osteen, to see if he'd be willing to help.

Osteen agreed that he would observe Gawande at work and provide feedback. The first operation he watched was one that Gawande had done a thousand times—as he writes, "more times than I've been to the movies." It went well, flowing smoothly and ending without problems. To quote Gawande, "I wondered whether he would find anything useful to tell me."

To his surprise, Osteen had a whole list of observations, things that were small but which, over the course of hundreds of operations, would be key to eliminating problems. He noticed that Gawande had positioned the patient perfectly for himself, but in such a way that his assistant's reach was limited, restricting his ability to help. He also noticed that Gawande was at times raising his elbows above his shoulders, instead of adjusting his position or choosing a different instrument, which ultimately reduced his precision. Says Gawande, "that one twenty-minute discussion gave me more to consider and work on than I'd had in the past five years."

Their coaching relationship continued, with Gawande taking in the feedback, practicing for a few weeks, and then meeting with Osteen once again. Sometimes, they went so far as to analyze video footage of his own or others' surgeries.

The result? Gawande's complication rates decreased. His operations became more efficient, he gained clarity on what to work on, and his patients had improved outcomes.

While a doctor with a coach may sound unusual, in the world of business, coaching is no novelty. There are executive coaches, leadership coaches, sales coaches, and life coaches. Most famous of all, perhaps, is Bill Campbell, dubbed the "trillion-dollar coach" for the value he added to the companies he helped. Campbell, former head football coach at Columbia, was a business executive who mentored, among others, Steve Jobs, Jeff Bezos, Larry Page, Sergey Brin, and Sheryl Sandberg. On paper, he was a board member and CEO. But off the books, he was a coach, helping leaders manage their teams and clarify their vision. At Google, he mentored then-CEO Eric Schmidt, sitting in on meetings and observing and providing insight. At Apple, he spent every Sunday walking and talking with Steve Jobs. At both companies, those in the know are effusive in their praise. Tim Cook, describing Campbell's impact upon his retirement, said that "He not only helped Apple survive, but he's led us to a level of success that was simply unimaginable back in 1997" (Apple, 2014). Members of the leadership team he helped mentor at Google have since stated that "without him, the company would not be where it is today" (Schmidt et al., 2019). All of this is in spite of the fact that he never took on a leadership position at the tech giant, nor was he compensated for his help. He was, in almost every case, an outsider, brought in to advise and support on an individual level. In other words, he was a coach.

While this is not well known, numerous sports coaches have also benefited from a mentor. Consider Pep Guardiola, one of the greatest football managers of all time, whose resume includes the treble and two Champions League trophies with FC Barcelona, three consecutive Bundesliga titles with Bayern Munich, and another Champions League title as well as multiple Premier League Championships with Manchester City. This is a remarkable list of accomplishments for a revered coach. But hidden behind the scenes, supporting Guardiola throughout his career, has been one man: Manel Estiarte.

They met on a soccer field, but Estiarte is not a soccer player—rather, he is a water poloist and is considered to be one of the greatest of all time. He has taken part in six Olympic Games, winning gold in 1996, and was also on the World Championship–winning team in 1998.

In 1991, the day Guardiola won La Liga as a player with FC Barcelona, Estiarte, an avid Barcelona fan, ran down onto the field to congratulate him. Over time, they became good friends, bonding over their shared athletic ambitions. In 2008, when Guardiola was appointed manager of the FC Barcelona senior squad, he felt that he was up against a new challenge, one that would require some help. He called his friend and asked him to be his assistant. Ever since then, Estiarte has been at his side, following him from Barcelona to Bayern Munich and now to Manchester City, where he is officially the Head of Player Support and Protocol.

But what can a former water poloist contribute to a soccer team in the strongest league in the world? In the book *Pep Confidential*, by Martí Perarnau, Guardiola himself has this to say about his trusted confidant:

> *Manel has an unerring instinct. He knows immediately if things are going well or not. He is quick to sense the slightest change in atmosphere and can tell me with absolute certainty whether or not the players are behind us. If there's a leak, he'll know about it.*
>
> *After five years working together he has learned to filter what he shares with me and I leave it to him to decide. I regularly say to him, "Manel, what's your take on this?" and can always rely on getting an honest, intelligent response. He interprets body language brilliantly, too, and knows exactly what a particular look or gesture means.*
>
> *The true greats all share this quality, this intuition. Other sportsmen do things mechanically, but to be truly great you need this extra ability. And Manel has it in spades. That's why I need him here working with me—all of that and the fact that we're good friends as well.* (Perarnau, 2014, p. 20)

When asked in an interview about managing egos at Bayern Munich, Guardiola said this:

> *Manel has helped me to understand that when I was going to make decisions about players of a very high level ... he would say to me "No, stop, not like that." Like in life, there are things that you have to treat differently, and he, with that, has helped me a lot. So much.* (Lee, 2016)

I've shared three stories of professionals from different fields who sought out mentorship and ultimately benefited from it. Despite each of them getting something different from their mentor, they all improved at their job. Atul Gawande was able to take advantage of a second set of eyes and instruction on how to get better, which resulted in fewer complications from surgeries. The Silicon Valley executives describe how Bill Campbell instilled courage, developed relationship skills, and fostered growth, leading to increased shareholder value. As for Pep

Guardiola, not only does he benefit from Estiarte's perspective and skill, but he is also supported emotionally. As he explained, "Managers are very, very alone. Very alone. It's very good for me to have him there. ... When I'm going through a difficult period, maybe even struggling with self-doubt, he is there for me" (Perarnau, 2014, p. 19).

Note that, in all three cases, the mentees went on to have extremely successful careers—far more successful than before their mentorship. Alongside his surgical practice, Gawande is now a professor at Harvard, an executive director and chairman at various think tanks and non-profits, and a government advisor. Schmidt, mentored by Campbell just after taking on the role of Google CEO, went on to lead the company through its initial public offering and subsequent 25-fold increase in market capitalization, making it the fourth-largest company on the planet and him a multibillionaire. And Guardiola, as mentioned, has gone on to set countless records, earning himself a spot on the list of the greatest football managers of all time.

These stories highlight the different roles a mentor can have: that of a teacher, who guides your development and helps you improve; that of an advisor, who helps you see things you might be missing; and that of a confidant, someone who you can rely on for support. But beyond the different roles of a mentor, we also see different levels of involvement. In a study of elite international coaches, researchers found that said coaches placed tremendous importance on mentorship, but wrote that "sometimes, this mentor was just someone they admired and tried to emulate, but no direct contact was necessary other than observation and writings of these 'mentor' coaches" (Mallett et al., 2016, p. 310). This is one end of the spectrum—a mentor with whom there is no direct contact. But on the other end, we have Guardiola and Estiarte, who maintain daily contact. In the middle, we have Gawande, who met with his mentor roughly once a month.

Mentors and mentees can also hold different degrees of decision-making authority. In some cases, a coach might work for their mentor (e.g. as an assistant coach), in which case they are not the final authority on important decisions. In other cases, however, a mentor might only advise, while the mentee coach makes their own final decisions. There is no one-size-fits-all formula.

Despite the significant and measurable benefits of mentorship and coaching for nearly all professionals, it is not a widespread practice. Why is this?

For one, it can be uncomfortable, even embarrassing, to have someone watch you work and point out your weaknesses. The best athletes in the world often have coaches for their entire career, but in our profession, the common view on development is black and white: you go through your training, and then you are done. You get your licenses, certificates, or qualifications, and then you are considered an expert, ready to coach and "gain experience." To submit yourself to judgment, evaluation, and instruction can seem infantilizing, an admission that you're not good enough.

This feeling—that if I seek out feedback, it means that I'm not qualified—often stops us from reaching out to colleagues or mentors. But even those of us who are open and vulnerable enough to be critiqued might worry about what our peers or even our players will think. Will our colleagues think less of us? Will our athletes assume that we aren't as good as the other coaches, those who don't "need" a mentor? The culture of performance coaching has not yet embraced mentorship, and the societal hurdles can be difficult to overcome. We'll discuss how to surmount these barriers in Chapter 7.

For those of us willing to bite the bullet, there is one final challenge: finding a mentor. Not only do they have to be qualified and accomplished, but they also need to have an awareness of *why* they are successful, so that they can help us. Furthermore, they have to understand what mentorship is, and then be willing (and have the time) to engage in it. Not many people fit that bill.

The difficulties are not trivial. But the fact remains: professional coaching works. Randomized controlled trials show that teachers who receive individualized coaching perform better, and their students get better grades (Kraft and Blazar, 2018). Coaches with mentors develop their skills, advance in their careers, and improve their players faster. When he was announced as the new head coach of Team USA, Steve Kerr had this to say about Gregg Popovich, his predecessor:

> *Pop has been my mentor for many years. Having played for him for four seasons, picked his brain over the last seven or eight years, the opportunity to work with him. I've learned so much not just about the game but about people, about culture. So a lot of what we do here in Golden State is based on what I learned from Pop. (Salao, 2021)*

In fact, finding mentorship and guidance at the right times might just be one of the most important things you can do for your coaching. Given that our profession involves dispensing advice and developing people's skills, to not seek out advice and guidance would be nonsensical. In Chapter 7, we'll discuss some best practices, including how to find a mentor and how to make the most of their time.

Part 2
Maximizing Our Own Development

In the last three chapters, I've made the case for seeing the coach as an athlete. Coaches are open-skill performers with a duty to develop not just their knowledge but also their abilities, and to bring the best of themselves to their coaching as often as possible in order to help their athletes.

In Part 2, we'll look at exactly *how* you can do that, the techniques and strategies that you can use to become an encyclopedia of your sport, an expert practitioner on the field, and a reliable performer in the moment. We'll start with Chapter 4, which lays the foundation for all your professional development, exploring the key beliefs, values, mindsets, and traits of coaches who reach their full potential. Developing these qualities will increase the effectiveness of everything else you do, including what is detailed in the chapters that follow.

Chapter 5 discusses how to improve the specific coaching skills you've selected, namely through deliberate learning, practice, and reflection. In applying this work, along with the psychological support of the qualities in Chapter 4, you can work toward a specific goal and see visible improvements in your day-to-day coaching as well as in your athletes' performance.

Once you understand how best to develop your coaching abilities, you can begin to think about how to perform at your best—how to get the most out of yourself, physically and mentally, in the short and long term. Chapter 6 introduces such notions as a coach's PPS along with strategies for how to achieve it, such as mindfulness training, visualization, and preparation, among others.

Finally, Chapter 7 addresses the topic of mentorship—the why, how, and what of a well-known but underutilized practice. In it, you'll learn how valuable it can be for performers like us, how to select and find a mentor, and how to get the most out of the experience.

As with Part 1, Part 2 is sprinkled with various brief learning activities. I *strongly* recommend completing them as you go, rather than skipping over them to return to later. You can write directly in the book—this isn't Hemingway—or make your own notes if you so choose. Either way, reading the book without doing the activities is a bit like going to soccer practice but never kicking a ball. Above all, make sure that as you read, you are reflecting on your own coaching and how you can apply what you're learning.

Ready? Let's go.

Chapter 4
Values, Beliefs, Mindsets, and Traits of Successful Coaches

Across the globe, locker room walls are plastered with inspirational quotes about the importance of attitude and mindset. In press conferences, athletes regularly make statements about their unwavering confidence and perseverant efforts. Time after time, we are reminded, at least by the media, of the role that one's mentality can play in success.

The reason these statements persist is because they are, by and large, true. A positive attitude will, generally speaking, allow you to overcome difficult periods that might stop someone else in their tracks. A strong work ethic will, on the whole, allow you to accomplish more in the same amount of time. In short, having the right attitude can help you overcome adversity and achieve more.

There is, however, more to the story. Our attitude doesn't just affect our longevity, our staying power. It also affects the way we behave, the way we interpret what happens to us, and the way we go about our day-to-day activities. There is perhaps no better example of this than what is often referred to as the Dartmouth Scar Experiment.

In 1980, researchers at Dartmouth University told 24 female undergraduate students that they were going to be looking at the effects of facial scarring on interactions with others (Kleck and Strenta, 1980). Using makeup, they placed realistic-looking scars on each of the participants' faces. However, just before the students left the room to meet the person they would be speaking with, the makeup artists, under the guise of "touching up" the scar, discreetly removed it, unbeknownst to the students. Despite now having a completely normal facial appearance, participants reported that those they interacted with stared at their scar or even made veiled offensive remarks about it. In the years since, similar studies have confirmed something that is now well understood: when we are primed to look for something, we will see it—even if it's not there.

Consider how this might manifest itself in a coach. If I believe, for example, that a certain team plays "dirty," then any act that is even somewhat ambiguous will likely appear unethical to me. If I believe that players with a certain style or technique have better potential, then I will likely look for evidence to that effect, while ignoring evidence to the contrary. Not only are these mental approaches unfair to those I am judging, but they also run the risk of hampering my coaching.

In the last two decades, more and more research has been conducted on the psychological traits and competencies underlying elite coaching. Some of those findings are included in Part 3, where I cover the fundamental skills of coaching. However, it's worth keeping in mind that the skills required to *perform* at a certain level (e.g. at the Olympic Games) are not always the same as those required to *reach* that level. In other words, while Part 3 covers where we want to go, Part 2 deals with how to get there, and this chapter is about the psychological base that will allow us to grow.

Based not only on research but also extensive observation and analysis of coach biographies, press conferences, and other literature, this chapter will present the key values, beliefs, mindsets, and traits of what I'll call *high-developing* coaches—that is to say, coaches who are continually improving and reaching new heights.

Values

Put simply, values are the things we prioritize over other factors. As such, they influence how *much* we engage in certain activities as well as *how* we engage in them. Across multiple decades and sports, the best coaches have consistently placed three values at the top of their list: high moral standards, hard work, and constant improvement.

High Moral Standards

Contrary to expectations, one of the notable findings from the myriad studies on Olympic medal–winning coaching is that the coaches studied were *not* win-at-all-costs coaches. In fact, they were almost always very clear about the importance of ethical leadership, and if they didn't state that themselves, their athletes did. These coaches made it clear that they believed they were role models and that it was their responsibility to cultivate ethical behaviors through their own actions and image. This value system manifests itself in a number of ways. For one, coaches with high moral standards make every effort to treat each member of their team fairly (though not necessarily equally) and communicate their rationale when having to make tough decisions. While they recognize that it's impossible to please everyone, they do their best to make sure that if they won't always be right, they can at least always be fair.

Paul Parker, who played under the legendary Manchester United manager Sir Alex Ferguson, recalls being told by his boss that the up-and-coming young players would soon be taking his place on the team:

> *Does it hurt? One hundred per cent. Do you form a hate against the manager because of it? I would be lying if I said it didn't, because you take it personally, you feel embarrassed; you turn up on a Saturday and feel like a spare leg, even if the team is winning and doing well. But Sir Alex told me the truth, and it depends how you accept it.*
>
> *I don't hold it against him, because I look at the decisions he made and he didn't make too many wrong. (Crafton, 2021)*

The importance of high moral standards is also evidenced by coaches' treatment of their staff and colleagues. They show them respect, trust, and kindness. Pat Summitt, one of the all-time greatest basketball coaches, was known for regularly involving her assistant coaches in pre- and post-game talks. John Wooden regularly sent congratulatory letters to other coaches after a big win.

Furthermore, while elite coaches recognize their passion and drive to succeed, they understand that it mustn't come at the expense of other people; they wouldn't take advantage of others in order to make it to the top. An analysis of NFL head coach press conferences by IBM's Watson supercomputer found that dutifulness (their definition of the term is "the extent to which a person takes rules and obligations seriously, even when they are inconvenient") and uncompromising ("the extent to which a person thinks it is wrong to take advantage of others to get ahead") were the third and eighth most common traits, respectively, of the coaches with the highest win percentages (Online Casino Canada, n.d.).

This value is perhaps best represented by the story of Clarence Walker, a Black second-string guard who played for Indiana State in the 1946-1947 season, when John Wooden was head coach. In the post-season, the team was invited to the National Association of Intercollegiate Basketball playoffs, with one caveat: Walker would not be allowed to participate. For that reason, Wooden declined the invitation. The next year, Walker was allowed to participate, but that didn't stop him and the team from running into trouble. At a Missouri restaurant on the way to Kansas City, Wooden was told, after the team had ordered, that Walker wouldn't be allowed to eat.

> *Wooden replied that if Walker couldn't eat there, none of them would. "You can't leave," the woman protested. "You already ordered."*
>
> *"Watch us," Wooden said. And they left. (Davis, 2014, p. 94)*

There were similar experiences throughout Walker's athletic career. While Walker admitted in his journal that he was, at times, disappointed in Wooden's reluctance to speak out publicly against the segregation of the time, Walker liked him deeply and respected Wooden for the way he treated him.

High moral standards can also be seen in coaches' interactions with fans and members of the public. In 1980, 25-year-old Steve Mitchell, born with Down syndrome, badly wanted a ticket to watch the Duke men's basketball team, the Blue Devils. His brother, a tradesman, happened to be working on Coach Mike Krzyzewski's house and mentioned his wish. Krzyzewski graciously arranged a ticket, right behind the bench. What started as a favor became a tradition, continuing for 37 years until Mitchell's death in 2017. Before every home game, Krzyzewski would turn to the seats behind the bench and shake Mitchell's hand and then the two of them would watch the Blue Devils running up and down the court, swearing and shouting with every turnover.

All in all, the best coaches value high moral standards. They believe that they are role models, and that they must carefully consider their actions and the way they treat their players, their opponents, and everyone else around them.

Hard Work

It should come as no surprise that coaches who make it to the top, place particular emphasis on the importance of hard work. Excellent coaches recognize that, as the adage goes, you must do the *extra* to achieve the extraordinary. In interviews, high-performance coaching is described as an all-in commitment, wherein coaches must work long hours behind the scenes to fuel their athletes' success. As one coach put it, "Commitment to athletes must be total. We ask them to take risks and to commit themselves wholeheartedly—and it's important for coaches to be made from the same stuff" (Mallett and Lara-Bercial, 2023, p. 109).

This commitment to hard work can take many forms. In some cases, it manifests as long hours on the job, working early in the morning and late at night, and coming in on weekends and days off. In other cases, it means doing work behind the scenes planning, analyzing, and watching video. For some, hard work may refer to the extensive amount of travel or the high level of pressure imposed by the media or by governing bodies. For others, hard work may simply mean having difficult conversations with athletes and parents.

No matter your role, to be a successful high-performance coach is to value hard work. This is especially important in the earlier stages of your career when you are constantly developing. In the words of one Olympic coach:

> *I know when I was younger, I had no issues with working on Saturdays and Sundays, I had no issues with working in the evenings, I had no issues with waking up early in the morning, I had no issues with setting aside a lot of other*

> *things in my life to further my coaching. (Mallett and Lara-Bercial, 2023, p. 108)*

Of course, the hard work doesn't necessarily stop once you get to a certain level. One of Sir Alex Ferguson's former midfielders, Nicky Butt, reports that "he used to tell a story about the head of one of the biggest companies in the world, a billionaire, he came in every day at 7am and was the last to leave. So he had that work ethic ingrained in him and he wouldn't accept anything less from his players" (Crafton, 2021).

At the same time, this wasn't just a standard for his athletes, but one standard that he lived and breathed himself. A 2021 profile of Alex Ferguson in *The Athletic* took a deep look at what made him successful, noting that "while [he] raged, his deployment of fury was strategic and fascinating to those watching on. He raised his own standards; increasing training, intensifying video analysis and applying all the same exacting standards to himself that he requested of others" (Crafton, 2021).

Constant Improvement

Finally, it should come as no surprise that every study of the best coaches in the world has found that they are, without exception, hungry to learn. In the words of Wooden, "Once I am through learning, I am through." This value—constant learning and improvement—manifests itself in three ways:

One study, by Werthner and Trudel (2009), described this phenomenon as "Always Thinking About." In other words, these coaches were constantly thinking about their sport and their coaching, wondering what they could be doing differently or better. This is reminiscent of Andy Reid's copious note-taking, John Wooden's cue cards, or Sean McVay's hours of practice review. On a similar note, research by Lara-Bercial and Mallett (2016) found that elite coaches were also obsessive *consumers* of their sport, watching it as much as possible in an attempt to learn just a little bit more.

The second aspect of this trait is what Din et al. (2015) called "analytic tenacity"—the rigorous and never-ending process of assessment, brainstorming, implementation, and review. This isn't just about learning about the sport, it is about tinkering with their process, maximizing every aspect of their coaching machine. The coaches in the Din et al. study were obsessed with finding the next edge, the 1% improvement that could help bring about stronger results:

> *I was always looking for that one and two percent in everything, all the time. ... It's there, you need to find it and never be complacent—never stop looking. (Olympic Coach)*
>
> *We were always brainstorming, trying to make ourselves better, trying to improve. ... If something wasn't going well Coach would ask us about it, what was happening, where we were going, it was a constant chatter. ... I think that was our greatest strength. (Olympic Athlete, Din, 2015, p. 599)*

The third piece of hunger for learning comprises a desire to learn from all possible sources. Across numerous studies, coaches at the highest levels of their sport have stated their openness to new ideas and their pursuit of multiple avenues of learning. In some cases, these insights came from other sports or even other industries. For example, Sir Dave Brailsford, a legendary British cycling coach, brought in psychiatrists and aerodynamics experts, while Sir Alex Ferguson recruited a vision scientist to improve his players' peripheral vision. In other cases, coaches learn from within their sport, again from a variety of sources: colleagues, mentors, books, videos, courses, and so on.

These coaches take their own development seriously. Consider Freddie Ljungberg, who transitioned from player to coach and eventually became interim head coach of Arsenal FC. At one point in his journey, he gave media interviews even though he wasn't required to, as he thought it was valuable for his development. Later on, he decided that he would learn Spanish in order to better communicate with the other coaches and athletes. In his words, "There are always challenges. I think the biggest challenge for me is to continue to learn" (McNicholas et al., 2019).

Beliefs

Beliefs are statements about how the world works that we hold to be true. Just as my belief in gravity fosters the confidence with which I walk down the hall, believing that most people have good intentions might foster grace and forgiveness. For coaches, three beliefs are essential to their success, and all three are related to the nature of our job.

We Have a Duty to Be Athlete-Centered

The first belief that is consistently found among elite coaches is that *we have a duty to be athlete-centered.* This means, first of all, that we must put our athletes' needs above our own and focus on the person before the athlete. There are times when a coach's needs and an athlete's needs might not match up completely—for example, when a coach might be trying to protect his or her job or, conversely, be tempted to self-promote, motivated by ego. In these instances, the best coaches take the high road and recognize that their athletes' interests are more important than their own. Furthermore, world-class coaches consistently stress that long-term success comes from consistently acting in line with what's best for the athlete as a *person*, not just a competitor.

For coaches who are transitioning from their playing career, this can be a challenge. As an athlete, it's important to look out for yourself and maximize your own performance. As a coach, your focus has to shift to those around you. In the words of Freddie Ljungberg:

> *I think as a player it's more of a dog-eat-dog world, just very competitive. ... When you're a coach, you really have to take a step back. It's not about me anymore, it's about the players and about how I can help them become better as players and human beings. That was the main thing for me: to put aside the ego—something you need to have as a player—and focus on helping everyone else. (McNicholas et al., 2019)*

The best coaches also endorse a long-term, holistic approach. They're not just focused on short-term gains, but also long-term success, and they're going after that success in a way that encompasses the personal and the professional, the mental/emotional as well as the technical/tactical/physical. Stanford's Tara VanDerveer, who has more college basketball wins than anyone in history, brought in the university's happiness expert to talk to the team every week, saying "I want to keep my players healthy—physically, mentally, and emotionally. I want them to have fun" (Anderson, 2023). She understood that in order to be successful as a coach, she had to put her athletes' needs first.

Our Job Is Important

The second belief that high-developing coaches have is that *our job is important*. We have a responsibility to our athletes. They are placing their hopes, dreams, and careers in our hands, and this is a trust that must be respected. Not only that, but we possess an outsize influence on our athletes—we have the potential to shape their viewpoints, perspectives, and morals through the life lessons that we teach.

John Wooden used to regularly recite one of his favorite poems, "They Ask Me Why I Teach", wherein the author, Glennice L. Harmon, depicts her students not just as boys and girls, but as future doctors, builders, farmers, teachers, and merchants. She may not live to see the impact of her work, but she treasures her role, finding joy in helping shape the world of tomorrow through those she teaches today.[7]

The vast majority of us work with young people—whether 8 or 18—and Harmon beautifully illustrates the impact a teacher can have in their formative years. Even those of us who are working with young adults must recognize that their athletic career will still only span the earliest stages of their life. Indeed, the work we do and the relationships we build can make a real impression in an athlete's 30s, 40s, 50s, and onward.

Sometimes, we are also representing our club, our region, or even our nation. The impact of our work is not limited to just our players. A successful high-performance program at a club can lead to increased registration and participation, benefiting future generations of athletes. Demonstrating excellence in a region can bring about funding and other opportunities, benefiting both participants and coaches, and of

7 The poem itself is beautiful – much more so than my shoddy summary. I'd include it here, but the rights holders won't get back to us and if I fight this battle any longer I'll either throw the book away or lose all my hair. All I can do is strongly recommend that you look it up yourself.

course representing your nation internationally not only contributes to the fiber of the country but can inspire confidence and pride across multiple domains.

Coaching is a responsibility—to parents, players, fans, and communities. Each of these responsibilities is a sacred trust. Our job is important.

You Can't Be Successful without a Work–Life Balance

Lastly, and perhaps controversially, the best coaches tend to agree that *you can't be successful without a work–life balance*. If, as we discussed in Chapter 1, coaching is a performance, then it's vital that we are physically and mentally fresh in order to perform at our best. However, there's another reason that work-life balance is important for coaching success: longevity. In this profession, you have to last long enough to be successful, because it's virtually impossible to reach the highest levels of the game in only a few years. You can't maximize your coaching development if you ultimately quit after five years. Work-life balance is crucial not only for performance, but also consistency and longevity.

That having been said, what that balance looks like can vary greatly from person to person. One of the coaches interviewed in Mallet and Lara-Bercial's (2016) study of serial winning coaches felt that he had a great work–life balance, despite being on the road 200 days a year. This may be because some coaches don't consider coaching to be *work*—it's a passion, and therefore sits on the "life" side of the equation. To quote a coach from another study:

> *I'll never refuse to assist anybody. It often means I'm on the water for hours a day and I enjoy doing it. I enjoy giving feedback. It's not hard for me; it's not work to be doing it. So, I guess you could say it's passion. (Mallett and Lara-Bercial, 2023, p. 147)*

On the other hand, there will be times of the year when the race is more of a sprint than a marathon—when bouts of intense work are required. This a normal part of the job, and the elite coaches recognized this, while ensuring that they could balance these times with periods of rest. Similarly, many coaches reported different capacities for hard work at different stages of life, mainly in relation to age but also other aspects of their personal lives. In these periods, elite coaches chose to embrace the long, grueling days, acting in line with the aforementioned value of hard work. At the same time, they recognized that there would be other times—months or even years—when they might need to slow down (Mallett and Lara-Bercial, 2023).

Ultimately, the belief in work–life balance is, funnily enough, balanced by a valuing of hard work. In other words, the best coaches in the world treat themselves the way they treat their athletes: they are demanding, they have high standards, but they also realize that physical and mental health are crucial to long-term success.

Mindsets

Mindsets are complex combinations of beliefs and values that influence the way we behave. Successful coaches generally adopt three: the growth, challenge, and solution mindsets.

Growth Mindset

By now, the words "growth mindset" are common parlance in the coaching industry. Put simply, someone with a growth mindset believes that their abilities can be developed and changed through focused efforts. This is in contrast to a fixed mindset, wherein one believes that their abilities are genetically predetermined and cannot be changed. As a coach, this may seem absurd to you. Of course our skills can be developed! But consider how many subtle fixed-mindset phrases make their way into our daily discourse:

- "I'm just not a numbers person."
- "I'll never be good at working with parents."
- "I can't coach girls."

High-developing coaches have a growth mindset when it comes to their coaching. They understand that coaching is a skill and that through deliberate, focused work, they can get better at the specific areas they choose to work on.

At the age of 45, Stanford Cardinal women's basketball team coach Tara VanDerveer decided that she was going to learn to play the piano. She bought a portable keyboard, a few books, and figured she would teach herself how to play. Her first attempts were fruitless (in her words: "I had no idea what I was getting myself into") but instead of concluding that it wasn't meant to be, that she simply wasn't good at music, she hired a piano teacher. She took lessons every week, practiced three to four hours a day while on vacation, and brought the keyboard with her on the road. According to her teacher, she wasn't just interested in playing a few songs: "She wanted to learn how to practice. She wanted to learn music theory." Now, 20 years on, she plays piano for her friends, family, and athletes, and even records CDs to give out as gifts. She has taken this approach to everything in her life, both personal and professional. For example, she studies the Stanford Olympic swimmers in order to learn from their form and regularly asks friends to give her feedback on her waterskiing technique (Smith, 2001; Jennings, 2024; The Daily Coach, 2024).

Of course, when Tara VanDerveer uses a growth mindset to learn piano, this doesn't exactly help her coach basketball. But in 2017, researchers from Sheffield Hallam University interviewed 12 coaches working at the highest level of their sport (e.g. the Olympic Games, world championships (Hodgson et al., 2017)). Among the many common themes identified, one is of particular note: conscious self-improvement. The researchers identified that the majority of coaches they spoke to believed that conscious self-improvement had helped them develop their abilities over the years. Specifically, "being able to identify areas of development and put in place action plans was considered highly important as it allowed coaches to engage in constant self-progression and, over time, gain increased self-understanding." These coaches self-reflected regularly, they analyzed videos of themselves, and they observed other coaches in action, all in the name of identifying things they could do better and formulating action plans for improving those skills.

Do these sound like the behaviors of someone with a fixed mindset? On the contrary, elite coaches are steadfast in the belief that their abilities are malleable and that, with deliberate practice, there is no limit to their potential development.

Challenge Mindset

High-performance coaching is ripe with challenges. Here are just a few examples:

- Criticisms from the media
- Criticisms from parents
- Dissatisfied athletes
- Disappointing performances
- Long hours
- Time away from home
- Comparisons to others
- Difficult conversations

In order to succeed, we need to be able to handle these challenges and handle them well. We need to be resilient, both to perform at our best and to have a long-lasting career. A challenge mindset is comprised of two beliefs: first, the belief that we can handle setbacks, and second, the belief that adversity makes us stronger.

The first belief of the challenge mindset—*I can handle it*—goes a long way toward helping us excel. After all, if I believe I can handle whatever comes my way, I will doubt myself less. As a result, I'll conserve mental and emotional energy, I will spend less time dwelling on challenges, and I'll act more confidently. The result will be that I'll be more focused and present for those around me, I'll have more time to focus on solutions, and my confidence will inspire others.

The second belief of the challenge mindset—*Adversity makes me stronger*—is also crucial for coaches who want to maximize their development. As mentioned earlier, elite coaches are always looking to improve, including during moments of difficulty. The best coaches recognize that adversity provides opportunities for development. For example, public criticisms provide an opportunity to work on mindfulness, difficult conversations are an opportunity to develop leadership, and long hours are a way to test focus. Coaches with a challenge mindset not only withstand adversity, they come away from it stronger.

In a 2023 article for CoachesVoice.com, Bartolomé "Tintin" Márquez, coach of the Qatar national football team, describes the ups and downs of his coaching career. He was fired from a number of roles before finally winning a major title, the Asian Cup, at the age of 62:

> *It was horrible, really. ... Two clubs as head coach, and two dismissals.*
>
> *I went back to Barcelona, where people kept asking me questions. Everywhere I went, or even in the street, Espanyol fans recognised me. "How are you?" they asked. "What happened? Why so little patience?" I know they did it because they were fond of me, but I felt suffocated. I had worked so hard to get the chance to coach at the elite level, and it had all gone wrong.*
>
> *At some point, I just couldn't take it any more. I made a decision. "I'm leaving," I told my family. "I can't live here, because I feel like I am drowning." I don't know what would have happened if I had stayed in Barcelona, but I suspect that things would have got worse. ...*
>
> *This time, I'm the one in the photos and on TV, lifting a trophy. A great trophy. I would like my story to be useful to all coaches who, like me, are fighting to win at least one title in their career. Many times it never seems to come, but you can't give up. It's a question of keeping going and going. (Márquez, 2023)*

Solution Mindset

Lastly, high-developing coaches have a solution mindset, which comprises two foci. First, they are focused on the solution, rather than the problem. We typically think of this with regards to the feedback we give—in other words, teaching athletes what *to* do, rather than telling them what *not* to do. The best coaches take that same approach with themselves. In difficult situations, they shift their focus from the problem to the solution. If there is a lack of resources, how can we raise more money? If there is a challenging parent, how are we going to address them? By shifting their focus this way, these coaches avoid wasting mental energy on parts of the challenge they can't control *and* they dedicate more time to specific action items, rather than general complaints.

A similar mindset—and one used by figures from Aristotle to Elon Musk—is known as First Principles Thinking. In it, one breaks problems down into fundamental truths, rather than relying on assumptions about what "is" and "isn't." For example, you might bemoan a lack of competitive opportunities in your area and accept it as is ("This is why our region can't develop good players"). Or you might take a First Principles approach such as this:

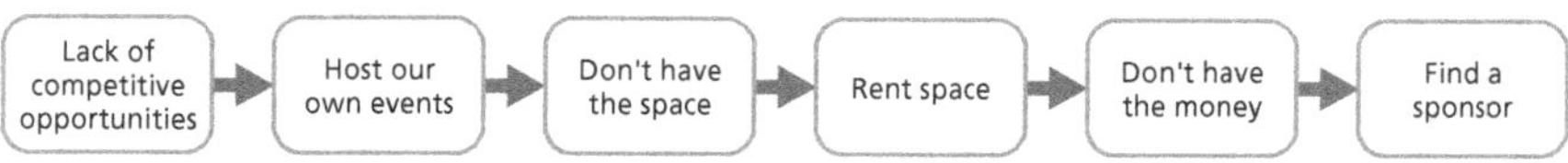

Figure 4.1. First principles thinking for creating competitive opportunities.

Ultimately, you may end up working on an item (e.g. finding a sponsor) that may seem quite removed from your initial goal (e.g. finding competitive opportunities for your athletes). However, if that's what is required, then isn't it what you should be doing?

A solution mindset also entails a focus on the future, rather than the past. While the best coaches are inclined to want to learn from past mistakes, their focus is generally on what they are going to do in the future. Sometimes, analyzing a past mistake can feel good, cathartic, even. However, it may only give the *illusion* of productivity. Picking apart a bad practice or a bad player meeting is not useful if it only leads to a list of things that went wrong. Any analysis of the past should quickly lead to action items for the future. Super Bowl–winning coach of the Seattle Seahawks, Pete Carroll, sums it up best in a behind-the-scenes video:

> *Most coaches are going to talk about the mistake that somebody made as the play's ending or what they should have done or whatever. ... We're really disciplined as coaches to always talk about what we want to see, the desired outcome, not about what went wrong or what the mistake was. We have to be disciplined and always use our language to talk about the next thing you can do right. It's*

> *always about what we want to happen, not about the other stuff. (Seattle Seahawks, 2017, at 3:27 of video)*

Elite coaches don't dwell on the past, or on the negative. Instead, they narrow their focus to the exact action items that will help them achieve their goals in the future.

Traits

Traits are personal characteristics determined partially by our genetics and partially by our environment and influences. Importantly, however, they can be changed through conscious effort. While there is some interesting research into what traits Olympic medal–winning coaches have in common, three in particular are most conducive to maximum coach development: conscientiousness, emotional competence, and reasonable self-doubt.

Conscientiousness

While it encompasses a broad array of traits and characteristics, conscientiousness is generally defined by psychologists as the tendency to be organized, deliberate, diligent, and disciplined. It's one of the five traits identified in the commonly used five-factor model of personality, and it has been studied extensively. People high in conscientiousness tend to think carefully before acting; they make clear plans; they are persistent in pursuing their goals; and they delay gratification (Thompson, 2008).

In their research into serial winning coaches, Mallett and Lara-Bercial (2023) found that both the coaches' self-ratings *and* the athletes' ratings of their coaches indicated that the coaches had higher-than-average levels of conscientiousness. In a series of interviews with 12 international-level coaches from a variety of sports, Hodgson et al. (2017) identified, among others, a theme that kept reoccurring: "conscious self-improvement." Given similar themes discussed throughout this book, it should come as no surprise that these coaches were deliberate in reflecting on their coaching, identifying areas of improvement, and carefully observing other coaches—all behaviors that demonstrate a high level of conscientiousness.

Along the same lines, in the aforementioned IBM Watson analysis, the single most common trait of the NFL coaches with the highest win percentages was what they termed "cautiousness," defined as "the extent to which a person carefully thinks through decisions before making them" (Online Casino Canada, n.d.).

Public interviews and profiles of world-class coaches paint the same picture. Pep Guardiola, upon taking over at Manchester United, imposed a number of changes highlighting his attention to detail, specifying the length of the grass and the frequency of watering, overhauling diets, changing the design of the lunchroom, and mandating that players enter and leave the field together, among other things. In the days before the internet, Tara VanDerveer would send her players postcards in the offseason with workout programs on them, expecting them to respond with their results so that she could keep abreast of their progress and send them new workouts. Andy Reid, one of only five coaches with at least three Super Bowl titles, is known for his extraordinary attention to detail. In interviews for *The Athletic* (Jenks and Sando, 2024), players recall his expectations for attire and appearance: shirt tucked in, no black shoes or socks, no hands in pockets, no leaning. Beyond that, his staffers describe his diligent note-taking—and not just the quantity, but the quality. As Brad Childress, assistant coach, says, "He's almost always able to see over the horizon. He was organized and methodical in the daily stuff, but he was always thinking ahead." Here's what fullback Anthony Sherman had to say:

> *We were so prepared for that first Super Bowl we went to. Everything was timed up. Everything was on cue, even so much so that I would do a pre-workout before every game, and [Reid] knew that. He was like, "Listen, make sure you time that pre-workout up right. You're going to get introduced and it's going to be another 20 minutes before kickoff, so time that thing up right." (Jenks and Sando, 2024)*

Read almost any profile of a high-level coach, and you'll see the same patterns emerge: these coaches have an elite attention to detail, engage in careful and considered decision-making, and persistently pursue perfection. The best coaches are conscientious to a fault, and this is what helps them get better every day.

Emotional Competence

Another finding from the research into Olympic medal–winning coaches is that they are exceptionally emotionally competent. In other words, they are highly aware of both their emotions and those of others; they understand what influences these emotions and what they, in turn, influence; and they can manage these emotions to maximize performance (Mallett and Lara-Bercial, 2023).

There's perhaps no better example of this than in the 2023 *Athletic* profile of Sean McVay, head coach of the Los Angeles Rams (Howe, 2023). Brandon Staley, then defensive coordinator, said that after 12 hours, "It was like we had known each other our entire lives." Zac Taylor, assistant wide receivers coach, said that "he has that effect on you, where you feel like you've known him forever, and you want to be around his energy." Liam Cohen, then the offensive coordinator, described having just started in his role and feeling in "way over his head." One night, McVay stopped by his office to say, "Hey man, I want to let you know how great of a job you're doing. I couldn't be more happy with having you part of this thing, and you're doing a great job."

These examples illustrate the extent to which a leader like McVay uses his emotional skills to motivate his players and staff and maximize their performance. It's clear that this competency is valuable for helping athletes and teams develop and perform at their best. However, it's also worth remembering the extent to which emotional competence is important for *you* to be at your best. After all, if, amidst a failure, you cannot step back and rationally assess your coaching, how can you identify what needs improvement? If you can't manage the distractions in your life and keep yourself motivated to put in the work, how will you get better? We can see the sort of self-reflection McVay engaged in after a particularly difficult season:

> *During the past offseason, as the Rams emerged from the wreckage of a 5–12 season—the worst record ever for a reigning Super Bowl champion—McVay needed a little more time to self-reflect. He needed to be confident in his*

> *own ability to be a leader for everyone in the building for another season. McVay was all in once he regained that confidence. (Howe, 2023)*

This is a perfect example of a coach engaging in emotional awareness (recognizing his uncertainty and lack of confidence), emotional understanding (knowing that it would negatively affect everyone in the building), and emotional management (taking time away from the job and engaging in self-reflection in order to rebuild his confidence).

Bill Walsh, longtime coach of the San Francisco 49ers, describes a similar process after a heart-wrenching Orange Bowl loss to the Miami Dolphins (edited for brevity):

> *Coaches aren't supposed to cry, but I'm not ashamed to admit that on the night flight back to San Francisco I sat in my seat in the first row of the plane and broke down sobbing in the darkness, ... contemplating whether I should offer my resignation. Most debilitating of all—devastating—was a gnawing fear that I didn't have what it takes to be an NFL head coach. ... Everything I had dreamed of professionally for a quarter of a century was in jeopardy just eighteen months after being realized. And yet there was something else going on inside me, a "voice" from down deeper than the emotions, something stirring that I had learned over many years in football and, before that, growing up; namely, I must stand and fight again, stand and fight or it was all over.*
>
> *And that was the instinct that slowly prevailed as we headed home in the middle of a very dark night. ... In my mind—or gut—and in spite of the pain, I knew I had to force myself to somehow start looking ahead—to overcome my grief over the debacle in Miami—or it would severely damage our efforts to prepare properly for the battle with New York; my comportment would directly affect the attitudes and performance of everyone who looked to me for answers and direction. I had to do what I was being paid to do: be a leader.*

> *... It took time for me to stop despairing and regain some composure, to settle down and start thinking straight, but gradually, during those hard hours on the flight back to California, I began pulling myself together. ... I can say with some pride that by the time we landed at San Francisco International Airport at 3:15 A.M. after a six-hour flight, I had pulled myself out of the hopelessness and begun working on the strategy we would employ against the Giants when they arrived in a week. I was wobbly but back up on my feet again. [...] I was able to summon strength enough to pull my focus, my thinking, out of the past and move it forward to our next big problem. It does take strength to shift your attention off the pain when you feel as though your soul has been stripped bare. (Walsh et al., 2009, pp. 33-34)*

Again, we see the same triad of emotional awareness, understanding, and management. Walsh wasn't dealing with his players' emotions. He was dealing with his own grief, fear, and uncertainty and responding to them in such a way as to perform at his best. And it worked—he went on to win five Super Bowls with the 49ers and become one of the greatest coaches of all time. Emotional competence isn't just about keeping your athletes on track, it's about keeping yourself on track throughout the long journey of coaching mastery.

Reasonable Self-Doubt

One of the traits that has appeared in multiple studies of successful coaches is confidence. A coach who communicates and acts confidently inspires belief in his players and doubt in his opponents. A confident coach makes decisions without hesitation and bounces back in times of adversity. The best coaches in the world, however, balance this confidence with something else, which Mallett and Lara-Bercial (2023) call "reasonable self-doubt." While these coaches have a strong belief in their abilities, founded on evidence, they also have a non-debilitating amount of insecurity, a persistent doubt as to whether they are in fact qualified for the job or whether they will be able to continue to deliver results.

Surprisingly to some, this state of insecurity is oftentimes beneficial for coaches in two ways. First, it drives them to continue to work hard and to push themselves. As one coach put it:

> *I want to know I've done everything[,] and I feel terrible when I feel like the other coach outworked me or out-prepared me, I can't stand that. I can't stand that anyone would do more in a summer than I would. (Mallett and Lara-Bercial, 2023, p. 63)*

Earlier in this chapter, we discussed elite coaches' propensity for hard work. For many, this comes from a desire to prove themselves—a perpetual state of dissatisfaction that pushes them to strive for more.

More importantly, however, reasonable self-doubt ensures that coaches do not become arrogant or complacent. Consider this: a coach who is overconfident, who believes she has all the answers, may still be driven to work hard. However, she likely won't see any value in questioning herself or seeking improvement. Coaches with a reasonable self-doubt, on the other hand, recognize the powerful effects of cognitive biases. They understand that sometimes they will be wrong. Sometimes, they will have made a mistake. Sometimes, their intuition and the data won't match up. They are constantly wary of deluding themselves. While confident in their skills, they are always reevaluating, examining the facts, and questioning their decisions. For the best coaches, the goal is to act based on evidence and rational thinking, rather than just emotion, gut, or ego. As one international-level coach put it:

> *So, when that happens and you win, you should make sure it does not turn into arrogance, that is a pitfall and the other pitfall is you stop being sharp, because you must stay sharp. That curiosity and keenness should absolutely stay present at all times. (Mallett and Lara-Bercial, p. 65)*

Chapter 5
How We Can Learn, Practice, and Reflect Better

The word of the decade, in our industry at least, seems to be *passion*. It's a word with a lot of different meanings: passion for competing, passion for the sport, passion for people, passion for winning, and so on. As we've seen throughout this book, the best coaches are passionate about *getting better*. They are consistently engaged in self-improvement, looking to develop themselves and learn as much as possible. However, the desire to improve is not always correlated to actual improvement. For example, consider the number of professional athletes versus the number of aspiring professional athletes. Bobby Knight referenced this fact with his famous quote: "The will to win is not nearly as important as the will to prepare to win." Backing up our passion with hard work is key, but even then, that's not all that's required—*how* we work matters too.

Professional development for coaches consists of three behaviors: learning, practicing, and reflecting. In this chapter, I'll outline some of the habits of high-performing coaches that we can apply to our own development.

Learning

There are three types of learning: formal, non-formal, and informal. Formal learning is exactly what it sounds like: there is a syllabus, students are tested or assessed, and it usually takes place in an educational institution like a school or university. Non-formal learning is less structured: there may not be a curriculum or any assessment, but it will usually be provided by an organization. Informal learning, also known as experiential learning, is unstructured, unmeasured, and spurred by intrinsic motivation. Examples of each of these as they apply to coaching are provided below.

Formal learning	**Non-formal learning**	**Informal learning**
University education	Clinics	Discussions with peers
Education/certification by sport governing bodies	Seminars	Self-reflection
	Workshops	Observing other coaches
	Conferences	Books, blog posts
		Podcasts, videos
		Journal articles, scientific studies

It's important that coaches access all types of learning, although the prevalence of each will wax and wane depending on the stage of a coach's career. There is a common misconception in some sports that formal education is divorced from reality, that what's taught in the classroom doesn't work on the field, and that the only way to really learn is to put in the hours. But in a 2016 study of "serial-winning coaches" (coaches who had won multiple Olympic or World Championship medals with different athletes or teams), coaches were very supportive of formal education, so long as it was "relevant and delivered by credible and capable coach developers" (Lara-Bercial and Mallett, 2016, p. 230). Of the 17 coaches interviewed, 15 held the highest level of coach certification for their country. Nine held sports-related university degrees, while another four had unrelated bachelor's degrees. Overall, these elite coaches felt that formal education had provided them with important foundational knowledge and mental models to help them process their own experiences as athletes and accelerate their on-the-job learning (Lara-Bercial and Mallett, 2016).

Non-formal learning—clinics, seminars, workshops, and conferences—was one of the most commonly accessed forms of education for these coaches, but it was not in their top four most preferred, the challenge being that it can sometimes lack relevance to your particular context. However, with the proliferation of video-conferencing technologies like Zoom, more and more webinars, workshops, and so on are being offered to coaches. For an enthusiastic coach with a deliberate agenda, there exists the possibility of crafting a curriculum suited to his or her own needs. This doesn't make up for the fact that non-formal learning is often impersonal and lacks assessment—factors that may hamper motivation and learning.

Thankfully, however, there are numerous opportunities for informal education, which serial-winning coaches consistently rated among their favorite modes of professional development. Coach observation and self-reflection will be discussed later in this chapter, and I've devoted another chapter to mentorship. But what about peer discussions, or learning from the reams of audiovisual content that are now readily available online?

Each comes with its own pros and cons. On one end of the spectrum, journal articles and scientific studies provide concrete, empirical evidence, but they may only be applicable in very specific circumstances. On the other hand, friendly discussions at the bar can surface advice that is easy to understand and apply but that may not be rooted in anything more than tradition—parables that have been passed down from generation to generation without a thought as to their validity. In the middle, DVDs, books, podcasts, and blog posts benefit from a slightly higher standard of accuracy while also being relatively easy to digest.

Ideally, you will learn from as many different sources as possible, weighing each one against its strengths and weaknesses and looking for overlap with others. When scientific theory aligns with common sense advice, or when multiple people come to the same conclusion independently of one another, that's a good sign.

When engaging in non-formal or informal learning, remember to be deliberate and carefully select what you'd like to learn and how. Like the serial-winning coaches described, at the start of your career you will benefit from formal education, which presents a curriculum to follow. As you progress, however, it will be up to you to take your learning into your own hands—even if you benefit from a mentor. Most coaches learn by happenstance; they attend a conference and are treated to whatever the speaker has chosen to present on, or listen to their favorite podcast and learn from the host's latest guest. There's nothing wrong with this, it just isn't the most efficient path to development. The more advanced you are, the more you benefit from (some would say require) specific education. When athletes are younger and less skilled, they usually take part in group classes or team practices. As they get older and more proficient, even if they are still part of a team, they will likely engage in individual practice following their own curriculum. Nothing sums this up better than this story about Kobe Bryant at a training camp before the 2008 Olympics, told by Dwayne Wade and Chris Bosh:

> *"We're in Las Vegas and we all come down for team breakfast at the start of the whole training camp," Bosh said. "And Kobe comes in with ice on his knees and with his trainers and stuff. He's got sweat drenched through his workout gear. And I'm like, 'It's 8 o'clock in the morning, man. Where in the hell is he coming from?'"*
>
> *Wade chimes in along memory lane.*
>
> *"Everybody else just woke up. We're still stretching and yawning and looking at [Kobe] like, 'What the f---?'" Wade said as he squinted into a frown and then burst into laughter. "We're all yawning, and he's already three hours and a full workout into his day." (Wallace, 2015)*

For a professional athlete striving to be the best, improvement is everything. Getting an extra edge, no matter how small, can be valuable, and oftentimes this requires a specific, individual approach. Why shouldn't it be the same for a coach? If you are truly passionate about being the best you can be, there comes a point where what you need in order to be better will be different than what your colleague needs. Take your learning into your own hands and seek out the information that will make you better. This is not to say that you will always know what you need—that's what a mentor is for. If I made it my goal to start learning about horse riding, I wouldn't even know where to start. As I learned about the different disciplines and events, I would then be able to narrow my focus to my specific areas of interest. Coaching is as broad as it is deep; it's an activity full of nuance and complexity. Pick an area to focus on and then dive into it. As you learn, shift your focus if necessary. If you don't know where to start, ask a mentor or colleague.

ACTIVITY: Set a timer for 2 minutes. Pick two topics you'd like to learn more about. Identify what type of learning would be best suited to you and these topics.

Gathering information isn't really learning, however. Learning starts when the information is stored in our long-term memory, when we can connect it to what we already know and apply it in our practice. Unfortunately, this isn't a guarantee. Most of the things we hear and read will be forgotten within a day. However, there are some best practices to enhance your learning and transfer your knowledge to the field.

The first will sound elementary, but bear with me: Take notes. Research has shown that students who take notes do better on both immediate and delayed tests, and the more notes students take, the better they do. Furthermore, the very act of taking notes, even without reviewing them, increases information retention. Harvard University has a set of guidelines for student note-taking (Friedman, 2014):

- Take notes in your own words. This ensures you are thinking about the content and prevents your working memory being taken up by transcribing every word you hear.
- Take notes in a structured, organized way. This helps you organize your thoughts and makes information easier to review.
- Review your notes early and often.
- Test yourself.

One of the traps learners fall into is to believe that understanding something when it's explained to them is the same as knowing it. This simply isn't true. When we are first taught something, it makes sense to us because it has been packaged and presented for that express purpose. Certain nuances may have been left out, certain tasks may be more difficult than they appear, and other elements may rely on information that you'll need to memorize. Explaining the concept of multiplication to a child can be quite easy, but it won't make them fluent.

When we take our newfound knowledge into the real world, we often realize just how complex things are. To make the transition from the classroom to the court easier, ask yourself these questions when you are learning something new:

- How would I apply this?
- When would I use this?
- Which athletes would this work for?
- How would I do things differently?
- How does this connect with what I already know?
- What potential problems might I run into when using this information?

The goal is to bridge the gap between practice and theory, to understand how what we've learned can fit into *our* coaching. Whether deliberate or not, this is a practice that all great coaches have engaged in, building their own methodology. In a way, they are making sense of the world. Legendary UCLA basketball coach John Wooden spent over 14 years working on his Pyramid of Success, which was the foundation of all of his coaching (Davis, 2014, p. 80). Pete Carroll of the Seattle Seahawks had his three rules (Carroll et al., 2011, p. 70):

1. Protect the team.
2. No whining, no complaining, no excuses.
3. Be early.

Bill Belichick's mantra at the Patriots was simple—Do Your Job—although there was no doubt a lot more thinking that went on behind the scenes (Rivera, 2024).[8] Whether you call this philosophy, methodology, leadership, or simply marketing, the fact of the matter is that these legendary coaches were taking in information and synthesizing it—making sense of different sources, data points, and influences—in order to formulate a method that would work for them and their athletes. The result was sustained success.

8 Bill Belichick had this to say about learning in his early days as a young coach: "I knew I had a better instinct for it than some of the older coaches on the staff. What I didn't know, I could learn–one of the things I had working for me was that I knew how to learn" (Halberstam, 2005, p. 117).

The last way to get the most out of your learning is to share with colleagues or teach others. As many before me have observed, the act of teaching can highlight for you those subjects you don't truly understand. Explaining something clearly requires a level of understanding above the intended level of learning (to quote physicist Richard Feynman: "If you can't explain something in simple terms, you don't understand it."). In *The Coach's Guide to Teaching* (2020), Doug Lemov recounts this advice from a coach:

> *Another coach told me it was helpful to occasionally coach players who were younger than those he was used to coaching. You could assume less and had to explain more—and more clearly—which was good practice. ... One of the challenges of being a coach—and once, presumably, a player who excelled and therefore learned easily—is that what's unclear to those who know less or learn less readily is often invisible to you. (Lemov, 2020, p. 108)*

Not only is it difficult to know what others know, it can be a challenge to know what we ourselves know until we are forced to explore it. Facing difficult questions, or realizing that your explanations might be a little unclear, will help you identify the gaps in your knowledge.

Practicing

If there's one thing I hope you take away from this book, it's the importance of deliberate practice for coaches. Not only does it make inherent sense (after all, it's exactly what we ask our athletes to do), but it's something that's already going on in small, elite groups around the world, in the domains of teaching, surgery, and yes, coaching. Deliberate practice might be the single most impactful thing you can do to improve your coaching ability, as long as it's done well.

I know what you're thinking. "Zack, practice sounds good and all, but I don't have the time! Plus, even if I did, what am I going to do? Hire actors to pretend to be athletes so that I can work on my coaching? It's just not feasible."

You're right, it's not. Thankfully, in this section, I'll show you how you can engage in deliberate practice by yourself, in very little time, without needing the help of anyone else. And, if that's still not doable, I'll tell you how you can develop your coaching while on the job—something researchers call deliberate *performance*. First, however, you'll have to choose what aspect of your coaching you will work on.

Identifying What to Work On

As emphasized throughout this book, coaching can be broken down into three large but simple steps: observation, planning, and execution. You watch your team perform, you decide what steps to take and how, you take those steps, and the process repeats itself as you observe the results of your actions. In evaluating your coaching, it may be helpful to start with this structure and pick an area to improve. Maybe your observation skills need work—your ability to analyze a game isn't where you'd like it to be. Or perhaps it's your planning—you think that you might be prioritizing the wrong things. Or maybe it's just execution—the plan is right, but the players aren't improving the way you'd like them to.

It may not be easy to decide what to focus on. A first step to narrow down the options is simple: self-reflect. Think about your successes and failures, including winning teams and losing teams, good practices and bad. Think about the feedback you've been given and the things you've learned from other sources, both formal and informal. What are your strengths? What are your weaknesses? To take the self-reflection a step further, you might consider watching yourself on video. While it's often an unpleasant experience, especially the first time, you'll almost always spot things that surprise you, resulting in a more complete picture of your coaching.

Observing others can also be useful. Notice the differences and similarities between their coaching and yours. What do they struggle with? What do they do well?

Lastly, ask for input, ideally from someone who is more experienced than you and who has seen you coach. In the absence of such a person, a trusted colleague or friend will do. Outside opinions are almost always useful, even if you don't have to listen to them.

Once you've identified an aspect of your coaching to work on, do yourself a favor and *be specific*. The art of coaching is vast and complex. Just as you would with an athlete, you may want to be very granular and specific when assessing what it is you'd like to get better at. Here's an example of what that would look like, both for a player and for a coach:

	For an athlete	For a coach
General	Attack better.	Maximize time.
	Miss fewer attacking balls.	Spend less time setting up drills.
	Miss fewer attacking balls when the ball is low up the middle.	Be more efficient with the words chosen when explaining drills.
Specific	Use the hand to create more spin on low attacking balls up the middle.	Have clear start and end cues so that athletes come in and out quickly.

When choosing how specific to be, aim to make the largest possible impact that is also achievable. Maybe I've already practiced using clear cues to signal breaks in practice, in which case I'd go one level up and focus on being more efficient with my words, which encompasses start and end cues but also includes avoiding filler words and using clear and concise explanations. In practicing this, however, I may find that I'm forgetting to use the start and end cues. In that case, I would go back down a level and make sure that skill is fully acquired before moving on to anything else.

Next, *name it*. In the example above, I might choose the simple term "clean breaks" to refer to using clear cues to start or end a stoppage. There are several benefits to this. First, giving specific coaching skills names allows me to store them in my brain as chunks, which helps me watch for them, modify them, and integrate them. Consider the word "car," a word that, despite its length, encodes a lot of information. Thanks to the name, I'm not only able to recognize cars but also identify variations (toy car, electric car, etc.) and related machines (e.g. trucks). This all sounds elementary, but without the term, I would be stuck with "four-wheeled vehicle powered by an engine that can transport people." Not only is this unwieldy and difficult to remember, but, funnily enough, it's arguably less clear. Does it include pick-up trucks? Golf carts? Having a term that is short, easy to remember, and intuitive makes learning that much easier. To tie this into my practice, a name like "clean breaks" might help me explore different types of clean breaks—for example, at the start of practice versus in the middle of practice. It might also allow me to observe clean breaks in other domains, like running a meeting or giving a speech. Naming the skill enhances your learning.

The other benefit to labeling our practice skills comes when we discuss them with others. For one, short names allow for easier and smoother conversation—two words are better than 15. But more than that, having what Doug Lemov calls a "shared vocabulary" ensures that everyone is on the same page. I could discuss "staying in the rally" with fellow tennis coaches, but for some that will mean neutralizing (going from a defensive phase to a neutral phase) while for others it will mean pure defense (just trying to survive and get one more ball back in play). You can see how a discussion might go awry if terms aren't clear. Imagine a discussion of coaching, a topic that has been historically underexplored. Clear terms are key.

Lastly, *identify success*. Not only do you want to be specific regarding what *you* will do, you will also want to be specific with what the *outcome* will be. What does success look like? What does failure look like? In my case, I might define success as getting players into the huddle, having them pay attention, and beginning my message in less than six seconds. Failure would be any of those elements breaking down: the players take too long to come in, they're not paying attention, or I waste words at the start of my message.

Doing this has two benefits: First, it helps me set goals for myself, which, as we know, not only increases my motivation but also gives me useful information about when to get extra practice or, conversely, when to move on. Second, it helps me anticipate what some potential challenges might be. This way, I can plan for them: how I'll address them in the moment, and how I'll practice them behind the scenes.

ACTIVITY: Set a timer for 5 minutes. Pick two aspects of your coaching that you'd like to get better at. Give each one a catchy name and identify what success would look like.

Speaking of practice ...

Practicing on the Job: Deliberate Performance

Just as we can give an athlete something specific to focus on during a game, we can challenge ourselves to practice a skill during a coaching session. This type of practice, known as deliberate performance, can be quite effective, especially in professions like ours where both time and human resources can be in short supply. Fadde and Klein (2010) define deliberate performance as "the effort to increase domain expertise while engaged in routine work activity" (p. 6) and propose four beneficial exercises, two of which we'll touch on here.

The first, *estimation*, is described as the act of making predictions. In our context, the two most obvious examples are estimating how long a particular drill will take to complete or predicting how successful an athlete or team will be at a new skill. These examples may seem trivial, but I'd argue that both abilities (each of which can be improved with practice) are crucial to effective coaching. Having a keen sense of how long an exercise will take is paramount to proper planning. If it takes too long, players may get bored, tired, or cold. If it is too short you may be left floundering, unsure what to do with the extra time. What's more, if you're trying to prioritize certain elements of the practice, then you don't want to run out of time because another drill went on too long. Conversely, you don't want the focus point of the session to be over in an instant.

Understanding your athletes' skill levels relative to different circumstances and tasks is equally important. Not only does it allow you to manage their emotional state by avoiding situations that are too challenging and that reduce confidence and motivation, it allows you to ensure the optimal environment for development, as we'll discuss in Chapter 8. Knowing exactly how challenging to make a drill makes for happier athletes, leads to faster improvement, and saves time.

To practice your estimation skills, you only need to do three things: make a prediction, observe the outcome, and take note of both. You can do this easily while on the job. Set up a task, guess at how long it will take, and then note how long it actually takes. Or, at the start of a drill, predict how successful you think an athlete will be. Will they succeed three times out of ten? Six times? Nine times? If you're already making lesson plans, you can add these predictions in, and then take 2 minutes at the end of practice to review them. Over time, as long as you give yourself feedback from observing the outcome, your estimation skills will improve, allowing you to coach more efficiently.

The second type of deliberate performance Fadde and Klein describe is *experimentation*. For coaches, this may be the most important type of practice. Experimenting with our coaching on the job allows us to try things out in a real-world setting, to see what works and what doesn't and to gain repetitions, confidence, and eventually automaticity. Donald Schön, in *The Reflective Practitioner* (1983), categorizes experimentation as either exploratory, move-testing, or hypothesizing.

Exploratory experimentation is when we try things out just to see what happens. For coaches, that could mean mixing up the normal order of practice or only giving positive feedback. It's hard to predict exactly what will happen or what the side effects will be, so we're exploring. These experiments can be interesting, but they aren't very scientific, which is why it's often more useful to go with move-testing.

Move-testing experimentation is when we try things out with a specific outcome in mind. I might give athletes a 5-minute break in the middle of a 2-hour practice, with the idea that they will come back physically and mentally refreshed. Or I might give athletes fewer total practice hours in a week but more one-on-one time, with the idea that this will accelerate their technical development. As with estimation, the key here is to take note of your goals as well as what actually happens. Over time, and with a bit of reflection, your skills will develop.

Hypothesis experimentation is when we compare two hypotheses. A coach working on decision-making might train one group with on-the-field tactical drills while training a different group with video analysis and theoretical quizzes.

One important note when it comes to deliberate performance: it's best used in situations in which you are already competent. Just as I wouldn't ask a player to change their forehand grip right before a tournament match, you probably shouldn't try a new training modality in a practice that already requires your maximum focus—in your first session with a new team, for example. The difficulty level has to be just right: tough enough to break you out of your comfort zone but easy enough that it won't interrupt your performance. For tasks at which you're more of a novice, that's where off-the-job practice comes in.

On-the-job practice has other limitations, unfortunately. For one, there's more pressure (no one wants to screw up in front of their team) and there are more distractions (coaches, athletes, drills, etc.). These can be overwhelming when you're trying to learn a new skill. What's more, in a real-life setting, we might not get that many repetitions (chances to practice the intended skill). If I'm working on what I say when players are exhausted, there may only be one or two moments during a session where that's appropriate.

ACTIVITY: Take the two aspects of your coaching that you identified as possible areas of improvement above. How could you practice them on the job? Jot down some ideas.

Practicing off the Job: Deliberate Practice

In Chapter 2, I shared the story of Maggie, the reading teacher who practiced handling unexpected questions during her class discussions. What would this look like for coaches? In her case, she had the help of a fellow teacher who could play the role of the student. But that's not always necessary.

On your own, there are a number of ways to practice your coaching—if you're creative. Here are some examples.

Objective: Better economy of language when setting up drills

Practice: At home, with your phone, audio record yourself explaining a drill. Listen back to it and transcribe it, writing down each word (including filler words, like "um" and "uh"). Rewrite it to be as succinct as possible, and then rerecord yourself. Continue until you're happy with it, and then practice with a new drill or exercise.

Objective: More confident body language during team talks

Practice: Film yourself giving a made-up team talk. Identify one area of body language to improve (e.g. posture, gestures, facial expressions) and practice in short chunks (e.g. 15 to 30 seconds) in front of a mirror or on video.

Objective: Focus on the lower body first when working on technique

Practice: Pick an athlete and, either by imagining them or by watching video, identify what technical changes you would suggest that they make. Write down what exercises you would use, what you would do if they struggled, and what you would do to progress things once they got it. Pick another athlete and repeat the process.

Off-the-job practice consists of two main exercises: mental rehearsal, in which you evaluate what you would (or should) do in different scenarios; and physical rehearsal, in which you practice the actual "doing." Together, these cover all three elements of coaching: observation, planning, and execution.

As you can imagine, both of these practices benefit tremendously from the use of video. There are two primary ways to use video to practice coaching. The first is to film yourself coaching. Ideally, in the video you are miked up, all the players are in view, and it's possible to hear them (at least when they're talking to you). Not only do you get to review what you did and said, but you also get to review the players' reactions. Where are they looking when you're talking? What is their body language when you give feedback? How does their energy change after you stop? How successful were they at accomplishing the task? You may have observed these things during your coaching, or you may not have been able to observe them due to other tasks, such as engaging with one particular athlete or modifying your practice plan. Rewatching your own video can give you information that you would otherwise be missing out on.

The second is to watch footage of other coaches coaching. This can be more challenging, but thanks to social media and "behind the scenes" features, it isn't impossible. As I touched on in Chapter 2, the best approach is often to do what I call ghost coaching—to imagine that you are coaching even when you aren't. As you watch the players or the practice, try to put yourself in "coach mode." What would you do in this situation? How would you progress things? When would you stop? What feedback would you give, and in what tone? As you go along, compare yourself to the coach you're watching. Were you on the same page, or did you take different approaches? Did the coach's approach work? How did the athletes respond? This sort of mental rehearsal is one of the best ways to get additional coaching hours without actually having to coach.

Video can be a powerful tool, but it's just that: a tool. The same fundamentals that apply to our athletes' practice also apply to us. One of the important rules to remember is that for any kind of practice, repetition is key. When working on a particular aspect of your coaching, consider that you might need to work on it for a few weeks, both off and on the job. First, you'll need the repetitions in order to figure out what works and what doesn't, to get past that awkward stage where the words don't quite roll off the tongue and your decision-making is a little slow. Then, you'll need the repetitions in order to make new behaviors automatic. This doesn't mean you should practice running the same drill or giving the same speech over and over again—on the contrary, you should vary your practice so that it accurately represents your working conditions. It just means that you want whatever you practiced to be so automatic that you can do it without thinking. After all, if you have to dedicate focus to it when you're working, you'll have to remove focus from another area, which will likely impact your performance. Repetition is the mother of all skills.

Another rule for practice is to get feedback. It may sound obvious, but it's incredibly rare. As we'll discuss in Chapter 7, a second set of eyes on your coaching practice can be an amazing resource, not only to spot things you might miss, but also to give you a perspective that you may not have considered. Of course, in an ideal scenario you would have a master coach, someone more experienced than you, to mentor you. But when it comes to practicing your coaching, there are plenty of reasons why having a colleague of equal or even lesser experience who can provide feedback may be just as good, if not better.

The curse of expertise states that as we become more knowledgeable, we forget what it's like to *not* know certain things. A highly experienced coach may not even know why they are good, or what it is that they are doing that's effective. And if they don't have experience in coach development, they may not know where to give you feedback. On the other hand, a colleague may have dealt with the same problem you're dealing with or may know you and your coaching context better. A less experienced coach may see things more through the eyes of a player, which could be exactly what you're looking for.

Ultimately, who you ask to observe you is not the most important thing. Far more crucial is to be specific with your request. For example, instead of asking, "Hey, could you watch me coach and give me some feedback on my team talks?" try, "I'm working on sounding more confident in my team talks. Could you watch me for 5 minutes and let me know what you think?"

You are already asking for someone's time, and you're asking them to do something they may not be entirely comfortable with. Don't forget that people can find it unpleasant to give feedback to people they know. Furthermore, it can be intimidating to be given carte blanche to provide any feedback they feel is necessary. Now not only do they have to observe multiple details, but they have to choose which ones to present to you.

Instead, do whatever you can to make it easy for them. Give them a specific duration (e.g. 5 minutes) and tell them exactly what to look for. Of course, depending on your relationship with them and their own personality, skill set, and level of expertise, you may find that you can ask them for more, or encourage them to use their own judgment. But it's good to start with a simple request to get them on board. A little feedback is better than no feedback.

Asking a colleague for feedback has other benefits. First, they may be able to give feedback on multiple occasions, allowing you to get repetitions and check if you're making progress. Second, you'll be forced to coach while someone watches you. Not only will this help you coach under pressure, it also will keep you from deceiving yourself by editing video or only selecting a "good" session.

ACTIVITY: Looking at those same two aspects of your coaching you'd like to improve from the previous activity, how could you practice them off the job? Take 5 minutes to write down some ideas.

Reflecting

I've spent a lot of time throughout this book discussing the first three elements of the open skill framework: perception, decision-making, and execution. But there is one final piece before the cycle repeats itself: reflecting on feedback. A tennis player perceives the incoming ball, decides how to respond, hits their shot, and then processes feedback—both from their sensation of the hit as well as the opponent's reaction—before resuming the cycle.

Reflection is critical for coach development. As the authors of the study on serial-winning coaches (SWC) summarize, "SWC deemed a deep level of self-reflection and self-awareness as necessary for any learning to take place." In the words of one coach, "You never stop thinking about it when you go home; about the things you could have done better to impact the outcome" (Lara-Bercial and Mallett, 2016, p. 231). Reflection is difficult, and it demands courage. Not only does it take time and effort, but it often requires confronting failures and weaknesses—sometimes painful ones. Nonetheless, these legendary coaches rated self-reflection as among the most powerful and lasting form of self-development.

For us coaches, reflection can take on many forms, from problem-solving in the car to sitting down with a pen and paper. Unstructured reflection can be powerful. Motivated by a specific goal or a particular problem, allow yourself to reflect freely, exploring any ideas or tangents that come to mind. You may find that unstructured reflection works best for you when you are also engaged in another task (e.g. driving, showering, or doing the dishes).

Structured reflection, on the other hand, can help make sense of a particular event (e.g. a tournament, a game, a practice, or a meeting) in order to learn from it. While there's no one-size-fits-all approach, no script to follow, the following structure has proven beneficial in my own practice:

- What?

  What happened? What did you do, and what did the athletes do? What did the opponents do? What about the assistant coaches? What drills did you run, and how did the game unfold? This is the time to record the details of what happened. Before you analyze, you must record.

- So what?

  What are the implications of what you observed? What does this tell you? What have you learned from this?

- Now what?

  What will your next practice or game look like? How will you adapt based on what you've learned? Is there more research you need to do?

Beyond unstructured or structured, reflection can also be specific or general. You may choose to reflect on a particular habit you have been trying to change, or a new type of drill you've been implementing. In such cases, you'll want to be specific, both in your observations and in your learnings. Or you may want to reflect more generally on your work: How does it feel? What do you like about it, and what don't you like about it?

Reflection can also be big picture or small picture. You might choose to reflect only on today's practice, or you could reflect on your team's progress over the last three months. Even with a specific topic, you could reflect on the warm-up you ran today (How responsive were the players? Did one exercise not work as well as intended?) or you could reflect on how the warm-ups have gone over the course of the season (Are the players benefitting from them? Are they too long or too short?).

Regardless of the type or style of reflection, one thing is clear: It has to lead to action. For the planning, doing, and reflecting cycle to work, reflection has to lead back to planning. In other words, ensure that the takeaways from your reflections are integrated into your plans. Hold yourself accountable for the changes you want to make. The learning from one reflection can become the focus point of the next one. In an article called "Challenge Accepted," Dawn Staley discusses the moment an assistant coach told her the team was tuning her out:

> *So I did step back and process things and really took Lisa's words to heart and I changed. I looked in the mirror and said "if it's me then I have to do something differently," and*

> *what I did was I talked less and listened more. I involved the team more in the preparation for games. I created a dialogue with the team and I brought them in individually and talked to them a lot more. I made them a part of the process and it worked out great. ... As leaders, you have to be able to know when you need to self-evaluate and when you need to change so you can reach the people you need to reach. I am always reflecting and really trying to get better. I am still always looking to be challenged. (Staley, 2018)*

Coaching happens primarily in the brain, which is why most of us can keep coaching well past our physical prime. In coaching, as in any other intellectual pursuit, reflection is central to learning. For coaches, it can be self-focused or centered on another coach; it can be structured or unstructured, general or specific, big picture or small. No matter how reflection occurs, the key to it is twofold: that you do it, and that you act on it.

Summary

- Learning can be formal, non-formal, or informal. Each type of learning has its pros and cons. Take what you can from each of them, but be deliberate in seeking out the information you'd like to learn.
- Take notes and try to see how you can apply what you've learned to your day-to-day practice. Form your own coaching methodology and discuss it with colleagues in order to get the most out of your learning.
- Coaches can practice just like athletes do. Identify what it is you'd like to get better at, give it a name, and define what success looks like.
- When practicing on the job, you can estimate or experiment. You can experiment just to see what happens, or you can experiment with a specific goal in mind.

- When practicing off the job, use video, get repetitions, and seek out feedback.
- All great coaches self-reflect. Reflection can take many shapes and forms, but what's important is that you do it and that you act on it.

Chapter 6
How We Can Perform Better

If you're anything like me, you've probably felt that some practice sessions are just better than others. Why is that? What makes for a great practice session versus an average one? No doubt some of the contributing factors include preparation, athlete readiness, drill selection, and so on. But have you ever felt that your *own* performance—your presence, attentiveness, and energy—was affecting the quality of your practices? Have you felt that some days, you are just "in the zone" more than others, spotting small details, bringing the right energy, and communicating effortlessly? The feeling of coaching with maximum effectiveness and minimum friction is the result of being in a peak performance state (PPS).

Just as each athlete has a PPS, so does each coach—just compare the soft-spoken John Wooden to the explosive Bobby Knight. Good coaches adjust their approach to the athletes in front of them, but they do so while staying true to themselves and their own style of coaching. Coaching in a way that isn't "you" will not only come across as inauthentic, it will likely make it more difficult for you to be at your best. Conversely, coaching in your PPS will be easier, lead to better results, and bring you more enjoyment.

First, we have to identify the key features of our PPS, and then we can learn to get into it.

ACTIVITY:

To find your coaching PPS, ask yourself the following questions about times you have coached at your best:

What does it feel like? Does it feel smooth? Organized? Fired up? Like I'm driving a race car or floating out at sea?

Answer:

What energy levels do I have? Am I at a ten out of ten, bouncing off the walls? Am I at a one out of ten, calm and quiet, hiding in the shadows? Or am I somewhere in between?

Answer:

What are the things I do? Am I more talkative at my best? Do I run more? Do I slow down and take my time? What are the key behaviors I carry out when I'm at my best?

Answer:

What do my players experience? Do they feel that I am there for them, that I love them? Do they feel my energy, my presence? Do they feel that they are independent and capable? What do they feel during my best sessions?

Answer:

What do my practices have in common? Do I do my best work on Fridays? In the afternoons? Is there a certain age group I do best with? Why do I coach better as a result of these things? Can I replicate these effects in other conditions?

Answer:

Your PPS can usually be defined by a few variables: your mood, your focus, and your energy. Take two minutes and circle the terms below that most reflect you when you're doing your best coaching.

Mood:

Angry	Content	Hopeful	Proud
Assertive	Creative	Irritated	Other
Calm	Curious	Loving	
Cheerful	Excited	Optimistic	

What are you focusing on?

The big picture	Keeping athletes' energy up	Taking time to explain	Athletes' moods
Specific teaching points	Maximizing time	Individual moments	Other

Mark with a dot the place you feel your energy is at when you are coaching at your best.

Energy:

Low High

Developing and Maintaining Focus

Once you've identified the key elements of your PPS, the question remains: How do you get into it? We can't simply wait to have a good day—we want to be able to put ourselves in a zone where we can perform at our highest level as often as possible. Thankfully, we can learn how from some of the best athletes and coaches in the world.

The job of a coach is multi-faceted: beyond coaching and competing, we're dealing with injured players, emails from parents, lineup changes, staff meetings, uniform orders ... the list goes on. Whether or not you consider these part of the job or distractions from the "real job" of coaching, the fact of the matter is that our attention is constantly being pulled in multiple different directions. This can be a problem when our success is dependent on our ability to perform in the moment while at the same time making sure others feel seen and heard. The slightest sign that we're not mentally or emotionally present can diminish trust and confidence. As such, being able to block out the noise and focus on the signal is critical. Thankfully, it's a skill that can be developed.

ACTIVITY: On average, for what percentage of a practice do you think you're completely focused on the task at hand? Draw a line on the scale.

One of the best methods for developing focus is *mindfulness training*, common to many forms of meditation. Such practices encourage the learner to be aware of distracting thoughts while simultaneously letting them go, returning focus to the task at hand. There is scientific evidence that supports the idea that continuous practice of this sort, by pushing one out of one's comfort zone, can lead to improvements in concentration (Semple, 2010).

To practice mindfulness, find a quiet place where you can sit and close your eyes. Set a timer for 10 minutes and focus on your breathing, counting each inhalation and exhalation all the way up to 10, and then back down to 1. Any time another thought enters your mind, don't fight it, just allow it to pass. If you suddenly find that you're thinking about something other than your breathing, just gently bring your focus back to your breath.

If you're unaccustomed to this sort of mindfulness training, you may note with some surprise how difficult it can be to stay focused. That's OK. With continuous practice, you'll find it easier to let go of distractions and stay on task. Over time, as your attentional control improves, you can increase the duration of your meditation sessions. If you want to develop your mindfulness in a more relevant context, you can monitor your focus throughout a practice. Every time you notice that your attention has drifted to something that isn't relevant, make a small tally mark on a piece of paper or in the corner of your practice plan and then reset your focus. Over time, see if the number of distracted moments decreases or if the time taken to refocus goes down.

On the topic of refocusing, *verbal and kinesthetic cues* can be particularly useful. Just as athletes in competition do, you can consider mantras (e.g. "right here, right now") or actions (e.g. a quick snap of the fingers) to help you return to the present moment. These will likely be unique to you. Verbal cues should be focused on the present moment, rather than the past or the future, and should be focused on what to do, rather than what not to do. Kinesthetic cues are usually short and sharp. Consider what we say when we're in a dreamy state: pinch me!

To make attentional cues even more effective, you can practice using them when you feel especially focused. By using them repeatedly when you are in a state of focus, your brain begins to associate the trigger with the desired state. Over time, using the trigger will help you enter this state.[9]

ACTIVITY:

Come up with two verbal cues you would feel comfortable using to refocus yourself during a practice or game:

-
-

Come up with two kinesthetic cues you would feel comfortable using:

-
-

These are not the only tools we can take from the athlete's toolbox. Pre-performance routines can help coaches get into the zone before a practice or competition. In 2015, *USA Today* spoke to a handful of NCAA basketball coaches and asked them what they do in the stressful moments before a game (Auerbach, 2015). The answers varied wildly, but everyone seemed to have a routine, whether it was drinking Pepto Bismol (Thad Matta), finding a lucky penny placed somewhere by a student manager (Tim Miles), or sitting in a quiet place to meditate and pray (Larry Krystkowiak).

9 While writing this book, I would often wear noise-canceling headphones and listen to white noise in order to block out distractions. Over time, I began to associate the white noise with a state of productivity, to the point that I would listen to it even in quiet spaces because it improved my efficiency.

One of the best anecdotes on the importance of pre-performance routines comes from Bill Walsh, former head coach of the San Francisco 49ers:

> *It was during this brief moment that I would remove myself mentally from the activities and considerable energy around me on the sidelines. I visualized that I was looking at the football field through a big plate-glass window, removed, in a sense, so I wouldn't get overly involved emotionally and could stay with what I had prepared prior to the game. Clear thinking and overly charged emotions are usually antithetical.*
>
> *I actually think my heart rate may have gone down as kickoff approached. A sense of calm came over me. If a person can be extremely intense, extraordinarily focused, and completely composed all at the same time, I guess that's the state I achieved through not singing the national anthem.*
>
> *By kickoff, I had blocked out crowd noise and all the crazy energy and activity on the sidelines, which are disruptive to good decision making. It may have been as pleasing a sensation as any I ever got as a coach.*
>
> *The state of mind I could achieve as a game was about to begin was pure, so free of dissonance—it was just the best. The ritual created it. It was the gladiator mindset, free of stress, distractions, and emotionalism, that got me ready for the competition and allowed me to work at my highest level. (Walsh et al., 2009, p. 154)*

Visualization and Preparation

Walsh's story is also a great example of two techniques that may not develop our focus, but can help direct our focus to the right things: *visualization* and *preparation*. Just like athletes, coaches would do well to visualize their own performance in advance of a game or even a practice. Take some time the night before to visualize the venue, the weather, the athletes, the equipment, and the opponents. Then, ask yourself some questions. What will it look like if the practice goes well? What will it look like if it goes poorly? How will I respond? What will I say at halftime if we're winning? And so on. The more you visualize and rehearse, the more the environment and the event itself will feel comfortable when you're in the moment, allowing you to stay in the zone.

ACTIVITY: Set a timer for 2 minutes and visualize, in as much detail as possible, what your next practice will look like.

All-time-great NFL coach Bill Belichick has a reputation for demanding (both of himself and of his team) an attention to detail and level of preparation that is legendary. In 2019, before the start of the Super Bowl, he was caught on camera questioning a referee as to when the stadium roof would be closed—a relatively innocuous detail to spectators, but an important one to Belichick, who recognized that any delay could lead to wind affecting the play on the field. In 2022, he gave an uninterrupted 5-minute answer to a question on game preparation, which included gems like this:

> *[The Arizona Cardinals] play a lot of different people. They have a lot of different personnel groups. So, it's kind of like, what are we calling this? What is this? So, as we're looking at it individually, you're calling it one thing, I'm calling it something else, somebody else is calling it something else. Wait a minute, how are we all going to talk about this, so we actually know what we're talking about? Like, that would be a big thing for this week. Same thing with, again, Arizona is a good example, some of the plays they run are not quite the same maybe. Okay, what are we going to call this play? Is this play really that play? Or is this play really a different play with this little variation to it? How do we want to present that to the players? Is it a pass? Is it run-pass option? What category does it fall into? How do we want to call it? How do we want to categorize it? So that part of the week of preparation is very important. So, when you actually start working on a team, you're not confused and everything's blurred. Alright, what's this? What's this? This kind of looks like this. This kind of looks like that. Where is*

> *this guy? Is he a linebacker? Is he a DB? Is he a defensive end? In this package, he's this. In that package, he's that. That type of thing.*[10] *(New England Patriots, 2022)*

American football is a notoriously complex sport, but this isn't to say that Belichick's rigorous preparation can't be replicated in other sports, or even that it should remain exclusively a game-day phenomenon. Of course, players and assistant coaches should be as prepared as possible when it comes time to compete, but what about you? What do *you* need to prepare for in order to be at *your* best?

Preparing for distractions, whether internal (worries, other obligations) or external (text messages, other coaches), can help block them out when they arrive. Some coaches include potential distractions in their weekly or daily plans so that they can anticipate them. Oftentimes, we are distracted because we are trying to remember too many things at once, or trying to make decisions on all of them at the same time. Consider making a list of everything on your plate, thereby freeing some space in your head, and then making a quick note of when you'll tackle each item, and how. That way, when that tricky parent meeting pops into your head, you can let it go, knowing that you're going to plan for it tomorrow morning.

In my own coaching, I'm often on the road at international tournaments, traveling from country to country and venue to venue. Sometimes, I return to familiar sights, but more often than not, I'm in a new environment. In the lead up to the trip, I try to prepare myself as best as possible: How many courts are there? Will they be available for practice? Are there other clubs nearby that we can use for practice? What balls will they be using, and where can I purchase them, if necessary? Will there be a physiotherapist on site? Is there a gym at the hotel? The answers to these questions and more go into a spreadsheet so that I can anticipate potential decisions and act quickly when I come to them.

This is not athlete preparation, like taking care of your body, eating well, or strategizing. This isn't game day preparation, like warming up, checking the weather conditions, or scouting an opponent. This is coach preparation. If coaching is an open skill, and therefore includes

10 Incidentally, this is another great example of the value of a shared vocabulary, as discussed in Chapter 5.

perception, decision-making, execution, and feedback, then it is about taking steps to make each of those elements as efficient as possible.

The same approach can apply to practice. I'm referring, of course, to lesson planning, which can be a contentious topic. One the one hand, there are those who remind us that failing to plan is planning to fail, that every battle is won before it is fought. John Wooden was known for his diligent approach to planning. Every session was reportedly planned down to the minute on a 3" x 5" cue card, and he tried to stick to his plan no matter what. After each day, he reviewed the plan to note what had gone well and what hadn't before filing it away. It was said that each day, he could go to his filing cabinet and look at his practice plan from that same day one year ago, two years ago, etc.

On the other hand, the vast majority of the world-class, highly accomplished tennis coaches I've met walk onto the court with one or two things they'd like to accomplish and only a rough idea of how they'd like to get there. Why the disparity?

For one, we have to consider Wooden's background. His training was as a teacher, where lesson plans are far more common, and he was meticulous and oriented toward writing and reading even in his private life. Meanwhile, although the quality of coach education is improving, historically coaches have not been expected to prepare through attention to detail or rigorous off-court work the way teachers have been expected to prepare for lessons. As such, it makes sense that coaches may not tend to plan as much.

We also have to consider that just because Wooden was inordinately successful doesn't mean one should copy everything he did. After all, he was a gifted speaker and motivator, his understanding of basketball strategy and team composition was very strong, and his success (along with the virtues of UCLA) allowed him to recruit the best talent that the United States had to offer. These factors may have contributed just as much (if not more) to his success as his approach to planning.

It's also worth thinking about the nature of our job. If you'll recall, coaching is an open skill, which means that what we do is dependent on what we perceive and decide. It's very difficult to predict what's going to happen over a year, a month, or even a session. You might plan a competitive schedule, only to be disrupted by injury, or more positively, results better than anticipated. You might plan a practice, only to find that your athletes aren't "getting it" and that more time is needed in a certain area. Flexibility is an asset in player development. Coaches of team sports, like Wooden, may not have as much wiggle room as those of us working with individual athletes one-on-one or in small groups, and may therefore place more value on a detailed practice plan.

At the same time, there is one big benefit to planning that often goes undiscussed: what it does to your focus. As I've mentioned previously—the human brain has a relatively small capacity for working memory, the part of our memory that stores information in the short term and uses it to complete tasks. For example, compare the amount of information stored in your long-term memory (e.g. birthdays, addresses, things you learned at school, names, routines) with how many numbers in a sequence you could remember and recite back to someone (around seven, for most people). Crucially, our working memory is the part of our brain we use most when coaching. We use our working memory to store short-term information (e.g. whether a player missed a shot) as well as to make decisions (e.g. whether to progress a drill).

Now let's imagine you're in the middle of running a practice. You don't have a plan and you're in the middle of an exercise when you start thinking about what drill you'll run next. What part of your brain are you using? That's right—you're using your working memory. As you consider what you'll do in a few minutes and take into account the different variables, the limited attention you have in your working memory is directed away from the task at hand (coaching your players) and directed toward the planning process.

A good analogy for this is driving versus parallel parking. Most people are at ease driving and talking to someone at the same time. After all, the basics of driving are stored in long-term memory, where someone doesn't really have to focus in order to follow the rules of the road. Parallel parking, however, is much more challenging for most people, and is *not* stored in long-term memory. It requires dedicated focus, which is why you see people stutter or even stop talking entirely when they begin to parallel park: their working memory is being overloaded. This is the risk we take when we fail to plan.

There are, of course, downsides and limitations to practice planning, mainly due to the variable nature of our job. However, I'd argue that the unpredictable elements of our job fall into two categories:

1. **Skill level/rate of progress.** No matter how well you know your athletes, you don't know exactly how they'll progress from session to session or how they'll be performing on any given day.
2. **Physical/mental/emotional energy levels.** Similarly, bad sleep, a surprisingly tough fitness session, or a disappointing result can all throw a wrench in the works.

Thankfully, both of these wild cards can be managed, to the extent that we can plan for different possibilities. I'd suggest that a normal session plan should contain the following elements:

1. **Objectives**

   What do you want to accomplish? How will you know if the practice session is a success?

2. **Priorities**

   What will you put ahead of all else? What will you spend the most time on? What do you want to do when the athletes are physically and mentally fresh?

3. **Main sections**

   Tied into your objectives, what are the building blocks of your practice? If the practice were a book, what would the chapters be?

4. **Observation points**

   What will you look for? What will you give feedback on? How will you know if the players are progressing the way you'd like?

5. **Progressions/Regressions**

   How will you make things easier or harder? What variations of exercises do you have up your sleeve if something isn't working?

6. **Possible deviations**

   What might go wrong? How will you adjust?

The exact *how* of your planning doesn't matter so much. Written out or in your head, digital or on paper, structured or not, what's important is that *you are planning the things that you need to plan*. What they are will depend on your sport, your role, and a host of other factors. Some days might require more planning than others. The only question you have to ask yourself after each session is: Was I adequately prepared to coach at my best?

Managing Distractions, Stress, and Anxiety

Lastly, on the topic of focus, I'd be remiss if I didn't mention one of the most ubiquitous and yet most dangerous threats to focused coaching: the smartphone. A 2023 study found that the mere *presence* of a smartphone reduced focus in test subjects, even when they didn't look at it or pick it up (Skowronek et al., 2023). Read that again. It's not just that smartphones are a distraction when they're being used—they're also a distraction when they're *not* being used. Not only do they buzz and beep with texts, calls, emails, and other notifications, but even when silent, their presence can be a constant reminder of everything that's going on, good or bad, outside of the here and now, pulling your focus away from those who need it most: your athletes. Putting your phone on "do not disturb" may be a good start, but for your most effective coaching, the best move is to leave it in the office or a duffel bag so that you can stay focused on your athletes without wondering about what you're missing.

On one hand, we have to develop our ability to focus. On the other hand, we also have to manage our physical, mental, and emotional loads so that the demands on our focus and energy aren't as high. Coach burnout is an issue that is starting to gain more attention. A 2023 CBS article covered recent coach stress and overload issues and featured a number of high-ranking coaches who had left their positions in order to feel physically and mentally healthier (Norlander, 2023).

While coaching doesn't require the same physical effort as playing, it almost always demands more time—planning practices, meeting with staff members and athletes, doing video analysis, and so on. A *Sports Illustrated* feature on Sean McVay, the youngest head coach in NFL history to win the Super Bowl, revealed that his days are often more than 12 hours long (Benoit, 2017). Whereas players only have to worry about their individual objectives and performance, a coach has to worry about each and every one of them, not only by showing them empathy but also by observing, monitoring, and adjusting elements of practice to suit their needs. And in many cases, all this work is done under the omnipresent threat of being let go for poor performance. Indeed, coaching is a mentally and emotionally taxing profession.

There are a great many arguments for why the current sport coaching climate needs to change to a model that is more supportive, both of athletes and coaches, and it goes without saying that an unhealthy environment is simply that—unhealthy—and our attempts to control what we can and thrive within such an environment will always be limited. However, these discussions are outside the scope of this book. My goal in this section is simply to provide you with some tools to help manage the load and stay fresh.

One of the simplest yet most overlooked techniques is rest. Coaches will preach rest and recovery for their athletes while at the same time working themselves to the bone in the name of "commitment" or "passion." But what's true for athletes is true for coaches, too: It's no use taking a break once you're already burned out. For longevity and maximum performance, periods of hard work should be interspersed with periods of rest over the course of a week, month, and year. Of course, different coaches will prefer different arrangements; for example, some will prefer longer days and longer breaks and others shorter days and shorter breaks. However, the key principles remain the same. This is not to say that high-performance coaching shouldn't be a demanding job. As we discussed in the introduction to Part 1, our athletes are trying to do something extraordinary, and we have a duty to support them. The job *should* be tough, and there's nothing wrong with doing tough things. We just have to make sure that we stay healthy in order to deliver our best performances consistently.

One of the challenges coaches have with taking time off is they fear that their athletes won't be taken care of. This brings us to another best practice: *delegation*. You may not have a team of assistant coaches, but that doesn't mean you can't get help from a colleague or parent. In so doing, not only do you conserve mental and physical energy, but your athletes benefit from a second set of eyes. Over time, the person you delegate to may develop their skills and take on more responsibilities, making them a part of the team.

No matter the support network you have, there's one person you can always delegate to: the athlete themselves. In fact, this may be one of the best moves you can make. Not only can this teach an athlete responsibility, it can also help them to develop autonomy and a sense of ownership of the process. An athlete who is actively involved in their own development may take it more seriously, appreciate how difficult it is, gain respect for those involved, and build confidence from knowing they've put in the work.

One of the other difficulties coaches discuss is the 24/7 anxiety—the racing thoughts that last late into the night, no matter the time of year. It's normal that someone who is engaged in a profession that is so mentally challenging would find themselves thinking about it nonstop. But that doesn't make it productive. The ability to *compartmentalize*—to choose when to engage with certain topics and leave the others behind, for another time—is essential. Many of the focus tools mentioned earlier can be of use here. I'll just draw your attention to one that is particularly relevant in this context: writing things down. As I mentioned, one of the reasons our heads swim with thoughts is because we are subconsciously worried about forgetting them. Writing them down solves this problem by allowing us to let go, knowing that they are stored somewhere safe. This is why sleep doctors and psychologists will recommend that some patients keep a notepad and pen by their bed—it works! Another reason we can find ourselves overwhelmed is because we are trying to solve a messy, complicated problem, such as who to cut from the team, what plays to run, or how to approach a difficult conversation. Writing our thoughts down can help us organize and clarify them, easing some of our mental tension.

Lasty, while somewhat cheesy, it can be good for us to *remember why we do what we do*. Hopefully, you got into this profession by choice—because you love your sport, you enjoy working with kids, or you want to make a difference. If you didn't, then hopefully you stayed by choice. As the days get longer and the stresses mount, it's easy to develop tunnel vision, to begin to believe that the issues facing us are the be-all and end-all. In those moments, take a second to remind yourself of your *raison d'être*. Some may have a poignant photo or quote on their phone's lock screen, while others may have a mantra to repeat. Just as the act of regular gratitude journaling has been shown to increase gratitude, reminding ourselves of a bigger purpose can help reduce our stress and anxiety.

ACTIVITY: Of the strategies listed above, which can you see yourself using to manage your mental load? How could you implement it in the next few weeks or months?

Staying Healthy

Finally, we can't discuss maximal performance without mentioning the same factors that affect the very athletes we coach: eating, drinking, and sleeping. As we've seen, coaching is a cognitive endeavor that requires a high level of focus, decision-making, and emotional control. Not only that, but it's a physical job—which involves demonstrating technique, projecting your voice, or running up and down the field, among other things—and your level of energy will oftentimes influence the energy of the practice. But how much of an impact can eating, drinking, and sleeping have?

In a 2021 review, researchers synthesized the findings from 46 peer-reviewed studies from the last 20 years and looked at the links between nutrition and neuroscience – specifically, the effect our diet can have on things like cognition, memory, learning, psychomotor processing, and inhibition control. The results are summarized below (Muth and Park, 2021):

- Helpful:
    - Complex carbohydrates
    - Monounsaturated fats
    - Polyunsaturated fats
    - Adequate protein consumption

- Harmful:
    - Simple carbohydrates
    - Saturated fatty acids
    - Trans fats
    - Over- and under-consumption of protein

As you can see, the impact of diet on mental function is vast. Similarly, a review of studies from 2011 to 2014 found that "even mild dehydration can lead to impaired concentration, slower reaction times, short-term memory issues, and negative mood changes" (Shabir, 2020). When it comes to sleep, a meta-analysis by Pilcher and Huffcutt (1996) determined that repeated sleep deprivation can significantly impair performance on cognitive and motor tasks, and negatively affect mood.

These findings shouldn't come as a surprise. After all, we're all in the business of human performance and the better our athletes eat, sleep, and drink, the better they perform. So why is it that a great many coaches fail to prioritize these aspects in their own lives?

One of the reasons is no doubt cultural. In a lot of high-performance sporting environments, coaches are expected to work long hours in stressful conditions. I wrote earlier of the *Sports Illustrated* article "24 hours with Rams Coach Sean McVay" (Benoit, 2017) in which he works a 12-hour day. By 2023, McVay was contemplating stepping away from coaching for a while, describing himself, without using the word itself, as burned out.[11] This is just one example of many.

Another potential reason we as coaches don't always prioritize our own health is simply that we don't value it. There's a belief that sacrificing our health is the sign of a good coach. We believe we are giving it all to the cause when, in actual fact, sacrificing our health just makes us worse at our job. There's no doubt that high-performance coaching requires making sacrifices and working hard. The crucial skill is being able to recognize when the well is running dry and it's time to refuel.

11 McVay's challenge was unique. Not only was he working a lot, but he had gone from being the youngest Super Bowl–winning coach in history in just his fifth season as a head coach to being the coach of a team that had failed to make the playoffs in the last two seasons. There's no doubt that these factors contributed just as much, if not more, to his feeling burned out.

At the same time, it's worth considering how we can be more efficient with our time so that we can afford to take time off. Coaching is a social profession—we often work closely with colleagues, and when we're not we're interacting with athletes, sponsors, parents, and officials. It can be easy to get sidetracked and lose track of time. In this area, it may be valuable to learn from some of the highest performing organizations, like Amazon and Google. These companies, and others, are acutely aware of how valuable each of their team members' time is, and that's why they're known for their extreme rules for meetings. At Amazon, latecomers are locked out (Chawla, 2023). At Google, Eric Schmidt and Jonathan Rosenberg had a similar rule about starting on time, with an added clause: If you finish the meeting early, don't fill the gap, just get back to work. Yet another rule shared between the two companies was that no side conversations were allowed during meetings. Participants had to stay on track (Schmidt and Rosenberg, 2014, pp. 163–165).

Of course, your days may or may not be filled with meetings. That's not the point. This isn't about meetings, it's about high performance. If we are to be high-performance coaches, then we should be *high-performance coaches*—coaches who perform at a high level. And to perform at a high level, we have to maximize our time. There are myriad productivity hacks available to everyone. Methods like the 5-minute rule or the Pomodoro technique can be useful, as can books like *Atomic Habits* or *Deep Work*. You will find what works for you. What's most important is that you squeeze the most out of your workday so that you can have shorter days. Work smarter, not longer.

ACTIVITY:

What are some things you could see yourself doing to nudge your mood, focus, or energy level toward your peak performance state?

Answer:

Chapter 7
Guidance and Mentorship

K. Anders Ericsson spent 30 years studying experts—people who were clear outliers in their domain, ranging from artists and authors to athletes and businesspeople. He and his colleagues pioneered the concept of deliberate practice, and their work inspired what Malcolm Gladwell termed the "10,000 hour rule" in his book *Outliers* (2008).[12] One of their less-discussed findings, however, was that in almost all cases, experts benefited from the services of a coach or teacher. As they summarize in an article for the *Harvard Business Review*:

> *Research on world-class performers ... has shown that* future experts *need different kinds of teachers at different stages of their development. In the beginning, most are coached by local teachers, people who can give generously of their time and praise. Later on, however, it is* essential *that performers seek out more-advanced teachers to keep improving their skills. Eventually,* all top performers *work closely with teachers who have themselves reached international levels of achievement. (Ericsson et al., 2007, emphasis mine)*

Remember, Ericsson isn't just talking about athletes here. He and his colleagues studied musicians, authors, CEOs, teachers, and others. In every case, they found that the best in their fields all worked with someone who could help them improve and perform at their best. The idea of nonathletic performers having coaches might seem unusual, but it makes intuitive sense. As Ericsson et al. (2007) write, "The development of expertise requires coaches who are capable of giving

12 It has since become clear that Gladwell either misunderstood or misrepresented Ericsson et al.'s findings with regard to the amount of time needed to become an expert. For more information, see Ericsson and Pool (2016).

constructive, even painful feedback." In their research, they found that the value of a coach for experts was twofold. First, a coach helped motivate and push them: "The elite performers we studied ... deliberately picked unsentimental coaches who would challenge them and drive them to higher levels of performance." Second, the best coaches helped performers identify which areas of their work they needed to improve in order to progress.

This idea—that the best performers should have coaches—is not only logical but, as we discussed in Part 1, backed up empirically by the number of professional sports coaches who had, or still have, mentors or other guiding figures. But as Ericsson et al. alluded to above, the role that this person plays can vary considerably, which is probably why public perceptions of mentorship vary greatly. For some, it's an extremely personal relationship, dealing with both on-the-job and off-the-job issues. For others, it's a purely professional relationship with strictly defined terms and conditions.

Cody Royle, author of *Second Set of Eyes: How Great Coaches Become Champions* (2023) and coach to multiple head coaches, advocates for a true coaching relationship. In other words, he believes that coaches should have their own coaches—someone dedicated to making them better, holding them accountable, and challenging them. It goes without saying that this is atypical in the sports world, even if Ericsson et al.'s research suggests it should be more commonplace. Coaches like Pep Guardiola, Steve Kerr, and Pat Summitt all had people they could go to for insight or to bounce ideas off of, but they were not coaches in the traditional sense, giving them instructions or holding them accountable. They were close confidants and mentors. This role is also common in the business world, where mentors can discuss challenging situations with CEOs without explicitly telling them what to do or how to do it. Another approach that some coaches use is to have a "board of directors"—their own group of trusted experts, each bringing their own individual experience and expertise to the table. Coaches can reach out on a case-by-case basis to the person most appropriate for the task at hand.

This is not to suggest that there is one right way to do things, or even to strictly categorize the roles that mentors will play. The truth is that the guiding figures you choose and what you rely on them for will depend not only on the stage of your career but also what it is you're looking for, and this can change throughout a week, month, or year. Generally speaking, coaches will look for one of three things from their mentors:

1. **Long-term support**. Coaching can be stressful as well as physically and emotional demanding. Turnover is often high, and burnout is a common risk. Too many coaches leave the profession too soon. In some situations, coaches will benefit from a mentor who can offer perspective, encouragement, and strategies for managing the workload. At the same time, mentors can also be on hand to offer career advice, increasing longevity and supporting growth.
2. **Skill development**. As I've stated numerous times throughout this book, coaching is a skill, and as both Royle and Ericsson et al. point out, coaches can develop their skills with the help of their own coaches.
3. **Performance maximization**. Some coaches will ask an expert coach to be a second set of eyes, to help them spot things they might miss, give advice on issues they might be facing in their day-to-day work, and generally make the business of coaching run more smoothly.

Regardless of how you see yourself benefiting from mentorship, both our knowledge of expertise and the empirical evidence from expert coaches around the world make one thing very clear: for high-performance coaching, having someone who can challenge or guide you (more than a friend or colleague can) is crucial. In this chapter I will discuss how best to find the right mentor and work with them in order to maximize your development.[13]

Choosing a Mentor

The first thing you must do is select the right mentor. While businesses and organizations will often assign an employee to a mentor, this practice is rare in the world of coaching. In some cases, coaches can benefit from mentorship as part of a course or grant, but these

13 While one could get picky about the words being used (coach, mentor, teacher, confidant, etc.), for simplicity's sake, I'll use the term "mentor" throughout the chapter.

opportunities are few and far between and are often constrained. As such, it may fall upon you to select and contact your mentor.

First, *pick someone who has accomplished what you aim to accomplish.* This may sound obvious, but sometimes coaches will find mentors who have impressive achievements but haven't done *exactly* what their mentee is looking to do. Examples are coaches who have been successful in one discipline of a sport, but lack experience in another, or coaches who have specialized in coaching men rather than women. While a lot of coaching skills are transferable, research suggests that teaching expertise is generally limited to the subject being taught (Sternberg and Horvath, 1995). It takes more work than you would expect to turn world-class math teachers into world-class science teachers. I suspect the same is true of sports coaching. This is not to say that fruitful collaborations cannot be built between coaches of different groups or of different sports. In such a situation, I would recommend clearly identifying what it is you want to learn, what your mentor will be able to provide, and how you'll be able to transfer these learnings to your coaching. However, the ideal scenario is to have someone who has achieved the goals you have set for yourself and who can therefore counsel you appropriately.

Similarly, try to *find someone who has done the sort of work that you are currently doing.* You may find a mentor who has reached the goal you have set for yourself (e.g. coach at the Olympics) but who hasn't done what you're currently doing (e.g. coaching at the regional level). Everyone follows a different path, and the sporting landscape is constantly changing. Not only is it important to find someone who has accomplished what you aim to accomplish, it's also vital to find someone who is doing (or has recently done) the sort of work that you are doing. In other words, if we envision coaching as a series of levels, someone who is successful at Level 4 may not know (or remember) how to be successful at Level 1 or 2. You want a mentor who can give advice that is actionable for you in your specific context, not theirs.

You'll also want to *find someone who is passionate about what they do and, more importantly, interested in sharing their knowledge and teaching others.* As outlined in Chapter 3, not everyone who is successful knows *why* they are successful. Furthermore, not everyone who knows why they're successful is interested in spending time (often unpaid) sharing their expertise with others. Pick someone who you won't feel guilty asking questions of, and who you think will be able to guide you the way a good teacher or mentor should. How can you identify these people? Oftentimes, they speak at conferences (which displays a desire to share their knowledge) or, better yet, they are already engaged in coach development. They may have mentored coaches in the past, or they might simply really like talking about coaching.

On that note, make sure your potential mentor is likely to be available! Although you can't know until you ask, consider how much time they might have at their disposal. Regular weekly discussions with an engaged mentor are better than biannual meetings with a world-class coach who can't remember what you last talked about.

Lastly, consider that your mentor probably shouldn't be a supervisor, or even work in the same organization as you. While employee–boss mentorships are common in many industries, they risk limiting your willingness to be completely open. For one, you may not be able to share some of the stresses of your work, either because your boss is responsible for them or because you don't want to seem unprofessional. You may also be uncomfortable discussing your weaknesses or failures with someone who exercises some control over your professional future. A mentor who holds no sway over you may be your best bet.

ACTIVITY: Take 2 minutes to make a list of potential mentors. Could different mentors help you in different aspects of your coaching? Do you have contacts who could potentially put you in touch?

Initiating Contact

Initiating contact with a potential mentor can be intimidating but also exciting. While you may feel uncomfortable approaching a stranger and asking them for help (something that some consider a sign of weakness), what you are doing will likely make them look kindly upon you. First, to ask someone to mentor you is to give them a compliment: you're saying that they are successful and have knowledge to share, and people tend to like people who give them compliments. Second, most coaches, no matter how busy or tired they are, have a degree of passion for the job and appreciate someone who is committed to bettering themselves. Even if they say no, chances are they will remember you as someone who went above and beyond in their dedication to the craft.

When reaching out to a potential mentor, be sure to do a few things:

- Introduce yourself. Don't just provide your name and background! While you might know a lot about your potential mentor, they might know nothing about you. Beyond the usual information, be sure to mention your current coaching context (ages, genders, levels, frequency, responsibilities), past experiences, and future ambitions.
- Be clear with what you are asking for. If they have not mentored before, they may not have any idea of what it entails. Be specific: What do you want to learn? How regularly do you want to meet, and through what medium (phone, Zoom, in person)? What topics would you like to discuss? What commitment will it take from them? Just like in any relationship, communicating clear expectations is vital.

Above all, don't be demanding. Flexibility is an asset when it comes to working with busy coaches. When I was 20, I moved across Canada to be mentored by a coach I respected. This, in and of itself, impressed him, but it wasn't until my first week working for him that he realized how serious I was. On Sunday night, I asked him when his first session of the day would be, and he said 7.00am. So on Monday morning, I woke up at 5.30 and took the bus in to watch him coach (at the time, I didn't have my driver's license). On Tuesday, I did the same thing. On Wednesday morning, when I again showed up at 7.00am, he asked me: "Are you going to do this every day?" To which I responded, "Of course." And from that day on he would pick me up and we would discuss coaching on the way to the club.

Of course, not every mentor–mentee arrangement works that well. I was young and single, and we both had an abundance of free time and passion. But I tried to make mentoring easy for him—we followed his schedule and I helped him out with busywork he didn't want to do. As a result, I was rewarded with hours of discussions and observations.

Making the Most of Your Meetings

The majority of your interactions with your mentor will likely take the form of one-on-one meetings. You may be lucky enough to have a mentor who will watch you coach and give feedback, or you may be able to watch your own mentor at work, but even if you do, these instances should still be supplemented by off-the-court discussions. Making the most of your time in these meetings is essential. Not only do you want to respect your mentor's time, you also want to get as much useful information out of them as possible.

To start, be sure to *have specific topics or questions in mind*. While long, flowing conversations are enjoyable, there's no guaranteeing that they will stay on topic or be relevant to your current issues. There's nothing worse than getting back onto the field after a meeting and realizing you forgot to ask about something that had been on your mind.

That being said, be willing to *ask follow-up questions*, rather than running through a list of questions like a pop quiz. Use each topic or question as a starting point and ask follow-up questions based on your own knowledge and experience. Remember: It's a discussion, not an interview. One of the best approaches is to try to anticipate what will happen when you implement their advice in your daily work. Think about how you might take what they're saying and do it your way. What problems might you run into? What are you unsure of? Try to ask follow-up questions based on these potential situations so that you don't have to try something, find it didn't work, and then wait another month before you can talk to them again.

On that note, *take notes*. Depending on your arrangement, you may have extended lengths of time between meetings, and the human brain is famously bad at remembering (even after a day, let alone a week or a month). Write down the topic or question, their answer, any actionable advice they give, how you'll implement said advice, and any questions you'd like to ask later.

At the start of your mentorship, you and your mentor may decide to set a mid- to long-term goal. In such cases, make sure to *review your progress* on the goal at each meeting or on a predetermined schedule.

Rather than jumping from topic to topic, you want to feel that the two of you together are aligned toward a common goal, following a clear path that will lead you to improved coaching.

Lastly, make sure to *have realistic expectations* regarding your mentor's commitment level. High-performance coaching is a demanding job, and they may only have limited time for you. Do not expect them to go above and beyond what you've agreed upon, and don't contact them outside of your agreed times. Ultimately, mentorship is sometimes more about guiding than teaching. In other words, the times without contact can give you the chance to self-reflect.

SIDEBAR:

While I think having a long-term mentor is often the best way to go, I'm also partial to occasional field trips—chances to step into a new environment and watch a master coach at work. It's something I've done on numerous occasions (one example is given at the start of Chapter 1) and each time I've left a better coach.

If you get the chance to watch a mentor coach, do the following:

- Have one or two specific things to look for in their coaching, but keep an open mind too—in a new environment, you may see things that you never thought to look for.
- If possible, ask for context. Try to understand what the coach is trying to do and why.
- Understand that you are only witnessing one session of many. What they do in this instance is not necessarily what they always do. Keep the session you observe in perspective.
- Ask questions, if possible during the session. Watching is useful on its own, but the formula for optimal learning in this context is Watching + Questioning + Reflecting.
- And of course, take notes. Otherwise, you will very quickly forget the small details of what you saw.

If a mentor coach gets the chance to watch you, do the following:

- Consider asking them to observe specific aspects of your coaching (things you may be struggling with) but also be open to general feedback. You may not even know what it is you're really struggling with!
- Give context, such as athlete background information, what you're working on, your intentions for the session, past experiences, and so on. Context will help shape your mentor's feedback.
- Do things as you would normally. Don't try to hide or avoid the bad—be as realistic as possible so that you can get the most useful feedback possible.

Applying What You Learn

The biggest impact of mentorship will not come from the discussions themselves, but rather how you choose to apply and practice what you've learned. It's easy to think that getting feedback is the hard part—it isn't. The hard part is going out into the real world and applying it, even if it's uncomfortable.

The most important rule to remember is simple: Do what they say. In their book *Practice Perfect: 42 Rules for Getting Better at Getting Better* (2012), Doug Lemov, Erica Woolway, and Katie Yezzi discuss a curious tendency we have, which is to want to discuss (and sometimes rebut) feedback before we try implementing it. Sometimes, the advice we're given doesn't seem natural or intuitive, but as they point out, if it was intuitive we would have thought of it already. Just as we ask our athletes to trust us and do things that are uncomfortable, we should do the same with our mentors. Do what they tell you to do, exactly how they tell you to do it, and *then* discuss and adjust. Not every suggestion you get will work—some will require changing and some will get thrown out. But be willing to step out of your comfort zone and try things out first.

Conversely, *don't put your mentor on a pedestal.* No one is perfect. They may not know exactly why they've been successful. And even if they *do* know, there's no guarantee that what worked for them will work for you. No two coaching journeys or contexts are the same. Show a healthy amount of respect and assume that they are right about what worked in their own experience. But don't be afraid to seek out second opinions or put your own twist on things. You are still in charge of your development.

In the early stages, *copying may be the best thing you can do.* To quote Louis Borfiga, former vice president of high performance for Tennis Canada: "A good coach is an idea thief." Expert painters spend their first few years of study copying the great paintings of the past. In doing so, they learn to use the same techniques, to appreciate the brush strokes, to feel what it's like to paint a masterpiece. Great authors like Hunter S. Thompson have been known to rewrite classics like *The Great Gatsby*, either by hand or on a typewriter, in order to become more familiar with great writing. Then, as they gained experience, these writers and painters learned not just the *what* but the *how* and *when*, and they combined and adjusted what they learned to suit their purposes. So it is with coaching. As you start out, copy directly—word for word or drill for drill can be good. As you gain experience and begin to understand why and how certain things work and don't work, you can exert some autonomy and find your own voice. No two people or coaches are the same; as you learn and develop, you will need to make changes and adjustments to suit your own personality, skill set, and context—and that's alright. The most important thing is that you can achieve the intended outcome, not that you can act like someone else.

Be sure to *take notes of your experiences* on the job, especially after implementing feedback from your mentor. Depending on the interval between meetings, you may find that you last worked on something nearly a month ago, and while your memory of how it went was fresh on the day of, now it's been a few weeks and you're starting to forget some of the details. Human memory is incredibly fallible—so much so that it's difficult to summarize in a few sentences. After an experience that's relevant to your mentorship topics, take note of how it went: what went well, what went poorly, how it felt, what you would do differently, any questions you have, and any other observations that might be relevant come discussion time.

If possible, you should also *use video*. Filming yourself coaching can be extremely valuable for your development, as discussed in Chapter 5, and if your mentor can't watch your work live, it's even more beneficial. If you decide to film yourself, try to do the following:

- Ensure that your voice can be heard, by making sure you're close to the camera, by using an external microphone connected to the camera via Bluetooth, or by recording your voice on a separate device and then joining the audio to the video in post-production.
- Edit the video to highlight the parts that are relevant to the aspects of your coaching you are working on with your mentor. Not every second will be useful, so editing the video not only saves you and your mentor time, but it also forces you to rewatch the video, allowing you to observe and reflect before your meeting.

Lastly, at the start of every meeting, be sure to *circle back to the topics you discussed in the previous one*. It can be tempting to start with a simple "What's new?" and then discuss any recent issues or dilemmas you're facing. But as we covered in Chapter 3, switching from topic to topic does not lead to lasting, long-term improvement. Stick to one or two things at a time until they are mastered, and then you can move on to the next thing.

Summary

- Mentorship is key to attaining expertise. Not only can a mentor help you develop your skills, they also can help you perform at your best and stay in the coaching game long term.
- Choosing the right mentor is important. Don't just pick someone who's good at their job, pick someone who can help you get good at *your* job.
- Make the most of your meetings. Have specific topics and questions in mind and take notes.
- Apply what you learn. Take and implement your mentor's feedback, but don't be afraid to also do things your own way. Take notes on your experiences and use video so that you can review your coaching.

Part 3
The Core Competencies of Coaching

If you've made it this far, you understand the importance of continuous professional development, as we discussed in Part 1, and you have become familiar with all the ways in which we can develop new skills and perform when it matters, as we discussed in Part 2. But there's no use starting the car if you don't know where you want to go. What exactly is it that you want to get better at? Which skills need developing?

Part 3 provides a map of the skill of coaching—an overview of the core competencies and the abilities that underlie them. We analyze our athletes' performance and skills in order to diagnose what needs improvement, so we should also do the same for ourselves! We need to be able to identify our strengths and weaknesses so that we can continue to develop. These chapters will help you do that.

In Chapter 8, I take a look at the concept of leadership, the foundation for everything that we do for our athletes. I explore the key outcomes of leadership, as well as the seven leadership behaviors that are crucial for success in high-performance sport, and the ways in which you can develop them.

In Chapter 9, I delve into the topic of skill development, be it technical, tactical, physical, or mental. I introduce both general and specific principles to help you develop any type of skill through the lens of the coaching cycle: observation, planning, and intervention.

Lastly, in Chapter 10, I look at how we can maximize game-day outcomes through the lenses of peak performance (how we can bring the best out of someone) and minimizing choking (how we can prevent collapses under pressure).

Throughout Part 3, I've aimed for more breadth than depth, providing an introductory level of understanding that will allow you to identify topics of interest for further research if you so desire. Unlike Parts 1 and 2, there is no real need to read Part 3 in order. In fact, I would recommend that you first navigate to the sections that appear the most appealing to you, whether they are strengths or weaknesses of yours. Then, either dive in or move over to a related subject. What's in these chapters is a jumping-off point—the first steps toward assessing your own coaching, learning more about a subject, and integrating it into your practice.

Enjoy!

Chapter 8
Leadership

There is perhaps no element of coaching more discussed, at least in the media, as leadership. Athletes and coaches regularly describe its importance in interviews, social media accounts fill their pages with inspirational quotes defining the qualities of a good leader, and business journals and magazines write articles about what CEOs and managers can learn from the leadership skills of elite coaches.

Almost everyone has, at some point in their life, experienced a good leader. In fact, if I asked you to, you would likely have no problem listing some of the qualities of one: they are caring, passionate, knowledgeable, and so on. Good leadership is somewhat unique—not only is it something that everyone seems to agree is important, it's also something most everyone seems to be able to identify.

However, clearly defining leadership is a challenge. After all, just within the limited context of competitive sports, we have different types of leaders: coaches, athletes, organization directors, heads of governing bodies, and so on. Each of these roles requires different skills and attributes, and while we can continue with our list of generic leadership qualities, there's no saying whether they will properly match each job description. This is the first issue with most definitions of leadership: they are vague lists of positive attributes, often incomplete and mismatched to the job at hand.

The second flaw in most models of leadership is that they often focus on either outcomes or behaviors, without linking the two. In these cases, it becomes difficult to measure leadership and identify areas for improvement. Take, for example, our earlier list: good leaders are caring, passionate, knowledgeable. These are great qualities to have, but what impact will they have on my players? If my team is lacking motivation, which of these qualities do I need to develop? I run into the same problem if I define leadership exclusively in terms of its outcomes—say, increased trust and cooperation. Without linking the behaviors to the outcomes, it's impossible for me to be truly athlete-centered—to identify the specific leadership behaviors I need to develop in order to bring about the intended outcomes. This chapter aims to bridge that gap—to define the key outcomes of good leadership, as well as the behaviors and skills that lead to those outcomes.

What is the ultimate outcome of effective leadership? This may be controversial, but I suggest that the answer is simple: goal achievement. Why do we hire coaches, CEOs, consultants, teachers, managers, or officials in the first place? To help us achieve a goal, whether we are athletes, coaches, shareholders, or employees. Of course, it's expected that they will also do this in a way that allows those they are helping to thrive and feel good—after all, if wellbeing decreases, so will performance. But wellbeing is not the primary objective of a leader, although increased wellbeing often comes about as a result of good leadership. The reason we engage and pay leaders is to help us achieve our goals.

But how do leaders do this? In the context of coaching, leaders help athletes achieve their goals by *creating the conditions for skill development and performance to occur as efficiently as possible.* On their own, athletes can still develop and perform, but our job as coaches is to make that process occur as smoothly and quickly as possible. Of course, we do that through the drills we run, the feedback we give, the meetings we organize—but there are other, subtler things we do that create the optimal conditions in which the entire coaching process can flourish. If developing a player is like growing a plant, then our on-court work is watering it and giving it sunlight, whereas leadership is ensuring the soil is fertile. Good leadership is at the base of everything we do, supporting all of our interventions and activities and accelerating the progress of our athletes.

That's what this chapter is about: creating the optimal conditions for player development and performance. So what are those conditions?

- Athletes need to believe in a vision.
- Athletes need to be motivated to pursue the vision.

- Athletes must believe in their ability to reach their goals.
- Athletes must be resilient.
- Athletes must trust in their coaching team.
- Player development requires resources.
- Player development requires the right environment.

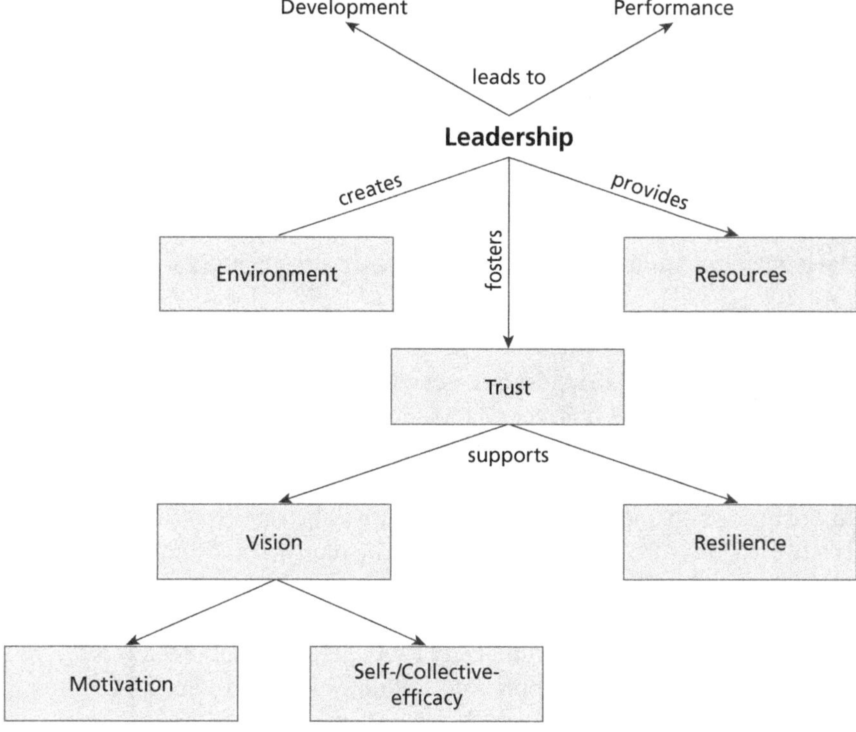

Figure 8.1. The seven conditions for optimal player development and performance.

Athletes Need to Believe in a Vision

Specifically, athletes look for a coach to provide them with answers to the following questions:

- What is our goal, both in terms of outcome (e.g. win the State Championships) and process (e.g. reduce turnovers)?
- How are we going to accomplish our goal? What are the steps we will take to make progress?
- What are our priorities? What are the most important things to focus on?
- What are each person's responsibilities?
- What is our timeline?

At the end of the day, every athlete is part of a team, whether they play a team sport surrounded by teammates, or an individual sport supported by a head coach, strength and conditioning coach, physiotherapist, parents, and anyone else who might contribute meaningfully to their development. For any team to reach a common goal, there has to be agreement on what that goal is. That's where vision comes in.

The coach's vision should be detailed and complex, accounting for every possible factor and obstacle. In *The Leadership Challenge*, authors Kouzes and Posner (2017) describe decades of research that ranks being "forward-looking" as the second most looked-for quality in leaders after honesty. In a study of Olympic and World Championship–winning coaches, both coaches and athletes independently discussed the importance of being able to predict what will be required to succeed in the future, but also being able to adapt the plan when circumstances change. Coaches described extensive, rigorous planning and analysis, while athletes described their coaches' ability to take an extraordinarily complex vision and present in a way that was simple and easy to digest. The authors called this "simplexity" (Mallett and Lara-Bercial, 2023).

However, it's one thing to present a vision and it's another to have athletes buy into it. How do we get athletes to believe in the vision? First, make your goal their goal. All but the most open of athletes will arrive with goals of their own, whether they know it or not. In some cases, our goals will align. In other cases, we'll have to do some convincing; we'll have to show them that accomplishing our goal will help them accomplish theirs. After all, the easiest car to sell is the one the customer already wants to buy.

For example, a tennis player might come to you determined to work on their backhand when, in your opinion, what really needs improvement is their forehand. With some discussion, you identify that they want to work on their backhand because it kept getting attacked in their most recent match. Now you have a common goal: to prevent this from happening again. With some good storytelling, you can explain how improving their forehand will allow them to hit better shots such that the opponent won't be able to attack their backhand. Not only that, but with a stronger forehand they'll be able to attack themselves and win even more points. Now you're selling them a solution that not only will accomplish their goal (stop losing so many points on the backhand), but promises them a bonus: more winners off the forehand side. They're convinced.

Second, paint a clear picture. No one buys their dream car without knowing every detail about it. Answer the questions above, but do it in such a way as to tell a story. What is the process going to look and feel like? What will the outcomes be? Be sure to account for everything, including possible obstacles or pitfalls. What do we have to avoid? How will we respond? Change involves risk, and no athlete wants to risk their game for a vision they can't clearly picture, so giving detail will help convince an athlete or team that the risk is being minimized.. You can even use video footage or stories from other athletes or teams to help sell the vision.

Lastly, back your vision up with evidence. Have the data to support your position to hand—where are we right now, and where do we need to go? Statistics can be convincing, even for those who don't like numbers. Evidence can also take other forms, such as carefully curated video clips or testimonials from other athletes who have followed a similar path. Sometimes, in order for an athlete to make a change, all they need to know is that their friend has done the same thing.

To summarize:

- Good coaches have extraordinarily complex and detailed visions that they are able to distill into simple, understandable plans for athletes.
- To get buy-in, try to align your vision with their goals.
- Paint a clear picture—answer all the questions they might have and back your answers up with evidence.

Athletes Need to Be Motivated to Pursue the Vision

Aligned with vision is our next key condition: *motivation*. Athletes must want to work toward the vision, and in the case of team sports, all the athletes in the team need to be aligned in that pursuit. Consider a man who is unhappy with his weight—he may have a very clear vision of what will be required to get in better shape ("If I cut dessert down to once a week, replace sugary drinks with soda water, and go for a 20-minute run three times a week, I'll be able to drop three pounds a month"). However, that doesn't guarantee that he actually wants to *do* this work. He may instead decide that, for the time being, he's going to set his focus on something more pressing—say, finishing his master's degree and his book about coach development.

What would motivate this mysterious character to take his diet and exercise more seriously? One model that may lend some insight is the cost of change model, which suggests that for any change in behavior to occur, the product of three factors—dissatisfaction, vision, and action plan—must be greater than the cost of said change. The latter two we've already discussed: subjects must believe in a clear vision and understand what steps they will take to get there. Those factors aren't my problem—I know how to lose weight; I've done it before. What I don't have, however, is enough dissatisfaction with the status quo. Why would someone go through the mental and physical effort of changing their behaviors and habits when they're already content with where they are? Dissatisfaction plays a big role in determining our motivation to change.

As coaches, our goal is not to break our athletes down, crushing their confidence in the name of increased dissatisfaction. That's why dissatisfaction has to be combined with the other two elements: vision and action plan. Good coaches can highlight players' weaknesses and shortcomings, while immediately bolstering their confidence by selling a vision and an action plan. In this way, athletes are left with a hunger to get better and a clear understanding of what they have to do to achieve this.

Of course, the initial motivation a player has when they are presented with a new plan can fade. After all, doing the work is much harder than just imagining the trophy. How do we keep players motivated on the practice court? The prevalent model supported by research in sport psychology is self-determination theory, which posits that an individual's motivation in an activity is dependent on three factors: competence (people want to do things that they are good at or that they are improving at), autonomy (people want to do things they choose to do), and relatedness (people want to do things that maintain or develop close personal relationships) (Deci and Ryan, 1985).

Coaches can, of course, have an outsized influence on each of these aspects. Perceptions of competence can be affected by both the selection of activities and their difficulty level. Selecting exercises that are too difficult or too easy for the player will only squash their motivation, while choosing activities in the "sweet spot" will allow them to strive for improvement. As mentioned, competence doesn't refer to just the desire to be good, but also the desire to improve. Thus, it's important to find clear measures of progress and reinforce those to athletes, highlighting for them their improvements and successes. This is also why good technical teaching ability is vital for coaches—an inspirational motivator can only go so far when their players don't improve. A coach who can teach effectively will not only help their athletes become more skilled, but also positively impact their motivation.

Autonomy can also be affected by the way we coach. Researchers Mageau and Vallerand (2003) have identified a number of coaching behaviors that can positively influence motivation and feelings of autonomy, including:

- Providing athletes with choices within certain rules or limits.
- Providing the rationale for tasks and rules that are assigned.
- Providing opportunities for taking initiative and doing independent work.
- Providing feedback on things that are within athletes' control.

Another principle we can use to increase feelings of autonomy is that of commitment and consistency, as outlined by Robert Cialdini in his book *Influence: The Psychology of Persuasion* (2007). In his own words, as human beings, we have a "nearly obsessive desire to be (and to appear) consistent with what we have already done. ... Once we have made a choice or taken a stand, we will encounter personal and interpersonal pressures to behave consistently with that commitment." The human experience abounds with examples of this principle—from gamblers who believe fully in their choice once they've put money down, to girlfriends whose relationship doubts fly out the window when they are proposed to. In other words, athletes who commit to a vision will internalize it as their own. The more they act in accordance with it, the more the consistency factor plays a role—it becomes a part of their identity and a behavioral habit.

Cialdini (2007) shows that the commitment and consistency principle works best when it is written down, in public, and some effort has been put in. Consider having athletes write down their goals, or what they will contribute to the team. Public swearing-in ceremonies can help make someone believe that this is their team now. Having athletes brainstorm elements of the vision—catchy phrases, keywords, logos, etc.—can help them make a commitment to the vision that you have worked so hard to sell, thus leading to feelings of autonomy and motivation.

Relatedness is a primary psychological need—a need to interact with and feel connected to others. In a sporting context, an athlete can feel relatedness with a coach and also with fellow athletes. Both aspects should be maximized in order to optimize motivation.

When it comes to interaction, the best coaches find the time to talk to their athletes. Sometimes they talk about their sport, sometimes they talk about life. Sometimes they talk during practice, sometimes they talk outside of practice. While it may sound simple, expert coaches know that they need quality one-on-one time with their athletes in order for them to feel seen and heard. Good coaches also give their athletes the chance to interact with each other, both in and out of practice. After all, the training environment is where athletes spend the majority of their time, so they need to feel they have a relationship with their fellow athletes in this environment. Being given the chance to chat, whether during a warm-up or a water break, allows for this.

At the same time, opportunities to interact outside of the practice environment are valuable. This is a well-documented practice in both high-performing businesses and elite sports teams; team activities outside of the sporting arena allow athletes to interact and build bonds. Sometimes the coach can be present, allowing athletes to build a stronger personal bond with them by seeing them outside a work context. Other times, it can be valuable for the coach to step away, allowing team members to create their own dynamic outside the confines of the coach–athlete or coach–team relationship. On that note, unsupervised free play or self-regulated games can be a great way for coaches to develop inter-athlete relatedness. Removing the coach from the picture can force athletes to interact more freely.

When it comes to feelings of belonging or connectedness, small gestures go a long way. At one of the academies I worked at, I decided I would greet students at the door of our facility before they walked onto the court to practice. This had a few benefits: first, it allowed me to greet each player, shake their hand, and exchange pleasantries. Second, it gave me the opportunity to sense each kid's mood and gauge which side of me they might need in the hours ahead. In this way, rather than having the players come in and immediately start their warm-up, I was able to have a one-on-one moment with them to build connection. I did the same at the end of practice—before leaving, each player would come see me at the door, where I could console someone who was in a bad mood, praise someone privately, or reinforce individual teaching points.

In team sports, these sorts of gestures are often already present in the form of team cheers and the like. But they don't guarantee automatic feelings of connectedness. Many coaches find it valuable to discuss and stress the importance of having a sense of being in a team, even going so far as to deliberately praise teamwork behaviors and reward team performances over individual ones. In short, as we'll discuss later, the feedback, language, and gestures we use go a long way toward shaping the environment we're in.

To conclude:

- For someone to want to make a change, the cost of change must be less than dissatisfaction × vision × action plan.
- Motivation can be divided into an athlete's feelings of competence, autonomy, and relatedness.

- Feelings of competence can be increased by teaching well, selecting activities of the appropriate difficulty level, and reinforcing and highlighting successes.
- Feelings of autonomy can be developed by providing athletes with choices, rationales, and opportunities for independent work, as well as by helping them make deliberate commitments to their goals.
- Feelings of relatedness can be fostered through opportunities for interaction, both among athletes and with their coach, as well as through small gestures and other activities that build connection.

Athletes Must Believe in Their Ability to Reach Their Goals

Our players now believe in the vision and are motivated to reach it. But do they *believe in themselves*? After all, why would I want to work toward a goal if I didn't think I could accomplish it?

In this context, what we're talking about is self-efficacy (or in the case of a team, collective efficacy). Self-efficacy, a term coined by psychologist Albert Bandura (1977), refers to one's "belief in their capacity to act in the ways necessary to reach specific goals." Self-efficacy is context-specific, whereas self-belief is more general. While self-belief (or self-confidence) can change over time, it's generally quite constant, like a personality trait, and may only experience slow, gradual changes. Self-efficacy, on the other hand, can fluctuate and change rapidly depending on the circumstances. Self-efficacy is so important for athletes because it significantly impacts the degree to which someone will be interested in pursuing a particular goal. Someone who believes they can reach their goals will not only pursue them more rigorously than someone who doesn't, they'll also keep going in the face of setbacks and more easily brush off self-doubt.

But what can we do to develop self-efficacy? If self-efficacy is the belief that one can accomplish certain goals, then part of our job is to give athletes the experience of reaching their goals. As Lara-Bercial and Mallett (2016) put it: "Belief is developed through close monitoring of performance metrics coupled with decisive and corrective actions when progress halts." In other words, two elements are required. First, we have to be competent coaches, capable of developing all the skills required for competition. If we aren't, then players don't improve nearly as quickly and they lose belief in their own ability to progress. Second, we have to measure what matters, both so that we can make adjustments and keep progressing, and so that we can reinforce to athletes that they are getting better. Measurement and communication are key to this process—the more athletes understand the link between "working on X" and "getting better at X," the more they will believe in their ability to accomplish their goals.

In fact, a great deal of self- or collective efficacy comes from our ability to facilitate an optimal learning experience. After all, assuming the athlete in question *wants* to get better, the only thing stopping them from believing in themselves is their experience of learning. As such, coaches who are good *teachers* will find themselves with athletes with a high degree of self-efficacy.

An athlete experiencing learning and development is having what's known as a "mastery experience," and this is the strongest source of self-efficacy. Another source is a "vicarious experience"—seeing a peer improve and succeed at a task (Kirk, 2007). While not as strong as a mastery experience, the effect is similar. To a certain extent, our brains are still wired the way they were thousands of years ago: we make inferences about the world based on what we see around us. "We're the same age, we train at the same club, and we have the same coaches. If *he* can develop and reach his goals, then so can I." Clubs and programs regularly promote their players' accomplishments online, through social media, and in person, through flyers, magazines, and posters. Of course, a great deal of this is marketing. But whether they know it or not, this self-promotion may also be contributing to self- or collective efficacy. The more members of a team see other members succeeding, the more they believe that they too can be successful.

Another source of self-efficacy that researchers have identified is *persuasion* (Kirk, 2007). Simply put, a coach can speak confidently about their athletes' skills and encourage them through the learning experience. It should be obvious that sarcastic remarks or put-downs will do nothing to encourage an athlete to get better, but excessive positivity won't help either. For one, athletes will tune it out over time, and for two, if it's not truthful, they won't believe it and you'll lose credibility. Coaches need to acknowledge the reality of the situation while truthfully expressing a belief that the athlete can overcome any adversity and ultimately reach their goals.

Similarly, coaches can demonstrate trust in their athletes' abilities without having to explicitly state it—for example, by substituting a player in at a key moment, or by naming someone as a starter. Facial expressions and tone of voice go a long way as well (see Chapter 10 for more on this). How do you react when a player is struggling to find their form? Do you act panicked, or do you show them that you know they can get over the hump?

Ultimately, self-efficacy is crucial to player development. Coaches should aim to:[14]

- Give athletes mastery experiences by teaching competently and efficiently.
- Give athletes vicarious experiences by celebrating the successes of the team.
- Speak confidently about their athletes' skills and their ability to develop.
- Demonstrate trust in their athletes.
- Focus on the process rather than the results.
- Give opportunities for independence and autonomy.
- Set SMART goals (specific, measurable, agreed-upon, realistic, timed).

Athletes Must Be Resilient

No matter how motivated, bought-in, or confident an athlete is, there will always be difficult moments. High-performance sport is physically, mentally, and emotionally taxing. Sporting careers are long, often

14 Kirk, K. (2007). "Self-efficacy: helping students believe in themselves." Available at: https://serc.carleton.edu/NAGTWorkshops/affective/efficacy.html

marked with extended periods of injury, disappointing performance, or doubt. One factor that has often been associated with success in sport is *resilience*: the ability to maintain wellbeing and performance in the face of adversity.

Researchers David Fletcher and Mustafa Sarkar (2016) have done extensive study in this area, identifying three main factors that contribute to resilience (also known as mental fortitude): personality, environment, and mindset. While personality can be changed, this process is often slow and gradual. Environment, however, is in the hands of the coach, and mindsets can be taught and developed. Therefore, that's where we'll focus our attention.

A training environment can be viewed as the product of two variables—challenge level and support level—and as such, it can be said to fall into one of these four quadrants:

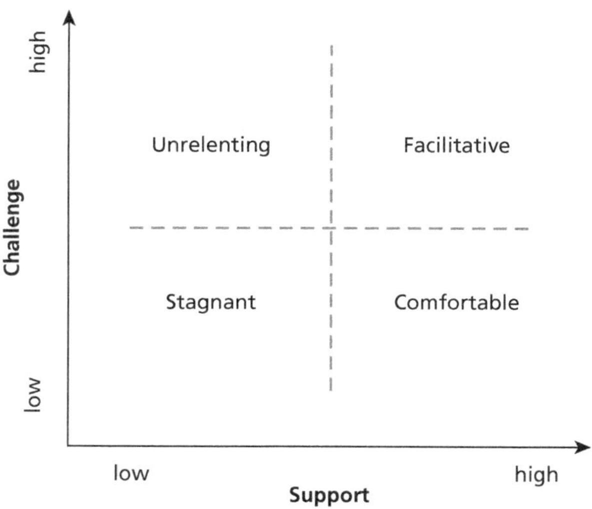

Figure 8.2. The challenge-support matrix for training environments.

For a training environment to encourage the development of mental resilience, both challenge and support need to be high (i.e. the facilitative quadrant). Think of it like the gym: for muscles to grow, they must be pushed to their limits. Push too hard and you get injured. Push too little and you don't see progress. In a comfortable environment, athletes are well supported but not sufficiently challenged, and so their mental fortitude never gets pushed to a point where it can develop. In an unrelenting environment, they are well challenged but not adequately supported, and they ultimately end up burning out. In a stagnant environment, they are apathetic, being neither supported nor challenged.

However, in a facilitative environment, athletes are pushed mentally—placed in adverse conditions—and yet simultaneously supported, both through emotional encouragement and through the teaching of mental skills, so that they can overcome the imposed adversity and become stronger. As the saying goes, "Comfort the troubled; trouble the comfortable."

But how do we show support? How do we teach mental resilience? Every athlete encounters stressors of different types: competitive (e.g. performance expectations, injuries), environmental (e.g. logistical issues, team conflicts), or personal (e.g. family issues, work–life balance). As a result, the athlete asks themselves two sets of questions: "How does this affect me? Do I care?" and "What can I do about it? Will it be enough?" Each of these evaluations can have an impact on a performer's ability to withstand pressure. If, for example, someone perceives a challenge as a threat ("If I play this tournament and lose, I might as well quit"), they are far less likely to be willing to face it. Similarly, if they do not believe they have the resources to handle the challenge, or they think the resources they do have are not enough, then they will, once again, struggle to face up to it.

The first step in teaching resilience is to raise athletes' awareness of their thinking patterns. Even the best of athletes will occasionally fall into dysfunctional thought patterns, examples of which are outlined below.

Table 8.1. Examples of Dysfunctional Cognitive Patterns

Pattern	Example
Catastrophizing	Blowing things out of proportion and thinking that the worst has happened or will happen: "I had a bad warm-up. This game is going to be terrible."
Overgeneralizing	"I always lose when I play against lefties."
"Yes, but..." thinking	Taking positive events and twisting them into negative ones: "Everyone told me my performance was good, but nobody said it was great."
Second-guessing	Making assumptions with negative repercussions: "Coach looks bored—he must not like me."
"It can't be done" thinking	"I'll never be able to improve."
Black-and-white thinking	Viewing the world in an either/or way, with no room for gray areas: "This is my only chance to prove myself."
Basing self-worth on achievement	"They said I could have performed better. I'm useless."
Perfectionism	Viewing any mistakes as unacceptable failures.
Blaming	Blaming other people or institutions for personal setbacks.
"Should and must" thinking	Believing that certain aspects of performance are *needs*, rather than *wants*: "I need to win this match"; "I have to get a good start."

Source: Adapted from Fletcher and Sarkar (2016).

Coaches should both observe their athletes and listen to their self-talk. When that's not possible, simply ask: "What are you saying to yourself right now? What are you thinking right now?" The first step is to point out when an athlete's self-talk falls into one of the categories outlined above.

Once an athlete can recognize that their thinking is flawed, then we can begin to teach them to control it. There are a few proven thought-regulation strategies, each of which we can teach:

- *Thought stopping*: This consists of abruptly interrupting a negative thought pattern with thoughts such as *Stop!*, *Wait!*, *Don't go there!*, or *Refocus!* Psychologists recommend thinking these thoughts in an assertive tone and using imagery, such as a red stop sign, for maximum effect.
- *Parking*: Parking a thought involves putting it aside for later reflection. This usually involves writing it down or telling someone about it.
- *Confronting*: Confronting a negative thought pattern can be done in a few ways:
    - A player can challenge their irrational thinking by questioning the assumptions they hold ("Have I really missed *every* forehand I've hit?"; "Is this going to mean as much to me in a month?"; "Is there another way I could view this situation?")
    - A player can imagine a dialog between themselves and someone they look up to or respect, where that respected person is confronting them on their negative thinking.
    - An athlete can imagine that a close friend is talking in the same way as the athlete is talking about themselves, and then imagine what rational encouragement they would provide them.
- *Replacing*: Negative thoughts can be replaced with positive ones. With assistance, athletes may develop their own preferred thoughts. Some may choose to focus on things they can control—the steps of a pre-performance routine, for example, or parts of their technique. Others may choose to focus on what they are experiencing in the present moment—sounds, sights, and sensations. Others still may try to raise their own awareness of what is positive in that particular situation—what are the *good* things they can focus on? Yet others may use positive phrases (e.g. "You can handle this") or images (e.g. a vacation on the beach) to alter their state of mind.

Through regular practice, athletes can develop these thought-regulation skills and, over time, build up their resilience.

To recap:

- Mental fortitude can be developed, both through the right environment and the teaching of mental skills.
- An optimal environment is one that is high in both challenge and support.
- Athletes must be able to recognize when their thinking is dysfunctional.
- Athletes can alter their thinking through thought stopping, parking, confronting, or replacing.

Athletes Must Trust Their Coaching Team

Each of the elements I have mentioned—vision, motivation, self-belief, and resilience—will be supported and influenced by one factor: *trust in the coach*. Specifically, trust that they are the right person for the job, the person who can be responsible for the athlete's career.

This kind of trust is special. I'm always reminded of Nick Saviano, legendary tennis coach, who described working with youth athletes as a "sacred trust" (Inside Tennis, 2014). This kind of trust is not just trust in a person—"Do I trust that they won't do me harm?"—although that is a part of it. This kind of trust is trust in a coach—"Can I trust them with my career? Can I trust them with my hopes and aspirations?"

In the domains of marketing, communications, and politics, this attribute has been studied extensively under the term "source credibility": the degree to which a communicator's characteristics influence the receiver's acceptance of a message. In fact, research into credibility can be dated all the way back to Aristotle, who defined three means of persuasion: *ethos* (character), *pathos* (emotion), and *logos* (logic).

These days, experts generally agree that there are three components of source credibility: competence, trustworthiness, and caring (McCroskey and Teven, 1999). I'll go through each of these and explain how they can be implemented and enhanced in the realm of coaching.

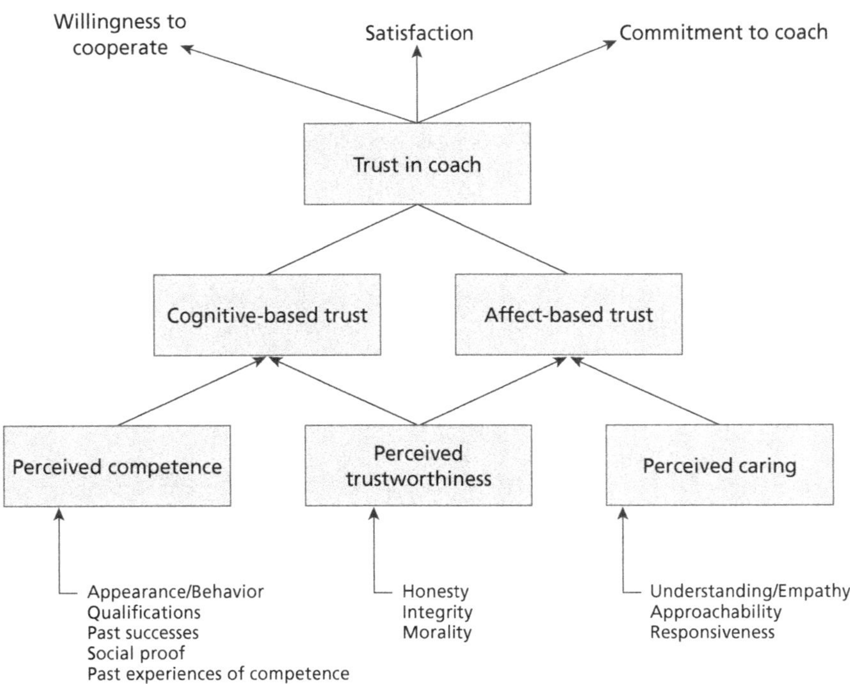

Figure 8.3. A comprehensive model of the determinants and outcomes of coach trust.

Competence

Competence refers to the extent to which athletes perceive that you are good at your job and that you know what you're doing. The perception can come from a number of sources, the most obvious of which is authority. Roger Federer, one of the greatest tennis players of all time, admitted that even his kids don't listen to him when he tries to give them tips (Tandon, 2023). In their eyes, he's not a coach; he's just their dad, and therefore a lesser authority than the coach. Of course, the coach–athlete relationship should not be based on a fear of authority—we don't want players doing things because they feel that we've ordered them to. However, it may be worth ensuring that you *project* authority, even if you don't call upon it. Looking the part is important—consider the role that a doctor's white coat or a pilot's uniform can play in assigning these people authority. Do you look (both in dress and appearance) like a credible coach? Do you behave like one? Do you speak confidently?

Another aspect of authority is qualifications, which is why doctors, dentists, therapists, managers, and many other authority figures display their degrees, diplomas, and qualifications proudly on their walls. That being said, the power of authority is diminished when it comes across as self-promotion. Be careful not to brag, but consider how you might make your qualifications visible.

More interesting, however, is the principle of social proof. As Robert Cialdini, author of *Influence: The Power of Persuasion* (2007), explains, in moments of uncertainty, we look to the actions of others for guidance. There is no context more uncertain than high-performance sport, where nothing is guaranteed and hopes can ricochet from 0 to 100 in a heartbeat. So how can we use social proof to increase our perceived competence? One of the ways this can be done is by acknowledging our past successes, either as an athlete or as a coach. Again, this shouldn't be done in a boastful way. Name-dropping and bragging are not only ineffective but also unpleasant. However, mentioning past successes, when relevant to the conversation, can help demonstrate competence. Another similar method is to put testimonials on your website or your social media accounts. The principle of social proof works best with people who are similar to us, so testimonials from people similar to those you are trying to convince (e.g. players, parents) can help convince people—"If it worked for them, maybe it will work for me!" In a study of athletes and coaches who had won Olympic or World Championship medals, social proof was identified as one of the two strongest factors influencing the athletes' belief in their coach (Lara-Bercial and Mallett, 2016). No one likes a self-promoter, but if you're good at what you do, make sure your athletes know it.

Lastly, one of the strongest "competence convincers" is simple: past experiences of competence. In other words, if you have previously demonstrated your competence with an athlete, they have an increased chance of believing that you are competent. That's why it's so important that you are at the top of your game for your first interactions with a new athlete or team. If, the first time you meet them, you can make them feel like you have improved them, then they are far more likely to trust and believe in you. If, on the other hand, you ask them for patience and begin a process that will take months to show dividends, you risk losing their faith from the get-go. That's why I've always tried, in my first sessions with a new player, to work on whichever area I think will give the easiest gains. That way, I can establish trust quickly and build momentum before tackling tougher tasks.

Trustworthiness

In the wake of recent disheartening scandals in elite sports, trustworthiness—the second factor in coach trust—is more important than ever. Trustworthiness, at least in terms of source credibility, can be broken down into three elements: honesty, integrity, and morality.

Athletes want someone who will be honest with them. Legendary Duke basketball coach Mike Krzyzewski (2018) was known to have two standards: "We look each other in the eye, and we tell each other the truth." Of course, there is a time, a place, and a way to have difficult conversations. Sometimes, the truth will need to be buffered by other supportive statements. But athletes don't want a coach who will bullshit them. Don't tell them they're good if they're bad, and don't tell them they're bad if they're good. They might need encouragement when they're down, and they might need an ego check when they're up. But you can do both of these things while acknowledging the facts, because at the end of the day, the athlete already knows the truth.

Integrity can be summarized as: you do what you say you will do. The first part of this is "saying." In every survey, athletes say they value clear communication, so clearly state your values, beliefs, and principles. How will your program be run? What are your plans, your vision? What are we going to do? Then comes the second part: "doing." Act in accordance with your stated values, beliefs, and principles. Act in accordance with the plans you laid out. If you can't do these things—if you say one thing but do another—how can athletes trust you with their careers?

Lastly, and quite simply, people judge a person as trustworthy when they see that they are a good person—that they act ethically. One of the elite athletes interviewed for Lara-Bercial and Mallett's (2016) study put it best:

> *Yes, I think when you don't know her, what drives you to her is her professionalism and the results that she gets, and then once you are working for her, you stay there because she's an incredible human being, she cares so much, and she really makes it about the process as well as the result.*

Players want to see that you are fair, kind, and honest. While some coaches will talk badly about competitors in an attempt to appear sympathetic, or encourage cheating in a win-at-all-costs approach, the vast majority of athletes soon recognize that what goes around comes around, and that such a coach could easily turn on them.

Caring

Finally, athletes believe in a coach who cares about them. As the saying goes, "People don't care what you know until they know that you care." But how does an athlete know that we care?

The first demonstration of care comes from a genuine attempt to understand and empathize with the player. Caring coaches ask questions and listen intently to the answers. Furthermore, caring coaches try to get to know the person first and the athlete second. Interviews with athletes reveal that the best coaches are those who take a holistic approach to development focused on the wellbeing of the person behind the performer. That means taking a long-term approach, ensuring work–life balance, and encouraging athletes to find meaning beyond the competitive results (Mallett and Lara-Bercial, 2023, p. 92).

Caring coaches are also described as being available, approachable, and easy to talk to. They are supportive while being demanding, and are even-keeled even in pressured situations. Their emotional stability provides confidence.

The second demonstration of care is responsiveness. Caring coaches don't just get to know their players—they respond to their needs. Again, in their research, Lara-Bercial and Mallett (2016) found that athletes who played for world-class coaches described a process of shared leadership, wherein the coaches collaborated with the athletes, allowing them "controlled freedom": the freedom to make certain choices within pre-established rules and limits. These elite coaches were also recognized as being adaptive, adjusting their coaching not only to the circumstances, but also to the individual athletes and their needs.

The power of caring also overlaps with Cialdini's principle of reciprocity, which can be of use for coaches. In his book *Influence: The Psychology of Persuasion* (2007), Cialdini explains that human beings naturally avoid feelings of indebtedness. Therefore, people are very strongly inclined to return a favor, even if the first favor was unprompted. This rule is very powerful, and we can see examples of it in all walks of life, from corporations giving gifts to politicians to grocery stores handing out free samples.

This gets interesting because, Cialdini notes, the effect is even stronger when what we give is tailored to the recipient—their circumstances, goals, needs, and so on. Thankfully, there is so much that we can give an athlete that shows them we care. It's no coincidence, I think, that two of the athletes I had the closest coach–athlete relationship with were two of the athletes I spent the most time in the car with. In both cases, at some point or another, their parents asked me to give them lifts to tournaments. Of course, these journeys provided opportunities for conversation, socializing, and bonding, but I think they also demonstrated my care and kick-started the principle of reciprocity. Both the athletes and their parents felt, in some way, indebted to me, and were thus more amenable to collaboration.

Of course, lifts aren't the only favor you can offer. As coaches, we have two things of great value that we can offer to people for free: our time and our knowledge! Nearly every athlete and parent wants more time from their coach, and they certainly want to feel that you are thinking of them. Taking some time to do a quick video analysis and sending it to them is an impressive gesture and shows them you care, while also encouraging reciprocity. Sending a link to an article you read with a note on how it could be relevant to them has the same effect.

These gestures may not be all that impressive to you. After all, we all know what a dedicated coach looks like. However, sometimes it can be easy to believe that coaches should go the extra mile only once they see that the athlete is committed to them. In reality, it works the other way around. When we show them how committed we are, they buy into us.

Remember:

- Trust in a coach is a combination of perceived competence, trustworthiness, and caring.
- Perceived competence can come from authority, qualifications, social proof, or past experiences of competence.
- Perceived trustworthiness comes from honesty (telling the truth), integrity (doing what you say you'll do), and morality (acting ethically).
- Perceived caring comes from: being understanding, empathetic, and approachable; being responsive to their needs; and doing unprompted acts of kindness.

Everything we've covered so far deals with the principles of leadership that affect the actual coaching process—what happens on the field, in the pre-game talks, when we're interacting with our athletes. But there are two more principles that aren't visible in our interactions but that ultimately affect the entirety of our work.

Player Development Requires Resources

The first of these principles is *resources.* Good leaders are good at procuring and providing resources. Consider the CEO of a department store. Her frontline salespeople need to buy into the vision, be motivated, believe in their own abilities, and so on. But she's not doing that work—her managers are; she might not even see her salespeople on a regular basis. But if they're overworked and need one more employee to cover a shift, she moves someone over from another department. If they need a more comfortable break room, she makes it happen. If the sales team needs new computers, she makes sure the money is there. That, too, is leadership.

Of course, not all coaches are CEOs. We don't always have ultimate decision-making power or access to the club's purse strings. That's why Lara-Bercial and Mallett (2016) talk about a coach's ability to "manage *upwards*"—to exert influence over their superiors, such as athletic directors, CEOs, or boards of directors. We can see examples of this in the professional game, from Bill Belichick acting as head of football operations and general manager with the New England Patriots, to Alex Ferguson acting as de facto sporting director at Manchester United. Influencing upwards, for those of us without the stature of the aforementioned coaching legends, is often about sales—convincing those who hold the purse strings that your way is the right way, or that you are deserving of extra resources.

Sometimes it's also about "schmoozing": getting along with people in what is, ultimately, a people profession. The height of schmoozing is what I call influencing *laterally*, which is equally important for high-performance coaches. Influencing laterally is working with donors, sponsors, granting organizations, and so on—anyone who doesn't exert power over you, but who could still be useful in the long term. Coaches skilled in the art of influencing laterally will often surprise you with their ability to conjure up money seemingly out of nowhere. These are the coaches with connections, with friends in all the right places.

Sometimes, however, we're *campaigning*—influencing *diagonally*. In these cases, we're extracting resources or enacting change through entities that are outside of our organization but that hold power over us—national or regional governing bodies, for example. Good campaigners can rally a group, make a convincing argument, and, equally importantly, know exactly who they need to get on board with.

Lyndon B. Johnson, 36th president of the United States, is known for his significant legislative achievements. During his presidency, he helped pass more than 200 major bills, including the Civil Rights Act, the Voting Rights Act, Medicare and Medicaid, the Higher Education Act, and the Immigration and Nationality Act, among others. His legislative success is often considered unparalleled in modern American history, but of course he couldn't do it alone; he needed the votes of his constituents, the efforts of his cabinet, and the support of his fellow politicians. Despite his sometimes controversial methods, he was an inordinately effective leader—as president, he vetoed 30 bills without a single veto being overridden by Congress. How did he do it?

Historians agree, first of all, that Johnson was a skilled gatherer of information, particularly with regards to those he was trying to convince. He would uncover their philosophies, their perspectives, their motivations, their values, their strong and weak points, and above all, what it would take to get their vote. Not only that, he was strategic in *who* he approached:

> *In the run-up to passage of the Civil Rights Act of 1964, he called the Washington Post's Katharine Graham, and pushed her to publish reportage and editorials advocating for a vote on the act. Knowing the influence of the United Steelworkers, he persuaded Dave McDonald, their president, to have his team lobby for the act, even having Dr. Martin Luther King, Jr. join this call with him in 1963. Realizing he needed Republicans, he partnered closely with Senate minority leader Everett Dirksen, appealing to him to honor the heritage of his home state of Illinois as the "land of Lincoln." And he worked closely with Dr. King and other civil rights leaders. Johnson knew that persuasion takes the work of multiple constituencies and always thought carefully of whose influence to employ. (Coleman, 2018)*

At the same time, he was psychologically and politically savvy; he understood that a favor done for someone now could lead to a favor in return. As Bruce Schulman (2018), professor of history at Boston University, puts it: "every member of Congress understood that cooperation brought benefits: invitations on foreign trips, influence on appointments, projects for the home district. When they voted against the president, recalcitrant members knew they would pay a price." At the same time, Johnson wasn't just about achievement through friendly cooperation—he also recognized when he was in a position to push and pressure in the name of forwarding his agenda.

Beyond his people skills, he was remarkably clear in his vision. To quote the man himself, "Your judgment is only as good as your facts" (Coleman, 2018). According to Jack Valenti, former special assistant to the president, on the evening of Kennedy's assassination, Johnson spent five hours with his team crafting what would become the defining movement of his tenure: the Great Society agenda. He was incredibly studious and methodical. Again, here's Coleman (2018):

> *Former Johnson aide Tom Johnson (no relation to the president) noted, "It's impossible to overstate his*

> *consumption of information." He'd immerse himself in the facts of a situation—reading hundreds of pages on a topic and speaking to everyone he could about it—so that he could make the most persuasive case possible. Then he'd obsess over the process of making the change. He knew the rules of government, the personalities and motivations of public officials, and the flow of the legislative process better than anyone. This mastery of detail was a hallmark of Johnson's effectiveness.*

Lyndon B. Johnson, like many great coaches and leaders, did not just influence downwards, by leading his staff. He influenced upwards, laterally, and diagonally, extracting financial, electoral, and political resources from people and entities all around him. While entire books could be (and have been) written about each of these skills (selling, schmoozing, and campaigning), some common strategies emerge from the stories of history's great leaders:

- *Know your audience*: Who holds power? What do they like? What motivates them? What is their communication style? What has or hasn't worked in the past?
- *Make their life easier*: It can be tempting to come to a meeting with a list of requests for things you want, but that doesn't make for a particularly convincing sell. Instead, make a clear case for how what you are requesting will be beneficial for *them*, the person you are requesting it from. You don't have to pretend that you aren't going to benefit, you just have to explain to them why *they won't lose*. Similarly, avoid presenting a list of problems—things that aren't as good as they could be. Whether these are your problems or theirs, dwelling on them won't fix them. Instead, propose clear, actionable solutions.
- *Be likable*: The principles of likability and reciprocity apply here, too. People are more inclined to help someone they like—someone they have something in common with, who compliments them, or who has cooperated in the past. And they're more inclined to help someone they feel indebted to—someone who has already done them a favor, given them a gift, or made a concession.

- *Tell a story*: Over the millennia, stories have been the means through which humans have derived and shared meaning. Stories are compelling, and you can use them to your advantage. Who is the protagonist, the main character, the person your audience should be rooting for? Give them a name, a face; let your audience get to know them. Who is the antagonist, the enemy? What is the conflict? Where's the resolution? Rather than simply making a request, tell a story, from beginning through the middle to the end. Build suspense, create engagement, and get your audience invested. Along those lines, present data to support your case. Not only does this show you've done your homework, it helps paint a clearer picture of your proposed solution. What is the scope of the problem? How much will the solution benefit us?

To summarize:

- Good leaders provide resources to their followers.
- To do so, they sometimes have to influence upward (sell an idea to their bosses), diagonally (campaign to influence change in outside organizations that hold power), or laterally (schmooze with donors, colleagues, or others who might be able to help).
- The best influencers know their audience, make their life easier, tell a story, and are likable.

Player Development Requires the Right Environment

Last but not least, great leaders create environments wherein each of the factors necessary for development can exist and flourish. After all, a player's relationship with their sport is not defined exclusively by the relationship they have with their coach—it is influenced by their interactions with other staff members and fellow athletes, their experiences of competition and training, and the subtle messages that each of these send. It is the responsibility of a head coach to ensure that each of these elements align to send the right message to the athletes.

Of course, you first have to be clear with yourself by asking, "What environment am I trying to create?" As the saying goes: "If you stand for nothing, you'll fall for anything." If you are not deliberate in deciding what culture you want to create, you will end up creating one nonetheless—it just might not be the one you want. I've already outlined in this chapter some starting points—athletes should believe in themselves and their coaches, be motivated and resilient—but you should still sit down and ask yourself what exactly you are trying to build. The environment that *you* create will be decided by a number of factors: your own personality, beliefs, and values, and also the unique interaction of your external environment (location, demographics, broader culture) with the backgrounds and personalities of your athletes. The environment you create with one group of players at a particular place and time may not be what's best suited to another group in another setting.

Once you've done this, recall that the environment doesn't exist without others. As Jim Collins put it in *Good to Great* (2001): "Get the right people on the bus." In our context, this means two things: first, aim to hire or bring on board the coaches and other staff members who will be able to support your vision. Primarily, this means engaging people who believe in your vision and share your values. Whether or not they have the right skills is, generally speaking, secondary, as skills can be taught. Their character and their willingness to join a team aligned to a common goal are what's critical.

Second, "get the right people on the bus" also refers to your athletes. Whether or not you coach a team sport, your players are always interacting with each other, in the locker room, the cafeteria, or the gym. Are there any bad apples in your bunch? If so, what impact are they having? Those of us who work with kids know that no child is perfectly behaved at all times. Junior athletes are deserving of second chances and opportunities to develop skills such as effort, focus, teamwork, and cooperation. At the same time, an athlete who has been given numerous chances to correct their behavior and who is, at the same time, influencing the behavior and performance of others, is not only *not* contributing to the success of the team, but in fact hindering it. Again, this applies both to team sports and individual sports; very rarely does player development occur in a vacuum. A big part of a leader's role is to either steer a follower's behavior in the right direction or, unfortunately, get them off the bus.

Once you're clear on your messaging, and you've got the right people on board, it's time to get to work. Within a coaching context, the environment is comprised of three things:

1. The feedback we give.
2. The language we use.
3. The small actions we take.

The first, feedback, may seem obvious, yet it's often overlooked by coaches. As an example, consider the coach who gives the following feedback after a series of tennis shots:

- "Great shot!"
- "That's too low."
- "Too low."
- "Not enough spin."
- "Good one."
- "Keep it out of the net."

The positive feedback ("Great shot," "Good one") is only focused on the outcome; there's no comment on what the player did to *make* it a great shot. The negative feedback is exclusively focused on what *not* to do (hit it low, in the net, with too little spin), as opposed to what *to* do. Continuous feedback of this sort will, ultimately, help to create a particular environment—one in which athletes are more focused on the outcome than the process and are motivated by the fear of making mistakes, rather than by the desire to improve or achieve a specific outcome.[15]

In any given situation, a coach has a number of options for what to feed back. Your team scores a goal. Do you celebrate the goal and nothing more? Do you congratulate the scorer or the player who made the assist? Do you point out why the play worked or what the opposition missed? Your decision about what to feed back shapes the environment you work in. Respond with "Great effort!" and people will start to look for effort. Respond with "Great teamwork!" and people will start to look for

15 Instead, a coach could give feedback focused on the solution and reward the process: "Try to let the racket travel further forward. Good, that one was longer!"

teamwork. Respond with "Way to score!" and people will look to score (for better or for worse). Your feedback shapes your environment.

The language we use outside of our feedback also speaks volumes. When I started coaching, a mentor pointed out to me that a lot of my feedback followed this format: "It's good that you did X, but you didn't do Y." It's only one word, but the "but" butts in and takes all of the air out of the initial praise (imagine telling your partner, "You're beautiful, but..."). Instead, I was taught to replace it with "now": "It's good that you did X. Now try to do Y."

One word can make all the difference. What do you call the different teams or subdivisions of your program? If the top level is the "champions" tier, what should those who aren't included in that tier conclude about themselves? We use language everywhere—in our greetings, our goodbyes, our explanations, our feedback, our social media, and our meetings. There are so many opportunities to review the words we use and question what messages they are sending and if there are any necessary replacements to be made.

Lastly, environment is set by the multitude of small gestures we make every day. If you spend more time giving feedback to one group of players over another, what message does that send? If your player calls you after a match and your first question is "Did you win?", what message does that send? If you want your athletes to be professional, but you arrive to practice a few minutes late and don't have all the equipment you need, what message does that send?

The New Zealand All Blacks are famous for, among other things, "sweeping the sheds": they leave the changing rooms the way they found them, if not cleaner. For them, discipline, excellence, and self-sufficiency are valued. Leaving the locker rooms dirty or disorganized would demonstrate none of those qualities, and so, even if it's a small gesture in the grand scheme of professional rugby, they sweep the sheds every day.

Beyond the feedback, language, and small gestures that we use to create and maintain a culture, there is one more piece of the puzzle for coaches: conscious and constant reflection and experimentation. There is no handbook; there is no formula. The only way to get good is to continuously reflect in a deliberate manner. What am I trying to achieve?

What have I tried so far? What is working? What isn't? Why did I choose these steps instead of others? Who am I targeting? After questioning yourself, don't be afraid to experiment. After a day or two of playing around with something, you will almost always have a good sense of whether it is helping, hurting, or having no effect at all. It's impossible to come up with the perfect plan on paper; culture is not created in the office, but rather out on the field. So ponder, reflect, and plan—and then go try things out.

In conclusion:

- Have a clear vision of the environment you want to create.
- Get the right people on the bus.
- Use feedback, language, and small gestures to create the environment.
- Constantly reflect and experiment.

Chapter 9 Skill Development

In this chapter, we'll discuss the ways in which coaches can go about developing their athletes' skills. To do so, we first have to define what we mean by the word "skill." I'll propose the following definition:

> **skill**
> *noun*
> a <u>developed</u> <u>physical or mental</u> ability to <u>do</u> something

You'll note that I've emphasized certain parts of the definition that I think are integral. First, the word "do": skill is about *doing*, not knowing—I covered this in Part 1. Here, we're talking about athletic skill, not coaching skill, but nonetheless the same principle applies.

Second, skills are not just *physical*, they can also be *mental*. The ability to focus is a skill, just like the ability to throw a football.

Finally, skills are abilities that can be *developed*. They get better through practice and often, but not always, through coaching or instruction. Some people are born with a naturally high level of ability, and that's what we'll refer to as "talent." But even talented athletes can develop their skills. That's why being tall isn't a skill (and neither does it demonstrate talent) but running fast is.

While this book is focused more on coach development than athlete development, the ability to improve a player or team's abilities is of such importance to coaching success that I feel it's essential to present some fundamental concepts. This information, which I have tried my hardest to present in a sport-agnostic fashion (that is to say, applicable to all sports), aims to help you in two ways.

First, it will help you coach better. Most everything in this chapter can be applied to any sport and, as such, addresses the foundational concepts that underlie skill development. As the old saying goes: "Think skill, not drill." Rather than being tied down to a list of exercises, drills, activities, or progressions, this chapter will give you enough knowledge to be able to identify the specific skill you want to improve and then design your practices from the ground up, planning according to the principles of skill development and *then* designing drills, rather than the other way around. Everything presented in this chapter is backed by years of scientific study and empirical evidence from some of the best coaches and teachers in the world. As such, a solid mastery of the concepts herein will equip you to develop better players, faster.

Second, it will help you identify areas of your coaching that could be improved. As you read, you'll no doubt come across topics that are less familiar to you. In these cases, you can make a note to do more research on your own. In some places, I've provided references to useful resources that explore the topic in further depth. Not only that, but when you reflect on your own coaching (as we discussed in Part 2), you'll be able to use the contents of this chapter as a rubric—a means of evaluating your strengths and weaknesses and determining what aspects of your coaching you'd like to work on.

This chapter will be divided into two sections. First, I'll outline general principles of skill development, which can be applied no matter the skill. Then, I'll discuss some specifics of technical and tactical development.

General Principles

As mentioned in Part 1, all coaching follows a cycle: observation, assessment, intervention.

First, we have to be able to accurately observe what is happening. From there, we must identify, out of everything we've observed, what needs to be developed, what doesn't, and how we will prioritize things. Then, finally, we can intervene.

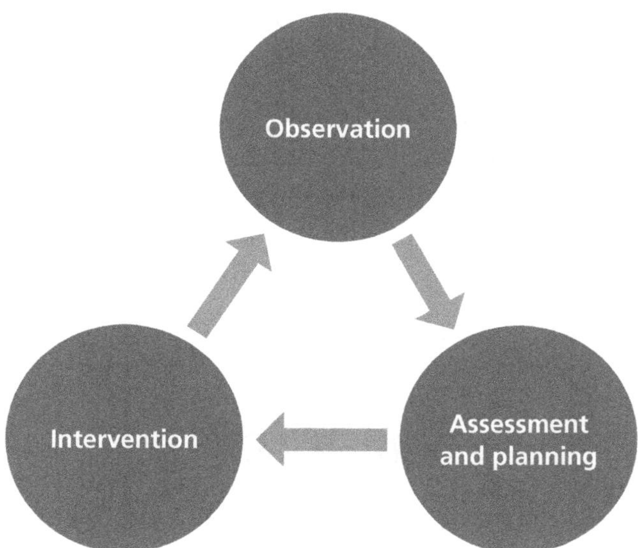

Figure 9.1. The Coaching Cycle.

Observation

In Chapter 2, I took an in-depth look at *how* to observe better. If you haven't read that chapter yet, I suggest you do. For some notes on *what* to observe, continue reading.

Identifying Areas of Improvement

In order to accurately observe our athletes and identify which areas of their skillset require development, we first need to have a robust awareness of standards—of both performance and development. What do I mean by this? *Standards of performance* are the normal ranges of *performance* that can be expected for athletes or teams of a particular age, level, gender, or discipline. For example, I probably shouldn't expect a soccer team to maintain a rate of possession above 80%. *Standards of development* are the rates of *improvement* that can be expected for athletes or teams of a particular age, level, gender, or commitment level. For example, I probably shouldn't expect an experienced sprinter to improve their 100m time by a full second in only two months.

Having a poor awareness of standards can be a real impediment, both for coaches and athletes. Setting goals that are too difficult, whether because they are impossible or simply too aggressive, can hamper athlete motivation or even cause burnout. Not only that, but it can also cause frustration and disappointment for coaches and parents. At the same time, setting goals that are too easy can lead to wasted time, a lack of drive, or boredom.

In addition, not knowing the norms for performance for different ages, levels, and genders will impede my ability to prioritize interventions. How can I pick what to work on if I don't know what's most important for my athlete? We'll discuss this in the next section on assessment and planning.

To strengthen your awareness of standards, identify the key performance indicators for your sport or discipline and record the norms for the age, gender, and level you are coaching at, the level your athletes would like to get to, and, if possible, every step in between. You may also want to observe (either in person or on video) what top performance looks like at each stage of the pathway, noting the differences between each stage. The better you understand what is required to perform at each level, the easier it will be for you to plan and intervene.

Identifying Root Causes

Another vital observational skill is the ability to identify the root causes of gaps in performance. In some cases, what appears to be one type of error may in fact be something else altogether.

Tactical (decision-making) errors may be just that—that is, errors resulting from a lack of knowledge. If someone does not know that there is a decision to be made or does not know what their options are, then they will more often than not make the wrong one. However, tactical errors can have technical causes. If I can't perform a particular motor pattern, what are the odds that I will choose to do it in competition? In such cases, tactical instruction (do X when Y) should be preceded by technical development. Tactical errors can also have physical or mental causes. Fatigue can cause lapses in decision-making, and anger or frustration can cause impatience and carelessness.

Technical errors can also have underlying causes. Some, again, may be purely technical (e.g. the athlete has not yet mastered the motor pattern). But some may be the result of physical limitations (e.g. fatigue, weakness, lack of mobility or coordination), while others may be the result of a particular mental state (e.g. stress causing someone to tense up and abbreviate their motion). And, of course, what appears to be a technical mistake may in fact be no mistake at all, if it is what the athlete intended to do (in which case it would be a tactical mistake).

Ultimately, when we observe tactical or technical errors, what we are actually looking at are *symptoms*, each with a variety of different causes.

Table 9.1. Root causes of observed mistakes

Observed mistake	Root cause	Description
Tactical	Tactical	True tactical error: lack of knowledge
Tactical	Technical	Technical flaws limit tactical options
Tactical	Physical	Physical flaws limit tactical options
Tactical	Mental	Mental/emotional state affects decision-making
Technical	Technical	True technical error: flaw in technique
Technical	Physical	Physical limitations impede technique
Technical	Mental	Mental/emotional state affects body
Technical	Tactical	Technique changes because athlete's intention changed

Of course, any cause can also have its own roots. If someone is making a true technical error, what is *its* cause? Someone making late contact on their forehand might do so because their preparation is too big, or because they don't see the ball early enough, or because their grip favors a contact point further behind them. Someone making a true tactical error is still having to make decisions based on a host of factors. The question we have to ask ourselves is what the exact error of judgment is that they are making. Are they not noticing the positioning of an opposing team member? Are they misevaluating their own skills or those of their opponents? Or do they have the wrong intention in this particular game situation?

Our goal as coaches is to identify the root causes of any gap in performance and then determine at which stage along the chain we should intervene. That's where the next section, assessment and planning, comes in.

To be sure of correctly identifying root causes, consider the following:

- Keep an open mind and consider all possibilities.
- Observe your athletes carefully, both in and out of practice/competition.
- Ask questions and engage in conversation with them.

Assessment and Planning

Once you've observed your athlete or team's performance in its entirety, you can begin to select which areas to focus on, and plan how and when to do so.

Maximizing Your Time

In the introduction to Part 1, I presented the idea that, as coaches, our job is to "beat the curve"—to speed up the rate of progress. Part of our job, when selecting which skills to work on, is to choose those that will have the greatest impact on development relative to the time invested.

Let me explain. I'm coaching Selma. Selma plays Calvinball, the fictitious sport from *Calvin & Hobbes.* Although, famously, in Calvinball there are no rules, let's imagine that there are a few key skills involved in the sport: running, kicking, jumping, and throwing. And let's say that I've assessed Selma and measured her ability *relative to her age group*, where a score of 100% would make her top in her class.

Table 9.2. Selma's Calvinball assessment

Skill	Ability
Running	82%
Kicking	73%
Jumping	79%
Throwing	95%

I must now make a decision: which skill do I work on? I could choose kicking, simply because it's her worst and has the most room to grow. But how much time would that take? And how much growth would Selma see? Let's imagine, for the sake of argument, that I can predict a 10 percentage point improvement in her kicking, but it will take six weeks of work. But I could also spend two weeks to see a 5 percentage point improvement in her running. Which one should I choose?

I also have to factor in the relative importance of these skills and their impact on the final performance. I might be able to make huge improvements to Selma's running, but what if Calvinball is primarily a kicking sport? A 5% improvement in running may only lead to a 1% improvement in final performance, whereas a 10% improvement in kicking might lead to a 5% gain in results.

A theoretical formula for choosing the best return on time invested could look like this:

$$\text{Value} = \frac{(\text{Potential improvement} \times \text{Relative importance})}{\text{Time required}}$$

Of course, there will always be other factors at play, such as logistics or equipment, or how soon the next competition is. Let's not forget, too, that you might choose to work on something that's less important but is easier to learn and will give the athlete confidence. The psychological aspects of practice are not to be overlooked.

Physical and Psychological Profiles

While success in sport can usually be quantified according to a selection of metrics, these key performance indicators will usually prescribe ranges of acceptability rather than precise values. Most sports require the successful combination of a variety of skills; the exact ratio depends on the circumstances, discipline, and individuals involved. Since every athlete and team will vary in their strengths, weaknesses, body types, personalities, and a host of other factors, we will often need to select which skills to develop based on their physical and psychological profiles.

Take tennis, for example. To break into the top 10 in the world for men, one needs to hold and break serve. And while the percentages for these skills combined must cross a quite clearly defined threshold (104%), their individual values are far more variable. Daniil Medvedev, for example, broke into the top 10 for the first time with a hold percentage of 84.2% and a break percentage of 27.9%. Diego Schwartzman, on the other hand, only held 71.7% of the time when he entered the top 10—a full 12.5 percentage points lower. But he broke serve 34.9% of the time—7% more than Medvedev (ATP Tour, 2025).

This might seem like random variation, but there's one detail about these athletes that I haven't shared: their heights. Medvedev stands at an imposing 6'6" (1.98m), allowing him to serve up aces, not only due to his height over the net, but also due to his long limbs generating racket speed. Schwartzman, on the other hand, is only 5'7" (1.70m) (ATP Tour, 2025). In 2017, he reached the quarterfinals of the US Open, making him the shortest Grand Slam quarterfinalist in over 20 years. His serve is not overwhelming, but his stature allows him to be fast on defense when returning.

No doubt each of their coaches understood what they were dealing with when shaping these athletes' games. It would not have made sense to prioritize Schwartzman's serve over his return. That's not to say that no time was spent developing his serve—after all, he still became one of the 10 best players in the world. It's just to say that one must recognize not only what limitations a player might have, but also what abilities they have that might make them special, and then allocate time accordingly.

The same can be said of personality. A team of rambunctious and outgoing soccer players might not be best suited to a patient, conservative style of play. And a more reserved, cautious player may prefer to play defense over striker.

When identifying skills to develop, it's not enough to evaluate the gaps between current and ideal performance. One must also consider the profiles of the athletes at hand and which styles of play will allow them to progress the most.

Stages of Development

Given that we operate in the world of player *development*, it may be valuable to consider the word "develop," the definition of which almost always includes the word "process." We can also look at the word "coach," which originally, in the mid-16th century, referred to horse-drawn carriages. It has taken on its current meaning because, in principle, just like the carriages, sports coaches take people from point A to point B.

My point in all this is that our mandate is not to provide quick fixes or cure-alls. We are not in the business of one-time transactions. Our focus should be long term, and our approach to planning should reflect that.

The concept of "windows of trainability" is the idea that there are periods in an athlete's life when certain types of training will have a greater impact than others (Balyi et al., 2013). This concept is well established in the realm of physical development—speed and flexibility should be prioritized at younger ages, while strength and stamina can be focused on in the teenage years.

When it comes to skill development, similar principles apply. When an athlete is younger, they have fewer repetitions in them and are more malleable, so changes are easier to make. At the same time, results mean less—there are no scholarships or Olympic spots on the line. As such, emphasis should be placed on building a strong foundation—in other words, teaching a broad variety of skills and focusing on solid technical and tactical fundamentals, rather than what will lead to a win next weekend.

As athletes get older, they develop their own styles and preferences, their techniques become more ingrained, and competition results begin to matter more. Throughout this developmental process, the priority can shift more toward depth rather than breadth—in other words, refining and enhancing a smaller subset of skills (specialized to the athlete's profile and what they need to win), rather than focusing on a wide variety of skills at a surface level.

It's also worth noting that some skills build off each other, even if they are technically different. One skill might incorporate an element of another, for example. If you know that you will eventually want to develop both, then doing so in order of easiest to hardest is the most logical. Allowing the athlete to rely on their knowledge of the first skill when learning the second one will speed up the process, while doing things in the reverse order has no benefit.

Stage of Year

Yet another factor influencing the choice of what to work on will be the time of year, or more accurately, the stage of the season. Generally speaking, the most important aspect in this regard will be proximity to competition. As mentioned earlier, certain skills will take more time to develop than others, whether due to their difficulty or due to the athlete or team's natural abilities. Either way, our planning must take into account our overarching goal: that athletes are at their peak level (physically, technically, tactically, and mentally) during competition.

After assessing an athlete or team and identifying areas for improvement, we must also be able to estimate how long each improvement will take. This is a concern because skill development, in most cases, does not follow a smooth, continuous curve; it is a stepwise function, where improvements are delayed and staggered. Both coach and athlete invest time and energy into the process of working on the skill, but a change in outcome is only seen after some time. Sometimes the plateau can be as short as a day; other times it's as long as a year. It all depends on the athlete and the skill.

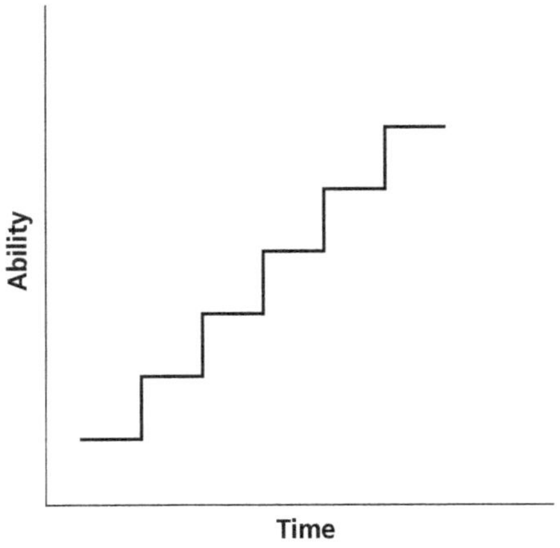

Figure 9.2. Stepwise improvements in ability.

It's also worth noting that oftentimes the improvement, once realized, is not always permanent. A skill may appear to have been acquired, but without sufficient repetition and maintenance, it can break down some time in the future. The Ebbinghaus forgetting curve shows us how skills and information are gradually forgotten over time. However, they can be regained with regular practice or review, which also delays the next period of decay.

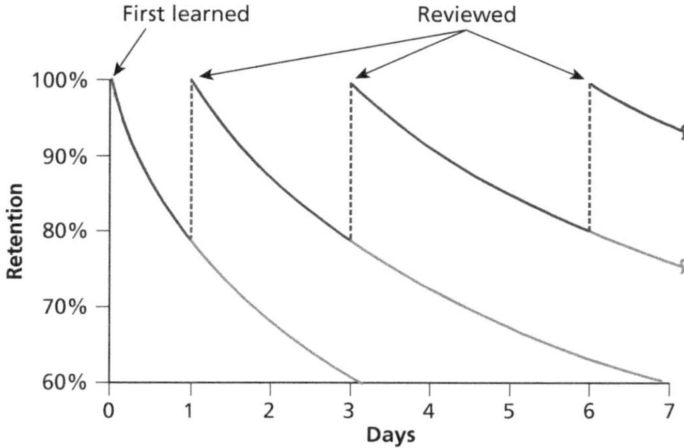

Figure 9.3. The Ebbinghaus forgetting curve.

Both of these principles—stepwise improvement and skill decay—make the point that we must be strategic with how we use our time in the lead-up to competition. Consider a scenario where the goal is to peak in two weeks' time. Imagine there are two options: Skill A, which is of less importance but should take two weeks to master, and Skill B, which is more important and will likely take four weeks.

I could choose Skill B, given its importance, and hope that even if this skill isn't fully mastered in two weeks, some residual improvements "stick" and manifest themselves in competition. But the best approach would likely be to work on Skill A. Even though it is of less importance, I am more confident that it will be mastered by the time competition comes around, thus ensuring an improved performance. *A small improvement that sticks is better than a large improvement that doesn't.*

We also must consider the psychological effects of working on skills when nearing competition. Some athletes may want to tweak things until the morning of their event, while others would rather groove and solidify the things they do best, sometimes for days or even weeks before a major game. Your choices should take both of these factors (time and effect on confidence) into account.

Time of Month/Week/Day

Another factor to consider is the time of the month, week, or day relative to the athlete's energy levels. Just as athletes are more responsive to training certain physical qualities at different ages, they are also more responsive to certain physical and technical stimuli at different levels of fatigue.

There are three factors to consider:

1. *Degree of complexity or coordination required*: On one end of the spectrum, you have skills that are multi-segmented or require elements of coordination such as dissociation, change of rhythm, or dexterity. On the other end, you have skills with fewer segments and simpler coordination.
2. *Degree of explosiveness*: On one end of the spectrum, you have skills that require explosive strength to perform well. On the other end, you have skills that don't.
3. *Degree of novelty*: What stage of competence is the athlete at? Is this a brand-new skill to them—something they've never done before? Or is it something they mastered long ago and just need to maintain?

Figure 9.4. Prioritization of skills in a session, day, or week, according to their demands.

As a rule, skills that are high in complexity, coordination, explosiveness, or novelty should be placed nearer to the start of the day or session, and skills that are simpler, more endurance-based, and already acquired should be placed nearer to the end. This is because there is a great deal of scientific research supporting the fact that, as athletes become tired, their coordination suffers, their nervous system doesn't form new motor pathways as efficiently, and strength and explosiveness gains are harder to come by.

This same logic can be applied to planning over a longer period, such as a week or a month—understanding that athletes will generally be more tired at the end of a week or training block than at the start. This doesn't mean that you can't do new stuff at the end, or maintain skills at the start. It just means that the ratio should flip as athletes progress through the training period.

Intervention

Once you've identified the skills to develop, selected which ones to prioritize, and scheduled when you'll focus on them, you can finally step into action and make them better. To do that, however, we first have to understand how skill development works.

The Four Stages of Competence

As I established in the introduction to this chapter, skills are abilities that can be developed, from novice to master. As they are developed, they pass through the four stages of competence—a model you might have heard of, but the implications of which are seldom discussed.

The model is often presented like this, without any further clarification of what each stage means:

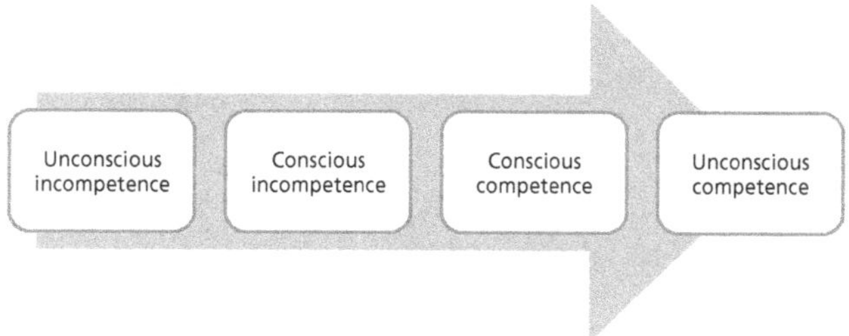

Figure 9.5. The four stages of competence.

Put simply, the four stages are:

1. *Unconscious incompetence*: At this stage, the performer can't execute the skill and doesn't know that they can't. Were I to begin learning, say, dressage, I would be at this stage. Not only do I not know how to ride horses, I don't even know what it is I don't know about riding horses. I imagine there are different methods, styles, techniques, and components of riding, all of which I must learn. I don't know them, and furthermore, I don't even know what they are. Parents may recognize this state in children—kids may flout social customs not because they lack self-control, but because they simply don't realize that there *are* any social customs.
2. *Conscious incompetence*: At this stage, the performer still can't execute the skill, but they are aware of their inability and have a better understanding of what the skill is. At various points in this book, you may find yourself in this stage—learning about a coaching skill that you have not yet developed.
3. *Conscious competence*: At this stage, the performer can execute the skill, but only when they are focused on it. Performance may also require ideal circumstances. Disruptions to concentration or changes in circumstances may cause performance to falter.
4. *Unconscious competence*: At this stage, the skill has become automatic—the performer can execute it without thinking about it, and often in varied circumstances.

With this information, we begin to more clearly understand skill development and the journey each of our athletes is on. However, where the four-stage model really comes into its own is when we consider the different roles we must play depending on the stage an athlete is at.

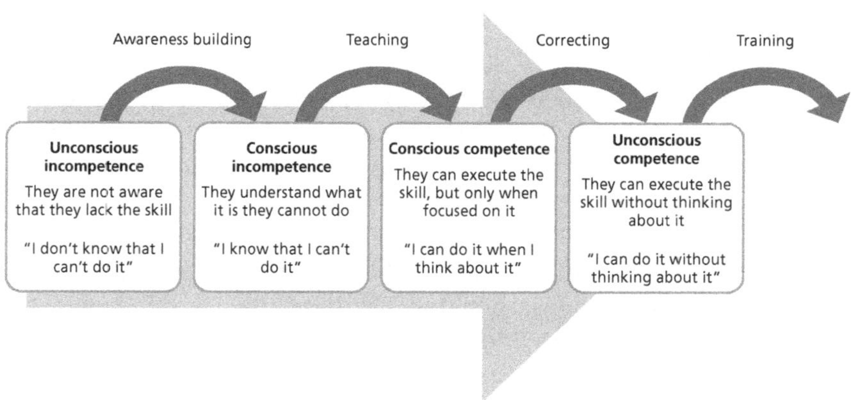

Figure 9.6. The four roles of a coach according to each stage of skill development.

Our job as skill developers is to help athletes progress from one stage to the next. As there are four stages, there are also four skill development practices:

1. *Awareness building*: Despite its simplicity, this may be one of the most powerful tools in a coach's toolbox. Anyone can stand in front of a player and point out their weaknesses, but awareness building is much more than telling someone what they can't do—it's helping them *feel* it, and with enough nuance that they can, to a certain extent, teach themselves.

   Suppose I am trying to teach a tennis player to make contact with the ball at the right spot relative to their body. Ideally, they would position themselves such that the ball is at a comfortable height and distance from them, but because they are a beginner, they are meeting the ball wherever it might be—too high, too low, too close, too far, etc.

   I could tell them: "Find the right contact point!" I could even explain to them: "You want to make contact at waist height. Right now you're making contact in a different position each time." In this case, I've given them the necessary information, but as we've established, execution matters more than knowledge, and if they don't know what a "good" contact point or a "bad" contact point feels like, then they will likely be doomed to repeat the same mistakes.

Instead, I could help them feel a "good" contact point by tossing a few balls to them in just the right spot, prompting them to think about the sensation. Then we could continue as before, but this time I could ask them to call out "yes" or "no" after each shot: "yes" if it was a good contact point, "no" if it was a bad one.

This simple exercise has multiple benefits. First, it allows me to determine how good or bad their self-awareness is, which will inform my next steps (if they're actually very self-aware, then I have to figure out why they still aren't able to position themselves in the right spot). Second, it allows me to intervene when they call out incorrectly—"yes" on a bad one or "no" on a good one. These are the moments I am looking for: chances to *build awareness*. In these moments, I can stop and correct them, allowing them to associate what they felt in their body with the feedback I have given them. Over time, as their awareness (not their skill) gets better (in other words, when their rate of correctly calling "yes" or "no" has improved, regardless of the number of yeses or nos), I can begin to ask: "Why was that a no?" Then I can see further into their awareness: do they recognize that the ball was too high? Or that it was too close? Or do they simply feel that the shot was uncomfortable? Once again, I can gently correct them, allowing them to connect different sensations with different pieces of information.[16]

Awareness is generally built in this way. First, the coach provides the relevant information ("yes," "no," "too high," etc.), then the player feeds back themselves and the coach affirms or corrects. But there are other methods as well—video analysis is quite

16 This is an example of what Doug Lemov and James Beeston call "binary feedback"–the only two pieces of feedback are "yes" and "no" (Lemov, 2020). Beyond giving us coaches useful information, binary feedback on its own can sometimes be enough to change behavior. As they receive the feedback, the athlete becomes aware of what they're doing right and what they're doing wrong and adjusts their actions accordingly. It should be noted, however, that binary feedback works best when there is a mix of yeses and nos. If there are only nos, then the athlete will not feel or understand a yes. Conversely, too many yeses suggests that the exercise is too easy and needs progressing.

common and is discussed later in the chapter. Guided self-reflection can also be effective.

Once the athlete is aware of what they're doing, they have progressed to conscious incompetence.

2. *Teaching*: The leap from conscious incompetence to conscious competence takes place through what I will term "teaching"—the essence of skill development. While awareness building is about helping a learner understand what they're doing and what the skill demands, and correcting is about automatizing and perfecting something that the learner can already do, teaching is about helping someone acquire a skill that they previously had no ability in. If the athlete, when attempting the skill, is successful 50% of the time or less, then they need teaching.

   When teaching, your primary objective is to help the athlete *feel* what it is to do the skill correctly. This means that you'll often either break the skill down into its component parts, or keep the skill whole but make the task significantly easier (e.g. by changing the target, the equipment, the movement). Coaches who are good teachers are often good at designing progressions, allowing the athlete to feel what success feels like right from the beginning, and then gradually ratcheting up either the difficulty or the realism, while maintaining correct execution.

   A mistake that coaches often make is to skip the teaching stage and go right to correcting, where the task is often more realistic and complete. When this happens, the athlete often struggles—not only are they not competent yet, they don't know exactly what they need to do in order to become competent. The result is a loss of confidence and stagnant, if not worsening, performance. Fortunately, the teacher has a variety of different tools in their toolbox, the most common being progressions, opposites, and constraints. These are discussed later in the chapter.

   Teaching generally occurs when the movement or behavior is unstable and unsuccessful. Once the performer can execute the skill 60% of the time or more, and their performance is stable (i.e. it looks roughly the same every time), they have progressed from conscious incompetence to conscious competence.

3. *Correcting*: Once the performer can execute the skill, there are a few things we must do. First, we need to give the skill enough repetitions that it becomes automatic. The correcting phase is marked by fewer stoppages and more repetitions. The task is made more realistic and complete, and the coach provides more opportunities for practice with perhaps less feedback.

   Second, we need to correct any small or infrequent mistakes that are still occurring. Correcting is about refining. The athlete is now successful 60% of the time or more—what's stopping them from getting to 100%? Our job is to identify the differences between the successful reps and the unsuccessful ones, and to continue to nudge our athlete toward optimal performance. Oftentimes, this is done through simple verbal feedback, but other tools such as questioning, analogy, and video analysis can also be used, as we'll discuss later.

   Third, if dealing with an open skill (see Chapter 2), we need to add elements of perception and decision-making so that execution can remain stable in more realistic game-like situations. We'll discuss this in the upcoming section on variability.

4. *Training*: This is the process of taking a skill that has already been mastered and improving it—making it, in the words of Daft Punk, harder, better, faster, stronger. The goal is not so much to change the skill as to optimize it. Training involves setting targets that are just outside the performer's abilities and then pushing them to reach these targets. The task should be complete and fully realistic, and less feedback should be given. The coach's main role is to encourage and motivate while setting challenges of appropriate difficulty.

With the four stages in mind, let's look at how we can create an environment that allows athletes to progress through them as efficiently as possible.

Creating the Appropriate Environment for Development

There's an old joke about a farmer who can't get his cows to produce milk. He asks everyone he can for advice, and when he's out of ideas, he goes to the physicists at the local university. They spend night and day working on the problem, and after a few weeks they return to the farmer with an answer: "We've got a solution," they say. "But it only works for spherical cows in a vacuum."[17]

No athlete practices in a vacuum. Everything they do is the result of their interaction with their coach, their teammates, the task at hand, the environment, and more. For now, we'll focus specifically on what kind of practice environment we want to create for skill development to occur.

Figure 9.7. The coach-performer-environment interaction.

In this case, we'll say that the environment consists of the motivational climate, the degree of variability, and the realism, quantity, and difficulty of the repetitions. The environment facilitates learning by playing two roles: the pillow and the stick. As the pillow, the environment supports the athlete by encouraging them—a well-designed task will reward a performer who makes progress. Similarly, a coach who creates an environment focused on mastery of goals and pushing oneself will find that athletes are motivated to learn and develop. At the same time, as the stick, an environment with challenging tasks and constant progressions can be demanding of an athlete, pushing them to step out of their comfort zone and get better.[18] The environment we create plays an outsize role in shaping our athlete's experience of their sport and ultimately accelerating or holding back their development.

Quantity, Realism, Difficulty, and Variability of Repetitions

As the saying goes: "Repetition is the mother of all skill." A big part of creating the appropriate environment for development is ensuring that athletes are afforded the opportunity to get repetitions on the skills they

17 This is the sort of joke that I love and my girlfriend hates. Too bad she's not the one writing the book.

18 Consider the environment in which a child learns to walk: it's motivating, in that there are so many places to go and objects to reach, and supportive, in that every adult in the room claps and celebrates when a step is taken.

are trying to improve. Without this, it's extremely unlikely they'll see any progress.

But how many repetitions should they get? Logic dictates that more is better, but that doesn't take into account things like fatigue or boredom. And what *kind* of repetitions should they get? Some would argue that the more realistic, the better—but is that always feasible? And how hard should practice be? How much variation should the athletes experience?

These are all good, important questions. As with most coaching questions, there is no one right answer. However, that doesn't mean that *all* answers are right, or that it's just a matter of personal preference. What it means is that each question can and must be answered in context—relative to the athlete, the sport, the skill, and a host of other factors.

Realism vs. Quantity

A repetition is realistic to the extent that it demands the same things of an athlete as competition does. These demands could be technical, tactical, physical, mental, cognitive, emotional, and so on. The most realistic environment is, of course, competition, but a practice environment can be realistic depending on the extent to which it applies the same demands.

It seems logical to some that the more realistic a practice is, the better. However, when taken to its extreme, this notion puts us all out of a job—after all, the most realistic practice is simply to play the game. If that were the best approach to development, there'd be no need for us coaches. Thankfully, few coaches take that approach, for two reasons. The first relates to difficulty: while playing the game is most realistic, it may sometimes present a difficulty level that is not optimal for development. We'll address this later. The second reason is that a more realistic scenario often presents fewer opportunities for practice.

Imagine a volleyball player working on blocks. Statistics tell us that there are somewhere between 1.5 and 2.5 blocks per set in competitive play. Even if we count "soft blocks" (blocks that don't immediately lead to a point), considering that there are six players per team and only one of them is doing the blocking, we are not left with very many chances to practice. So while playing a set might be most realistic (in terms of where the ball will come from, the mental stressors, physical state, etc.), it would not provide very many repetitions on blocking.

In most cases, realism and quantity lie at opposite ends of a spectrum: the more realistic an environment is, the fewer repetitions it provides, and vice versa.

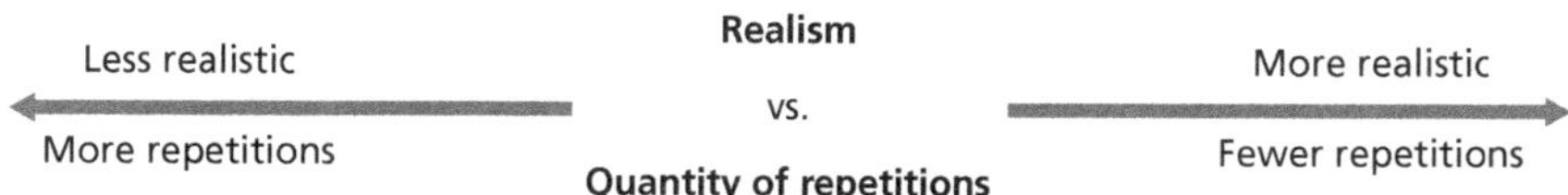

Figure 9.8. Realism vs. quantity of repetitions.

So how do we choose how realistic (or repetitive) to make our environment? The best way is to refer back to the four stages of competence, with repetitions starting high and gradually decreasing, and realism starting low and gradually increasing. In the unconscious incompetence stage, a learner is processing new information and needs lots of opportunities to learn and become familiar with the skill. In the conscious incompetence stage, they still require repetition as they practice and make adjustments. At the same time, as the skill is new and their level of ability is low, too much realism (i.e. extraneous information) will overwhelm and hinder them.

Conversely, in the later stages, as the athlete progresses through conscious competence and unconscious competence, repetitions can be decreased. Once the skill reaches a point of stability, fewer repetitions are required as the performer becomes more and more skilled and needs less work to maintain their level. This is again demonstrated in the Ebbinghaus forgetting curve (see Figure 9.4). At the same time, as the skill stabilizes and the performer becomes more competent, it becomes increasingly important to ensure that the skill will hold up in a more realistic environment.

This outlines the broad concepts, but exactly how many repetitions should we be aiming for? How much is too much? How much rest should athletes be given? It's understandably difficult for researchers to pinpoint the exact number of repetitions required to master a skill. Similarly, it can be difficult to determine where the "sweet spot" is for how many repetitions to give in a practice. One thing we *do* know, however, is that there is often a point of diminishing returns, after which very little progress can be made without rest.

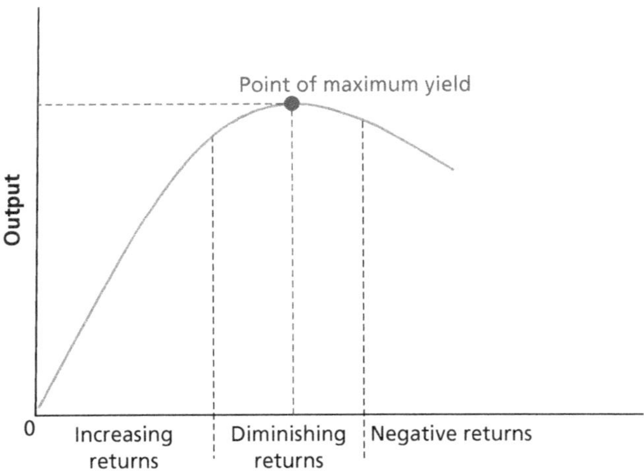

Figure 9.9. Diminishing returns in skill development.

As coaches, we have to monitor how the athlete is responding to our feedback and to the task. As time goes on, you may notice that they are making less and less progress; this can be for either physical or mental reasons (or both), and it is the point at which you want to take a break and, if possible, switch to a different task. Continuing to practice beyond this point will, at best, be a waste of time, and at worst cause frustration, burnout, and a drop in performance. In other words, our goal is to get as many *productive* repetitions as possible, but no more.

Research is also very clear on the benefits of rest for skill development. When the brain is resting from practice, whether sleeping or not, it is binding together the memories required to perform the skill and strengthening the neural pathways. Contrary to popular belief, the real improvements happen between practice sessions, not during them. Giving athletes sufficient rest in between repetitions, sets, and sessions is crucial for development.

Difficulty Level

Not only should repetitions be of the appropriate realism and quantity, they should also be of the appropriate difficulty. While this might sound simple, the ability to adjust exercises and activities to the level of the athlete may be one of the most important a coach can have. There are conflicting viewpoints on this topic, at least if we are to listen to social media. One school of thought is that players should experience success, learn to win, and gain confidence. Another is that players must be pushed, challenged, and brought outside their comfort zone. Of course, both are true. The question, as always, is when should each be applied?

In the 1930s, psychologist Lev Vygotsky developed the notion of the zone of proximal development (ZPD) (Vygotsky, 1978). In his view, there are three zones of learning. In the first, tasks are easy enough that the learner can perform them without any help. In the third, tasks are so difficult that the learner cannot perform them, even with help. In the middle, the ZPD, learners can perform the skills if given a little bit of assistance.

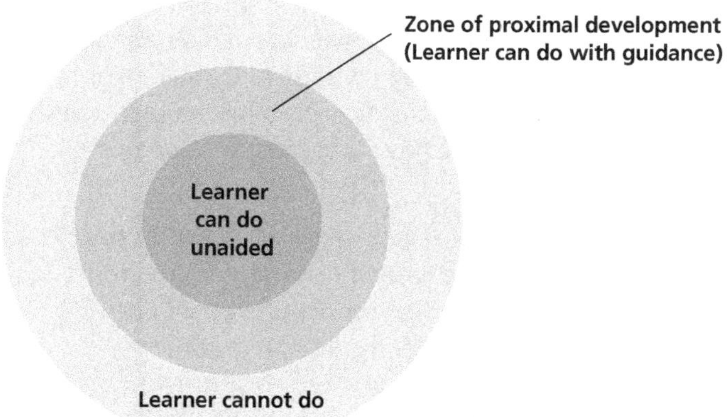

Figure 9.10. The Zone of Proximal Development.

Research in education has repeatedly demonstrated that students given tasks in their ZPD improve the fastest. Intuitively, this makes sense—practicing a task that they can't perform, no matter how much help is given, will lead nowhere. And practicing something that they can already do, without any challenge, won't help much either. Our job, when developing a skill, is to set tasks that are at the maximum level of difficulty that is still achievable with some assistance.

In schools, assistance is as simple as providing instruction or guidance. But what does that look like for *us*? In sports, assistance can come directly from a coach via feedback, instructions, or guiding questions. But it can also come from the task and the environment via modified scoring systems, progressions or regressions, or altered equipment or spaces.

For optimal progress, our aim should be for players to succeed at the task between 50% and 70% of the time. Below 50%, motivation decreases. Who wants to fail more than they succeed? Above 70%, things start to become too easy; not only will some athletes lose interest, but those who remain engaged will not be sufficiently challenged to improve.

Of course, the 50-70% sweet spot is only a guideline. Some players need reassurance and feelings of success, while others love a challenge more than anything. Also, the difficulty level you set may well vary according to the time of year, your goal for the activity (development, maintenance, or training), the mood of the athlete, or any other number of factors. But this 60% success rate—or the idea that the "sweet spot" for learning is in the zone between what you can already do and what you can almost do—is present in many facets of life. Consider this story from leadership coach Kelli Thompson about when she gave a presentation to her company's leadership:

> *"How are you justifying the sales and expenses estimates?" the CEO asked. My face glowed red as I stuttered. My heart rate skyrocketed and my throat tightened. ... Instead of taking over from me when I was facing tough questions, [my boss] Valerie let me figure my own way out of the discomfort. I did muddle through it, albeit not as well as I would have liked, but in a way that left me better prepared for my next meeting with him. ... I remember Valerie as a good boss because she often gave me developmental opportunities like these. The stakes were usually low like that small, internal meeting, where everyone knew I was still green and would be supportive. Valerie was present but in the background, allowing me to succeed or stumble but learn from the experience either way. [Her] approach that day with our CEO didn't feel good at the time. But had she intervened, I wouldn't have learned how to respond to*

unexpected questions or later reflected on how to better prepare for executive presentations. (Thompson, 2023)

Think about it: if you're succeeding less than half the time, how likely is it that you're progressing? And if you're succeeding 80% of the time or more, are you really progressing, or are you just doing what you can already do? For maximum skill development, we should aim to create an environment where athletes are successful around 60% of the time. If they aren't, then we make it easier. But once they acquire the skill and start getting better, then we make it harder again.

Variability

In coaching, "variability" means having athletes perform the same task multiple times, but with certain variables changed between each repetition.[19] Here are some examples:

- *Baseball*: Instead of doing batting practice off the same type of pitch every time, practice batting against random pitches.
- *Tennis*: Instead of hitting only rally forehands, hit a mix of rally, attacking, and defending forehands.
- *Basketball*: Instead of practicing 50 jump shots from the same position, change position each time.

Generally speaking, the scientific literature is supportive of this kind of practice. The logic is that it is not only rare but almost impossible to execute the exact same motor pattern twice in a row. As a test, take a piece of paper and a pen and a draw a brief squiggle:

Now try to draw over that line repeatedly, tracing it exactly. Chances are, you'll end up with something like this:

19 Sometimes it can refer to variability in the *order* or *type* of activities in a practice. This is known as "interleaving" and we'll address it shortly.

Somewhat like an expensive machine being calibrated, variability in practice can help our brain develop a better awareness of our body and the way it moves, thus leading to better control and stability.

Often, discussions of variability involve the terms "blocked" and "random" practice. Blocked practice is what you'd think of as traditional "old-school" practice: doing the same thing over and over again. Random practice involves varying each repetition, forcing the athlete to adjust their technique to solve each new problem. But there's a third, less discussed kind of practice: "serial" practice. In serial practice, the repetitions are varied, but predictably.

So, if blocked practice looks like this:

1 1 1 2 2 2 3 3 3

and random practice looks like this:

1 3 3 2 1 2 3 1 1

then serial practice looks like this:

1 2 3 1 2 3 1 2 3

or this:

2 1 2 1 2 1 2 1 2

From a cognitive perspective, blocked practice is easier than serial, which is easier than random. Given what we know about difficulty levels and the ZPD, we can use this information to help us decide how to approach our practices.

The first question we have to ask ourselves is whether the skill we are trying to teach is *open* or *closed* (as outlined in Chapter 2). Open skills are performed in a cycle: perception (the athlete perceives relevant information), decision-making (the athlete uses that information to decide what to do), execution (the athlete performs the skill), and feedback (the athlete assesses how it went). Closed skills consist only of execution and feedback.

For years, the common belief held by coaches and players alike was that "practice makes perfect." As time went on and our understanding of motor development advanced, the saying shifted to "practice makes *permanent*." The idea is that practice, in and of itself, is not sufficient to master a skill. Practicing the *wrong* thing will just make you better...at doing the wrong thing. Deliberate practice, with feedback, correction, and other factors interspersed, is required for true progress.

Unfortunately, this idea—that practice makes permanent—is itself only partially true, and those of us who coach open-skill sports will likely have seen evidence of this: players who execute a skill flawlessly in isolation, but crumble in a more complex game situation. Why does this happen?

Part of the reason, setting aside psychological factors like stress, is what's known as "perception–action coupling." In open-skill sports, actions are linked to specific perceptual cues—"If this happens, I do that." When players fail to execute a skill they can do in practice in competition, it's often because the game situation presents specific perceptual cues that were not present in practice (e.g. the presence of an opponent). Coaches must create practice situations that present similar perceptual and decision-making opportunities so that players can learn to associate the right actions with the right situations. That's where variability comes in. You see, variability for the sake of variability will not necessarily help players of open-skill sports transfer their skills to competition. Variability must be introduced systematically. Thankfully, there's an easy formula for opening up a skill—one, the other, alternate differentiate:

1. *One*: Teach the skill you are trying to improve. As Czyz and Coker (2023) write, athletes at the beginning stage of learning a skill (conscious incompetence) "should not only practice one skill at a time but should initially do so under conditions that do not require decision-making." If they can't do it in simple conditions, why should we introduce variability? Practice this skill until the athlete can do it at least 7 times out of 10. Then, move on to step two.
2. *The other*: Practice another skill—one that is different but related to the first one. The two skills should occur in a game situation such that the athlete might have to choose between them. Practice this skill until it is as good as the first one. You can skip this step if the second skill is already acquired.

3. *Alternate*: Alternate between the two skills. The goal here is to develop the player's *differentiation* ability—their ability to organize their body to produce two different motor patterns. Everyone likes to get into a groove, but in open-skill sports this is rarely possible. Players have to switch between techniques frequently and may spend long stretches of time in between repetitions of the same technique. A tennis player may only hit a drop shot once every 15 minutes; a soccer player may go an hour between headers. But when it's time, each has to be able to find the appropriate motor pattern. Alternate until the athlete can execute the skill correctly on demand.
4. *Differentiate*: Differentiate between the two skills. Introduce an element of perception and decision-making: if this, do that; if that, do this. At first, keep the decision down to one variable, until the player is not only making the right decision but also executing the technique correctly. Then add a second variable (if this *and* this, do that; if that *and* that, do this, etc.). Continue this process, ensuring the athlete is deciding and executing correctly, until it is sufficiently realistic for competition.[20]

For coaches teaching closed skills, steps 1-3 can still apply, albeit in slightly different ways depending on the sport. In sports that are closed but demand a variety of movement patterns (e.g. golf, which is self-paced but requires a player to be able to hit woods, irons, putters, and more), players don't have to make split-second decisions, but they do have to be able to find the right swing when it counts, without the ability to warm up or get into a groove. Having players practice going from one technique to another (i.e. serial practice) can help.

In sports that are closed but demand roughly the same movement pattern every time (e.g. swimming, track and field, shooting), practicing with what is known as intra-skill variability can enhance a performer's precision or accuracy. For example, learning to pot a billiard ball from multiple different angles and distances, while requiring essentially the same motor pattern each time, will enhance the player's skill by building

20 This process—one, the other, alternate, differentiate—can be likened to blocked, serial, then random practice. However, I prefer the former simply because I find the term "random" to be misleading. Variability must be introduced systematically for skills to transfer to game settings.

their body awareness. That being said, there is still a place for blocked practice in closed sports when it is for the purpose of training—pushing the physical or mental limits of a skill.

But the concept of variability doesn't just apply on the micro level, mixing things up on each repetition. It can also be applied to how we structure our sessions, mixing up the order or type of activities within a practice. This is known as "interleaving," and extensive research on the subject has been conducted both in classroom and sports settings. The result? Interleaving two tasks, even if it means spending less time on each one in total, can lead to greater improvements in both tasks than when they are practiced separately.

Why does this work? There are a couple of cognitive mechanisms at play. For one, interleaving allows learners to compare and contrast tasks (recall the concept of awareness building), building their cognitive and physical knowledge and enhancing learning. Another important mechanism is recall. When a learner returns to an activity after abandoning it earlier in the session, their brain is forced to recall what it was doing from *long-term* memory. This process of bringing the skill back from *long-term* memory into *working* memory (the part of our memory that processes and uses information) strengthens that neural pathway, engraining the skill in our memory and making its performance more efficient in the long run.

Once again, the key to all of this is not so much the *what* or the *how*, but the *when*. I'm reminded of the John Wooden (2009) quote: "Don't mistake activity for achievement." There isn't much value in running around from activity to activity just for the sake of interleaving. Instead, here are a few best practices:

1. *Make each block productive*: Learning should occur in each block. If the time spent on one task is too short, the athlete will not have the chance to make any progress. Remember that interleaving works because the performer's brain recalls what it has learned and builds on it. If no learning occurs, there is nothing to recall.
   That being said, the blocks don't need to be long enough for the learner to *master* the skill. Aim to get them to a point where they have made progress but the skill isn't yet "solid." Remember that spending too much time on a task defeats the purpose of interleaving.

2. *Choose tasks of appropriate similarity*: The other principle at play in interleaving is that of contrast. If the two skills are too similar, performers will not learn anything from the differences between them, and neither will their brains be forced to recall anything stored in long-term memory, since all their time will be spent in working memory. If the tasks are too different, however, performers might get confused or overwhelmed, hindering learning. While it's a somewhat subjective target, aim to interleave skills that are 50% similar. Not twins, not strangers, but siblings.

Non-Linear Pedagogy, the Constraints-Led Approach, and Other Methodologies

Lastly, no discussion of a practice environment would be complete without mentioning the constraints-led approach (CLA)—one of a few pedagogies that have gained in popularity in recent years. This chapter is not the place for a full-scale discussion of the pros or cons of this approach, but I'd like to provide a brief overview of the pillars of the CLA, connect them to what I've already written, and offer suggestions for best practice.

The CLA stems from the principles of ecological dynamics, which propose that any performer's behavior adapts and evolves in response to the demands of the environment they are in. Non-linear pedagogy is an approach to teaching and coaching that has emerged directly from these principles, advocating for a more player-centric and exploratory approach, as compared to the more coach-centric and directive approaches of the past. Among the tenets of non-linear pedagogy are:

- Representative learning design: The idea that training environments should be representative of the game environment.
- The promotion of an external focus of attention (as opposed to an internal one).
- Variability: The idea that "blocked" repetition of skills without any variation is less optimal than repetition with variation.
- Information–movement couplings: The idea that motor patterns should be linked to perceptual information gathered by the athlete.

- Manipulation of constraints: The idea that the task, performer, and environment can be constrained and manipulated in order to bring about learning outcomes.

Each of these principles is based upon a solid theoretical framework backed up by varying degrees of empirical evidence. To start, the benefits of having an external focus of attention (i.e. the intended effects of a movement) over an internal one (i.e. the movements of body parts) have been well established for decades. A 2021 systematic review of more than 70 studies with more than 3,000 participants found overwhelmingly that external foci led to better performance and learning of motor skills when compared to internal foci, regardless of age, health, or skill level (Chua et al., 2021).

When it comes to representative learning design, experimental studies have found that, generally speaking, training environments that are more "game-like" encourage a greater transfer of skills (Müller and Rosalie, 2019; Seifert et al., 2016). However, as Champion et al. (2023) highlight, the more realistic the practice environment, the higher the cognitive and physical demands placed on the athlete. In some cases, this is exactly what we want. In other cases, the increased load can cause breakdowns, whether cognitive (e.g. confusion in decision-making or inability to acquire a skill) or physical (e.g. fatigue, loss of coordination). As discussed earlier, keeping athletes in their ZPD is crucial, and adjusting the representativeness of the environment can help to make that happen.

These same principles apply when we talk about information–movement couplings. All tasks sit on a spectrum of representativeness and information density. A player kicking a soccer ball from a stationary position at an empty goal may not be experiencing a full game condition, but his environment is still more realistic than if he were to kick a ball in a lab. A softball player batting a ball tossed gently to her is not perceiving as much information as she would be in a game, but still more than when she hits the ball off a tee. This is important to recognize because the addition of perceptual or informational cues will almost always make things more difficult. Kicking a ball to a fixed target is easier than kicking one to a moving target. Observing one defender is easier than observing two. Intercepting a ball rolling on the ground is easier than catching it when it's bouncing. The addition of information to the task will increase the difficulty level—and once again, for skill development to occur, athletes must be challenged just the right amount.

The same principle applies when it comes to variability. As discussed earlier, using variability is not so much a question of *if* as of *how* or *when*. In the earlier stages of skill development, blocked repetition can be useful. The athlete cannot perform the task consistently, so in a sense they are supplying their own variation—adding more will just make things too difficult. As they progress, some variation can be included (ideally in a predictable pattern), before eventually opening the skill up completely (true game-like variation) when it has been acquired.

Advocates of a CLA also often endorse what is known as "discovery learning": a process by which students learn by exploring a problem. In *pure* discovery learning, students are given little to no guidance from a teacher, whereas in *guided* discovery, students are provided with "hints, direction, coaching, feedback, and/or modeling to keep the student on track" (Mayer, 2004). Numerous studies with students split into pure and guided discovery groups have found that those in the guided discovery group learn faster, remember more, and better transfer their knowledge to new problems (Fay and Mayer, 1994; Lee and Thompson, 1997).

Every sport is inherently difficult, and competitive sports even more so. When athletes are presented with a challenging game situation and given no guidance for how to overcome it, three things are at risk of happening. First, it is almost guaranteed that the athlete will spend more time than necessary trying solutions that don't work. This period of trial and error doesn't make the athlete smarter (after all, we don't teach kids what 2 + 2 *doesn't* equal) or more capable of solving problems (because without being told what to look for or being given necessary background information, they haven't learned anything); all it does is waste time. Second, there is a chance that the athlete will find a solution that works in the short term (e.g. because the environment wasn't perfectly designed, or because their training partners are weaker than them) but won't work in the long term (e.g. when they get older, or their opposition gets better). In such cases, you'll then have to spend time convincing the athlete *not* to do something they've found success with.

Third, there is a chance that the athlete will not be able to accomplish the task on their own and, without guidance, become frustrated and lose motivation. Pure discovery learning is inefficient at best and ineffective at worst. Guided discovery, however, can be used effectively, with the right environment, constraints, and cues.

When it comes to the use of constraints, a nuanced approach is required. On the one hand, a recent meta-analysis looked at 18 studies and found that the majority had results that supported the use of a CLA (Clark et al., 2019). On the other hand, most of the studies were also of low quality. This isn't all too surprising when you consider that the CLA is a relatively new pedagogy in sports, and testing its effects against another approach is incredibly difficult. Not only do you have to compare groups and ensure that they are being coached in distinctly different ways, you also have to clearly define what CLA coaching looks like compared to other methods (no easy task), and account for possible differences in the groups (e.g. maturation, athleticism, access to opportunities, other environmental factors). In other words, constraints can be a powerful teaching tool—the art is in understanding the how, when, who, and why.

There are many different types of constraints, and they each have value. You can constrain the environment, making a space bigger or smaller or changing it altogether. You can constrain the equipment used, or change the rules to reward one action or discourage another. You can physically constrain an athlete's movement in order to encourage a certain technique.

Coaches sometimes fall into black-and-white thinking: an approach is either good or bad. In reality, the best coaches use a CLA as a tool like any other—in different ways, at different times, with different people. That's not to say that there aren't any guidelines for using a CLA, or that we're free to do whatever strikes our fancy. Given what we already know about learning and motor skill acquisition, there are some overarching guidelines that can help to inform our use of a CLA:

1. *Manipulate the constraints, but don't expect them to do the teaching for you*: In some cases, a constraint can engender the exact change in behavior you're looking for, but in others, the constraint will only serve as a source of motivation. Not every athlete can figure out what adaptation to make given

the circumstances—that's where we come in. Manipulate the constraints to create a demand, but offer guidance to those who need it so that they can meet that demand.

2. *Remember that there are good and bad adaptations*: It's rare to design the perfect environment with exactly the right constraint. Oftentimes, different athletes will meet the demands of the environment with different solutions. Be aware that some of these solutions might be productive and helpful, but some will hinder their development in the long term. Be careful with the constraints you establish and guide athletes, if necessary, toward a solution that will serve them well as they continue to develop.
3. *Remember that your instructions are a constraint*: The instructions that we give shape our athletes' perceptions of their environment. Therefore, we don't always need to change the environment, the rules, or the equipment. A simple cue like "Look for the open space" or "See if you can push the opponent back" can be enough of a constraint to change behavior and lead to development.

In summary, given what we already know surrounding the ZPD and open and closed skills, we can see where the CLA and associated methodologies fit in:

- Representative learning design: The environment should be as realistic as possible while allowing for enough repetitions. This balance depends on which stage of the four-stage model the athlete and the skill are in.
- Relevant perceptual cues should be present, but only enough to ensure the optimal level of difficulty. Elements of perception and decision-making should be added systematically (i.e. only one at a time, and keep it the same) and progressively (i.e. only once the previous one has been mastered), keeping the athlete in their ZPD.
- Variability should also be introduced systematically and according to the level of ability of the athlete and their mastery of the skill.
- Constraints should be used, but they do not relieve the coach of their duty to teach.

- Discovery learning should generally be limited in order to maximize time, avoid negative impacts on players' confidence, and prevent maladaptation.

The theory underpinning the CLA and others can be aligned with what is already known about human learning and motor skill acquisition. The question of CLAs vs. more traditional approaches is not a question of either/or, but rather of when and how. As Bobrownicki et al. (2023) articulated: "ecological approaches ... are insufficient to guide effective talent development and coaching practice in their entirety. ... [They] are not the whole answer for coaching and instead represent useful tools to be deployed within coaching practice. Indeed, ecological approaches represent theories of human movement, not of coaching and performance."

Learning Styles

I've worked really hard to ensure that everything presented in this book rests on a solid foundation of evidence—mostly from empirical scientific study, but when that's not possible, from the years of experience gleaned from experts around the world. My goal is also to make this book as actionable and informative as possible while remaining succinct, so I'll be brief: there is overwhelming scientific evidence that learning styles do not exist.

This may come as a surprise to you. As a coach, you may have been taught that different students learn best in certain ways. A recent systematic review found that 89% of teachers still believe in learning styles (Newton and Salvi, 2020). As a student yourself, you may have found that you prefer to be taught in a certain way. Nonetheless, the evidence is clear: learning styles are a myth (Dekker et al., 2012; Blanchette et al., 2019).

It's important to define what we mean by "learning styles." Students tend to have preferences for how they receive information. This is not being questioned—different people prefer to be taught in different ways. However, the idea that individuals can be classified by learning style and that they learn better when taught in a style that matches theirs is entirely without proof. Over the last few decades, numerous studies have researched the validity of learning styles and found that there is absolutely no correlation between educational achievement and the use of learning styles in teaching.

But wait! If players express a preference for being taught in a certain way, what's the harm in catering to them? There isn't any. At least, not necessarily. But a few things should be kept in mind:

1. Are you making the best use of your time? Given the lack of evidence for learning styles, any attempt to cater to an athlete's preference shouldn't take time away from the things we know *do* help learning. One example would be an "auditory learner" whose coach decides to spend extra time talking and explaining things in minute detail—time that would be better spent practicing. Other athletes may claim to be visual learners, and while watching game film or technical analyses can be useful, we must ensure it isn't taking away too much time from the actual practice.
2. Are you catering to the whole group? Most of us work with teams or groups of athletes. Attempting to cater to each individual's preference will either fail or be extremely inefficient. As they say, trying to please everyone results in pleasing no one.
3. Are you helping them "feel" it? All athletes could really be lumped into one category: kinesthetic learners. Teachers are in the business (mostly) of information transfer. Coaches are in the business (mostly) of skill development. Our job is not to get players to *know* what they have to do; our job is to help them *do* what they have to do. And to do that, they have to *feel* it. There's nothing worse than a player who tells you, "I know what I'm supposed to do, but I just can't do it!" All the time spent with auditory or visual approaches would be better invested in helping an athlete develop body awareness so that they can feel what they are supposed to be doing.

When shaping our learning environment, it's important to take into account each athlete's personality and preferences. However, the biggest favor we can do an athlete is disregard learning styles in favor of approaches that will actually help them get better.

Feedback

Oftentimes, our perception of coaching is reduced to simply giving feedback. In the car ride home, parents ask their kids, "What did the coach say?" On the court, coaches repeat the same instructions over and over, hoping that time is all it will take for the message to sink in. Of course, coaching is so much more than giving feedback, as this chapter hopefully illustrates. Even skill development, which is only a part of coaching, involves shaping the environment, organizing activities, observing and planning, and more. But giving feedback is nonetheless an important piece of the puzzle, and like anything else, we should strive to be as good at it as possible. Giving feedback is so much more than just telling people what to do—there's a great deal of nuance in the what, how, and when.

On the Type of Feedback

Whenever possible, feedback should be *externally focused*. Internally focused feedback directs attention to the movement of specific body parts. Externally focused feedback directs the athlete's attention to the impact of those movements. For example, instead of saying, "Bend your knees more," you could say, "Get low to the ground." Instead of saying, "Snap your wrist after the forearm fires," you could say, "Let the tip of the racket come through the ball."

Sometimes, it will be impossible to bring about the intended result without focusing attention on the body—and that's OK. But research has shown that externally focused feedback leads to quicker improvements, which is why we want to use it whenever possible.

Feedback should also be *solution-oriented*. Rather than tell an athlete what they did wrong, why not tell them what they should do instead? Note that this is different from praise. We don't have to look only for the positive, or never comment on mistakes, flaws, or weaknesses. But when we do discuss something that could be better, we can feed back the solution, not the problem. For example, instead of saying, "Don't hunch your back," you could say, "Keep your back straight." Not only is problem-focused feedback inherently negative, it doesn't actually tell the athlete what to do. Furthermore, research has found that performers who are consciously telling themselves *not* to do something end up subconsciously doing that thing under pressure.

Speaking of praise vs. critique, for decades researchers have studied and attempted to define the different types of coach feedback. Most feedback that you give will fit broadly into the following categories:

Table 9.3. Types of coach feedback

Type	Description
Instruction	Guidance on what to do or how to do it
"Hustle"	Anything to activate or intensify previously instructed behavior
Positive modeling	Demonstration of what to do
Negative modeling	Demonstration of what not to do
Verbal praise	Compliment
Verbal scold	Expression of displeasure
Non-verbal praise	Smile, pat on the back, etc.
Non-verbal scold	Scowl, despairing gesture, etc.

Source: Adapted from Gallimore and Tharp (2004).

A study of legendary basketball coach John Wooden found that over 75% of his feedback contained instruction (either direct instruction, hustle, modeling, or a combination of these) (Gallimore and Tharp, 2004). Numerous studies of other successful coaches have found that while the numbers may vary, the rankings don't. In other words, instruction is by far the most common type of feedback given by successful coaches, and praise is more common than scolding (Becker and Wrisberg, 2008; Markland and Martinek, 1988).

On How You Give Feedback

Focused

So your feedback is externally focused, solution-oriented, and instructional. What's next? Ensure that it is *focused*—in other words, directed at one thing at a time. In the words of Dave Hadfield, "If you chase five rabbits, you catch none" (Lemov, 2020, p. 99). Coaches often make the mistake of giving feedback on whatever they see—or even if they have a deliberate plan for what they want to focus on, they can get too excited and try to correct every mistake at once. Athletes who are given too many different pieces of feedback will either pick one to focus on and ignore the others (thus teaching them that it's OK to ignore their coach) or try to focus on all of them and end up achieving none. Keep your feedback focused on one thing at a time.

Economy of Language

Teaching expert Doug Lemov uses a phrase that I think is too good not to steal: "economy of language" (Lemov, 2020). One of the reasons I love this phrase so much is that the word "economy," in this case, carries two meanings. First, it means frugal or sparing ("economical"). The idea is that the more we talk, the more time we take to do so, and we risk muddying the waters and distracting our athletes from the intended focus. Consider this feedback: "Make sure that at the moment when her racket makes contact with the ball, you make your split step so that you're in the air when she touches it and you can react quickly, OK?" Now compare it to: "You split when she hits, OK?"

Second, "economy" refers to financial markets and the idea of supply and demand: as supply increases, demand decreases. Consider the tennis coach who would like her player to turn his shoulders when hitting a forehand. Her feedback might look something like this: "Turn your shoulders! Good. Turn! Again, turn your shoulders! Turn your shoulders! Come on, turn your shoulders! Turn! Come on, turn your shoulders! Turn your shoulders! That's it, turn your shoulders!" This is focused feedback—there's no doubt what she wants out of her athlete—and it's arguably instructional, but what do you think happens in the mind of the athlete as he hears this? How long do you think it will take for him to completely tune out his coach? As the amount of feedback (particularly the same feedback) increases, the student's demand for it decreases. Just as saying a word repeatedly makes it sound like a jumble of letters, repeating the same feedback almost guarantees that it will no longer mean anything to the intended recipient.

As coaches, we have to treat our feedback as a precious commodity: too much and it loses its value; too little and no one knows that it has value. Choose your moments to intervene, and when you do, choose your words carefully.

Cues

Cue words or phrases can work miracles, accomplishing much in little space. For one, they allow you to keep your words to a minimum, which, as we've just discussed, is key. For two, they are often easy for athletes to remember. And for three, they can very often be used to "chunk" multiple concepts together so that they appear as one to the athlete.

Let's imagine I've been working with a tennis player on hitting an approach volley—a volley hit from around the service line, in transition to the net. First, I had to teach them the right footwork: to get their outside foot behind the ball, then to get low with their legs in order to be stable, and finally to make contact a little bit closer to their body than they're used to. Once each of these concepts has been acquired, I could feed back each point individually: "Get your outside foot behind the ball! Stay low! Contact point further back!" But I could also group them into one cue: "Get close." If the athlete does anything wrong—steps with the wrong foot, stands up too tall, makes contact too far in front—they'll be too far from the ball. So while it's only two words, "get close" actually reminds my player of three things. The beauty of this is that it happens without them knowing it. To them, it's just a feeling—the feeling of getting close to the ball. This reduces the amount of feedback I have to give and helps them get out of their own head, making skill execution more automatic and helping them perform under pressure.

Of course, if I keep using "get close" but notice that one particular element of the movement (e.g. the footwork) is breaking down repeatedly, then I can shift my focus to that element and give more specific feedback. It should be noted that in the earlier stages of learning, more specific feedback will likely be required—chunking feedback into cue words works best when each element has been acquired. But if I just want to refocus someone on the feeling of a successful execution without making them think about all its complicated parts, cue words do the trick perfectly.

Tone of Voice

The tone of voice you use when giving feedback can influence how your message is perceived and also create the right atmosphere for development to occur. Consider a phrase like "kick with the laces" and imagine all the different ways in which you could say it: demandingly, casually, supportively, encouragingly, dismissively, and so on. Like anything else, we should be deliberate about the tone we use.

In the early stages of learning, an athlete is pushing themselves out of their comfort zone. They want to feel safe and supported as they go about doing something that they've never done before and will probably be bad at. As such, our tone of voice should communicate encouragement and a lack of judgment. When they have mastered the skill and need to be pushed to new heights, they need to be motivated and energized. As such, our tone should be demanding, energetic, and upbeat. In between the two ends of the spectrum, when athletes are gaining in competence but still require refinement, our tone should probably be focused and neutral, celebrating improvement while concentrating on the process.

One of the mistakes coaches can make when giving their feedback is to infuse it with a sense of judgment or disappointment. Sometimes this is intentional (under the guise of "tough love") and other times it's accidental (either a default tone that the coach doesn't realize comes across this way or some inner frustration coming to the surface). Feedback given with such a tone is almost never effective—not only will the athlete focus on the emotion rather than the message, thereby ignoring the feedback itself, they will feel disappointed or ashamed, killing all motivation and learning in the process. Coaches should monitor their tone to ensure that even harsh feedback communicates encouragement and belief.

On the Timing of Feedback

Relative to an athlete's execution of a task, feedback can be given during execution (*concurrent*), immediately after a single repetition (*immediate terminal*), after a series of repetitions (*delayed terminal*), or later in the day or session (*postponed*). Feedback can also be given as an instruction *before* the execution of the task—we'll call this "priming" feedback. Which is best?

The answer, of course, depends on your objectives. Generally speaking, if you know what you want your players to focus on, tell them in advance! Rarely is there a benefit to letting athletes practice without purpose and *then* giving them feedback. Instead, tell them what to focus on from the beginning, and then give feedback and adjust it based on what you observe.

When it comes to the choice between immediate terminal and delayed terminal feedback, it's usually best to go with immediate terminal. The reason for this is something called the "feedback loop": the athlete executes, receives feedback, and then executes with new information. Research has shown that the shorter the gap between execution and feedback, the more information people retain. This is because the execution is still fresh in their memory and they are the most motivated to learn. Consider the training of a dog—not much is accomplished by putting him outside 30 minutes after pooping on the rug. This is why postponed feedback is usually the worst kind, because memories and motivation have faded, so very little of the key message is likely to stick. The other benefit to immediate terminal feedback is that it allows for *more* feedback loops—in other words, the athletes get more opportunities to execute, receive feedback, and implement it, which means not only more iteration and development, but also more opportunities to practice learning.

Note, however, that research has shown that *instantaneous* feedback—feedback given the very second a movement is complete—has less effect than feedback given after a delay of a few seconds (Swinnen et al., 1990). By pausing for just a moment, we allow the athlete to process their own internal feedback before comparing it to ours. This self-evaluation has been shown to be beneficial for both learning and retention.

Following that same logic, concurrent feedback has been found to have positive effects in the early stages of learning—that is, when the athlete does not yet have a *feel* for the motor pattern. However, continuous concurrent feedback creates a dependency and limits self-evaluation. In a study comparing concurrent feedback to terminal feedback, participants given the latter significantly outperform those given the former when it comes to retention tests (Armstrong, 1970). That's why it's best to provide concurrent feedback at the very early stages and then quickly graduate to terminal feedback.

We also have to consider the frequency of our feedback. The research in this area is not totally conclusive—while experts have studied the topic for decades, there are so many variables to account for (e.g. task complexity, stage of learning, participant age) that it is difficult to establish black-and-white rules. However, there are a few things we know for sure.

The first is that two approaches—providing feedback on all repetitions (100%) or none (0%)—are both equally ineffective (Winstein and Schmidt, 1990). The former creates a dependency and limits self-analysis, while the latter provides no guidance at all. The research is inconclusive regarding the ideal ratio, but it is probably somewhere between 25% and 66%—in other words, give feedback on two out of every three to eight repetitions. A number of studies have found that "summary" feedback (i.e. allowing a learner to make multiple attempts before giving feedback on each of them) and "average" feedback (i.e. giving feedback on the average performance from a series of attempts) are both more beneficial than feeding back on every trial (Lavery, 1962; Schmidt et al., 1990). In fact, in a series of baseball batting experiments, Schmidt et al. (1990) found that the optimal series length was five repetitions and then feedback, although they note that there are a number of factors that may influence this number. Summary or average feedback work because they prevent dependency, allow for self-assessment and awareness building, and enhance movement stability since the learner is not overcorrecting on every repetition.

Research also shows, interestingly enough, that learners do better when they are the ones requesting the feedback. This effect is not due to the frequency with which they request feedback (usually between 10% and 30% of the time). One theory for this is that when the learner requests feedback, they will be more receptive to it. Another theory is that learners request feedback after *good* repetitions, because they want to know what they did in order to replicate it. This leads us to a final point on feedback: provide feedback on the good repetitions as much as (if not more than) on the bad ones. Not only does this have a motivating and encouraging effect, but it teaches athletes what *to do* as opposed to what *not* to do.

Some final things to consider when giving feedback:

1. What are you trying to accomplish? What stage of learning are they at? Are you trying to teach something brand new, or just

ironing out some kinks? While the research is inconclusive, some experts think feedback frequency should be at its highest (say, 70% of the time; Schmidt and Lee, 2014) in the earlier stages of skill acquisition and then taper off as the athlete gradually masters the skill.

2. Is the athlete *trying* to do the right thing? If so, your feedback may not be necessary. Let them try. On the other hand, if they're clearly trying something that won't work, your intervention may be necessary.
3. Are they making progress? If they're getting better with every repetition, you might not need to say anything other than to encourage them. But if they're starting to hit a plateau, you might need to jump in.
4. Will they be able to figure it out on their own?
5. How new is this skill? How much time have they had to try it out? How naturally athletic are they? How patient are they? All of these factors may influence the degree to which you choose to guide them.
6. Will they be receptive to your feedback? Are they tired of hearing your voice? Are they stubborn and in need of more time? Or are they eager to learn and looking for help?

On the Use of Questions

Questioning is a valuable tool for any coach. Its benefits are numerous and include increased retention, greater sense of ownership, and improved problem-solving abilities. Expert coaches and coach developers have written about different approaches to coaching and how they impact questioning (e.g. cooperative vs. autocratic), and about the format of questions (e.g. binary, leading, open-ended).[21] These topics have been written about in far greater detail than I can cover here, but in this section I'll present a less discussed topic that may be of equal or even greater importance: *when* should we be asking questions, and *how* should those questions differ depending on the situation?

21 This section is adapted from Ohlin (2020).

First, we have to consider what it is we are trying to achieve by asking questions. There are four main objectives:

1. To check for understanding, or to practice recalling information.
2. To raise awareness, either of the body or of tactics.
3. To guide thinking toward solving a problem.
4. To find out what the athlete is thinking.

In line with these objectives, there are four main types: retrieval, awareness-building, problem-solving, and probing questions.

Retrieval Questions

Retrieval questions have two purposes: to solidify information in the athlete's memory and to gather data about player learning. Let's imagine that on Monday I introduce a new theme and give the players some key teaching points—e.g. the step-out footwork when volleying. On Tuesday I might ask the group: "What kind of footwork do we want on our volleys?" Or if I want to be more open-ended: "What's the key teaching point on our volleys?" By asking the question, *I'm forcing the players to recall the information from their memory.* This is called "retrieval practice," and studies have shown that it increases long-term retention of information (Moreira et al., 2019). Just like exercising a muscle makes it stronger, recalling previously acquired knowledge solidifies it in the memory. In contrast, simply telling the players, "We're working on our step-out footwork" doesn't engage them mentally and doesn't do much to increase the chances of them retaining the information.

That's not the only benefit, though. Retrieval questions can also be used to gauge what percentage of the team has learned something. I could, for example, ask, "What's one of the six tactical intentions?" and call on players randomly. If I call on four players and only one of them has a correct answer, then that gives me a pretty good indication that we need to review the material.

Retrieval questions are best used when the answer is objective (i.e. there is only one right answer) and has already been taught. Here are some more examples:

- "What do we call it when...?"
- "What is the most important...?"

- "Remember: why is X important?"
- "How do we Y?"

Awareness-Building Questions

Just as awareness building might be the most overlooked stage in the four stages of competence, awareness-building questions might be the most forgotten type of question. However, they might also be the most important. This type of question helps an athlete gain an understanding of either how their body works or what is happening tactically. *Awareness-building questions are so valuable because they directly influence the athlete's perception of reality*, and it is this perception that influences their actions. Therefore, if their perception is inaccurate, their response will likely be inappropriate.

One of the simplest and most effective forms of this type of question is not even technically a question: the "yes/no" drill. In tennis, I might challenge a player to make contact with the ball when it is at the peak of the bounce—the highest point after it touches the ground, before it starts to fall. The drill is simple: after each shot, the player calls out "yes" if they made contact at the peak and "no" if they didn't. The question being asked implicitly is: "Did you make contact at the peak?"

The benefit of awareness-building questions is not just that they require thinking from the student, but that they allow the coach to be more deliberate with their feedback in the future. If a player answers yes when the answer was no, two things happen. First, the coach gains information about the player's level of awareness, which can go a long way to explaining future mistakes or roadblocks. Second, the coach is given the opportunity to correct the answer with an explanation. For example: "Actually, that was a no. You made contact on the rise on that one." The result is that the player can compare the coach's feedback with what they felt and gain a higher level of body awareness. This is why awareness-building questions are best used when players aren't "getting it." If it seems that the feedback isn't landing, it could well be that the athlete's awareness is off.

Here are some more examples of awareness-building questions (with apologies for my tennis bias):

- "Where on the racket did you make contact?"
- "Where did your opponent's return land?"

- "Which foot did you jump off of?"
- "Where were you on the court when you hit your first volley?"
- "What did your opponent change in the second set?"

Problem-Solving Questions

These sorts of questions guide a student toward solving a problem on their own. In contrast to the coach providing the solution directly, problem-solving questions have three main benefits. The first is that allowing the player to solve a problem can increase their confidence and self-belief. *A player who feels they are regularly producing solutions to the challenges they face will be more inclined to believe they can handle difficult situations—in or out of sport.* The second advantage is that being exposed to the problem-solving process can implicitly teach students how to go about solving problems independently in the future. For example: if a coach's approach is to ask questions that first assess the mental, then the tactical, then the physical, and finally the technical aspect (in that order), then players will be more likely to follow that same approach when the guidance is removed. The final benefit is that problem-solving questions often give the athlete a more complete understanding of the answer. Rather than just knowing the ideal solution, they understand the logic behind it and the steps taken to arrive at it.

This does not mean, however, that problem-solving questions should be used any time a coach wants to deliver information. Players must have enough background knowledge to be able to arrive at the correct answer if guided. Without sufficient background information, the net effect can actually be negative. Players who cannot arrive at the answer will begin to doubt their own abilities, and the interaction between player and coach will inevitably take longer, wasting valuable practice time. Problem-solving questions should only be used when the students have enough baseline knowledge but don't know the answer.

A few examples of problem-solving questions:

- "What options did you have in that situation?"
- "What could you have done to give yourself more time?"
- "What do you think is most important to focus on in this situation?"

Probing Questions

Finally, probing questions are questions you ask to figure out what the athlete is thinking. Oftentimes, the answers to these questions are the impetus for mental or tactical coaching. For example:

- "What are you feeling right now?"
- "What are you saying to yourself?"
- "What did you see there?"
- "What made you choose that shot?"

Coaching mental or tactical skills without asking probing questions is like driving to work with a blindfold on. *We can never know what an athlete is thinking without asking them.* We can't rely solely on what they did, since it's possible they were trying something else but failed to execute it. Without asking questions, we can only assume—and giving feedback based on assumptions is irresponsible.

When teaching tactical skills, probing questions are essential in determining what a player was intending to do. Giving tactical feedback without knowing for certain what the player was thinking has two potential risks. First, the player can accept the feedback, which at best will be useless, and at worst will hurt them. Second, the player can ignore the feedback, which will weaken the coach–player relationship.

Probing questions are equally important in coaching mental skills. As we all know, human behavior is complex, and we can't simply use actions to infer thoughts or emotions. Conversing with players and understanding the root causes is critical, not just to improve performance, but also to strengthen the bond between coach and athlete.

Specific Principles

I will outline in the sections below some principles relevant to technical and tactical development. While physical and mental skills can also be developed, the former is outside the purview of this book, and the latter will be discussed in more depth in Chapter 10.

Technical Development

Teaching Methods

While there are thousands upon thousands of drills, they all fall into only a handful of categories, which I call teaching methods. I'll outline these now.

Progression

To begin with an easier or simpler version of the intended skill and then gradually make it more difficult or complex

The ability to progress or regress a skill may be one of the most important for a coach to have, as using appropriate progressions will allow athletes to spend more time in their ZPD (see our earlier discussion on difficulty level). Oftentimes, coaches use progressions simply because they have seen another coach use them, or because they were taught them on a course. But to really be successful in skill development, we have to understand why we're using a particular progression.

Most often, as stated, we're progressing or regressing the *task* in order to find the optimal difficulty level. In such cases, it's important to keep in mind that any task can be progressed in any number of ways. The best framework through which to look at this may simply be the four performance factors: mental, physical, technical, tactical. A drill may be made harder by manipulating any of these. For example:

- *Mental*: Changing the scoring system, adding an element of pressure or distraction, challenging focus.
- *Physical*: Inducing fatigue in the athlete before they have to perform the skill, increasing demands on strength.
- *Technical*: Raising the standard for what is considered an acceptable execution, sparring against tougher opponents, adding complexity (e.g. combining with other skills), changing equipment.
- *Tactical*: Adding elements of perception or decision-making.

Each of these options is always available to us as coaches. But does it matter which one we choose? The answer, of course, is yes. When observing an athlete perform, we have to take note of the conditions under which a skill is breaking down, and also *why* it's breaking down.

Your progression or regression should then focus on that area. A player who is struggling technically but is aerobically fit will not win more thanks to a progression that tires them out. Neither will a technical progression improve tactical decision-making. Your progressions must be targeted to the specific performance factor you are aiming to improve.

Task progressions are most often used when a skill is in the conscious competence or unconscious competence stages—in other words, when we are making small adjustments (correcting) or pushing limits (training). In some cases, however, we progress or regress the technique. This means the task remains largely the same from progression to progression, but the technique used to accomplish it changes. In this context, the focus is less on creating the optimal challenge point, and more on helping the athlete feel a particular motor pattern by starting simple and gradually making it more complex.

Technique progressions are most often used when a skill is in the unconscious incompetence or conscious incompetence stages—in other words, when we are teaching the fundamental movements (building awareness or teaching). An example of this would be someone learning to skate. They might start off by pushing themselves along the side wall, before graduating to taking small steps. Then they might start pushing off with one skate and sliding on the other. After some time, they will use the other foot, and eventually they will develop the confidence and ability to take longer strides with alternating feet. Throughout the process, the task has remained the same—skate forward—but the technique has evolved from a very basic pushing action to a more advanced skating action. Furthermore, at each step, the new motor pattern has built on the previous one. This can be contrasted with progressing the *task* of skating: one could start with skating backward, then skate backward and use crossover steps, then skate backward and stickhandle. In this case, the motor patterns do not build on one another; rather, the task is changing and becoming more complex. In a technical progression, the task remains the same, while the technique builds on itself.

No matter the progression, a coach's knowledge of their player and their player's skill level will go a long way. Starting with a progression that's too difficult and regressing it can make an athlete lose confidence, while spending too much time on an easy progression can infantilize them or cause boredom. Being able to pick the correct starting point right from the beginning is a valuable skill.

When using progressions, consider these best practices:

- Be precise with what you want to progress.
- Start at the right level of difficulty.
- Be deliberate about whether you want to progress the *technique* (when in awareness building/teaching) or the *task* (when correcting/training).

Skill Transfer

To take a skill the athlete can already do, and then transfer part of it to a new skill

Skill transfer is the process by which an athlete takes a skill they can already do and transfers part of it to a new skill. For example, a golf student who has played baseball might be asked to swing a baseball bat but pretend the ball is on the ground. In this way, they transfer part of the baseball swing (the biomechanics) to their golf swing.

Skill transfer doesn't have to come from other sports—it can also come from within the same sport. For example, in tennis, the feeling of chipping a forehand return of serve can be compared to the feeling of hitting a forehand volley.

There are two ways to use skill transfer. The first is through analogy, as I illustrated above (the golfer "pretends" they are swinging a baseball bat). The second is through direct transfer: having the student perform the donor (original) skill a few times and then immediately perform the new skill. Ideally, athletes should be made to go back and forth between the two skills, and their attention should be drawn to the key feelings or sensations that they are meant to transfer over.

Skill transfer is generally best used when a skill is in the conscious competence stage (when we are correcting).

Opposites

A form of awareness building, to engage the athlete in the process of performing a skill at each end of a spectrum (e.g. slow vs. fast, big vs. small)

Opposites can be particularly powerful because they develop awareness in the performer. To use opposites in skill development is to engage the athlete in a process of performing a skill at each end of a spectrum. A runner might be told to take the smallest steps possible and then the largest steps possible. A volleyball player might be told to set the ball as gently as possible and then as forcefully as possible.

When using opposites, it's vital that we *let the athlete do the wrong thing*. The immediate goal is not for them to develop perfect technique, but rather to develop a more complete awareness of what their body can do and is doing—and the only way for them to do that is to experience both extremes. Don't be afraid to let them do something "ugly." As long as they don't do it for hours every day, it won't stick. Push them to experience both ends of the spectrum, and then, once they are comfortable with both extremes, you can direct them to the "ideal" technique, which lies somewhere in the middle.

Opposites are best used when a skill is in the conscious incompetence or conscious competence stages (when we're teaching or correcting).

Remember:

- **Be specific about which aspect of the technique you want them to feel.**
- **Don't be afraid to exaggerate.**
- **Ensure they get good at each end of the spectrum before going to the middle.**

Analogy

To draw a mental image in the mind of the athlete and elicit a physical response

Analogies have been used in coaching for decades (e.g. "imagine there's a wall behind you—your racket can't touch the wall"). The goal when using analogies is to paint a mental image that is translated by the athlete into a sensation that then elicits a physical response. Whether in a sporting context or not, analogies are a way of drawing a connection between something that your student is familiar with and something they aren't. For this reason, analogies can be powerful—instead of providing new information, they rely on information already encoded in the performer's brain.

However, not all analogies will translate into a feeling for the athlete. In these cases, the athlete will understand what they should do, but they still might not be able to do it. That's why the choice of analogy is so important, and also why other, more direct approaches to skill development are sometimes necessary.

Analogies are best used in the conscious competence or unconscious competence stages (when we're correcting or training).

When using analogies:

- Use an analogy that the athlete intuitively understands.
- Use an analogy that targets the exact movement you'd like to see.
- Turn the analogy into a cue word.

Direct Verbal Instruction

To verbally tell the athlete what to do

Direct verbal instruction is the act of simply telling the athlete what they should do. It is generally the least effective teaching method. Of course, it will inevitably be used in conjunction with the other techniques. In a progression, I may tell someone, "For these next ten, start with your elbow already up." When using opposites, I may tell them to "take the biggest swing you can!" These are verbal instructions, but they are combined with other interventions that help the athlete feel what they need to do.

Elite athletes may possess such a high level of body awareness and athleticism that direct verbal instruction can occasionally be the most direct route to a technical improvement. However, in the vast majority of cases, telling someone to "hit your forehand like Federer" will not help.

Overusing direct verbal instruction when it is not effective can not only waste time, it can also have more harmful effects. For one, it tends to be the wordiest of the teaching techniques and also the one that leads to more thinking than feeling. This can lead to slower progress (as we saw earlier with external vs. internal feedback) and can also worsen performance under pressure (see Chapter 10). For two, given that verbal instruction is so ineffective, overusing it can lead to frustration or even resentment from athletes.

Video Feedback

Another form of awareness building that can help athletes see what they are doing but might not help them feel it

The use of video analysis software in coaching has grown tremendously in the last 15 years, sparked mainly by its accessibility. Video feedback can often be a great way to build awareness.

Depending on your sport, you may associate video with a particular use case. In some environments, the use of video is primarily tactical—for noticing the positioning of a defender, the decision-making of an attacker, and so on. In others, video is used for technical or biomechanical analysis. In still others, video is used to teach valuable lessons on teamwork, energy, attitude, and so on. In all cases, however, there are a few key principles to keep in mind:

1. *They don't know it like you do*: You've watched video for years. Even if you're a new coach, you've likely watched more game footage than your athletes simply by virtue of being older. When you take into account your coaching experience, you might as well be watching two different videos.

   Consider the Invisible Gorilla Test, which you may have already taken part in. If you haven't, the basic premise is as follows: test participants are presented with a video of a group of people wearing either white or black shirts, passing a basketball back and forth. The participants are told to count how many passes the team in the black shirts makes. The video runs for a few minutes, during which time a man in a gorilla suit walks slowly across the frame. Afterwards, participants are asked how many passes they counted and if they noticed anything out of the ordinary. In the majority of tests, more than 50% of people do not report seeing the gorilla.

This phenomenon, known as "inattentional blindness," tells us that what we are looking at is not always the same as what we see. More specifically, our ability to notice things is highly dependent on what we are already looking for. For this reason, it's important to ensure that athletes are seeing the right things when watching a video.

To do this, first tell your athletes what to look for. You can choose how prescriptive to be ("Pay attention to your positioning" vs. "Notice how you are positioned too far away from the sideline"), but be sure to give them a general area of focus *before* watching the footage.

Second, when watching video, use the pause and slow-motion functions liberally. Not only do your athletes not know the video as well as you do, they are also learning as they are watching—their brains are already working. Pause or slow down the video to let them process what they are hearing and seeing.

Lastly, show them the video multiple times. The more they watch it and pay attention to the relevant details, the more they will perceive automatically. A study of chess players found that grandmasters could recall the position of every piece on a board shown to them for just a split second, whereas amateurs couldn't. However, when participants were shown other images and asked to remember objects' positions, there was no difference between the grandmasters and the novices. The chess experts didn't have special memory or vision skills, they had just developed domain-specific expertise that allowed them to perceive more in a shorter time, because they knew what they were looking for. We coaches don't realize all the things we are noticing subconsciously because we've been in the game so long. That's why we have to slow it down for our athletes.

2. *Engage your athletes mentally/cognitively*: The goal of using video is to teach your athletes something, but as we know, learning can only occur if the student is mentally engaged—so engage them! This can take a few forms:

    a. Ask them what they see.
    "What do you notice here?"

"What are you looking at?"
"Which way is he facing?"

b. Ask them what will happen next.
"Where is she going to hit?"
"Which way is he going to move?"

c. Quiz them on what you've discussed.
"What is this an example of?"
"What stance are you using here?"

3. *Remember basic teaching principles*:

   a. *Keep it simple*: Again, "If you chase five rabbits, you catch none." When you show a video, use it to make just one point. Or make your one point, review it, test your athlete to make sure they understand it, review it some more, and then use the video to make a second point. A player watching footage while a coach narrates a list of flaws will either tune out due to boredom or become overwhelmed and forget the majority of what is said.

   b. *Repetition is the mother of all skill*: Show the video. Show it again. Show it a third time. Practice the skill. Show the video another day. Practice it again. Chances are, your athlete won't understand the lesson fully after the first video session. And if they do, they still won't be able to apply it properly until they've practiced it repeatedly. You may need multiple video sessions accompanied by multiple practice sessions. Repetition is the mother of all skill.

4. *The video won't do the teaching for you*: Just like creating the right environment, using video is only part of the equation; it is the first step, but not the only one. The teaching really starts once you've shown the video. After all, if "video knowledge" was enough to be an elite athlete, I wouldn't be writing this book (I'd be playing tennis on tour). The knowledge athletes acquire in video review is the precursor to the skills we will hopefully teach them out on the court, pitch, field, or track. As such, make sure you're tying your video work in with your practical work. If you are reviewing technical concepts, make sure you then take them onto the field and help your athletes feel and then practice what they've just

seen. If you're reviewing tactical concepts, make sure they're given the chance to practice perceiving the right cues (in real life) and making the right decisions, and do this enough times to make it automatic. Video will help them *know* it, but it won't help them *do* it.

Constraint

To shape the environment to discourage the "incorrect" behavior or encourage the "correct" behavior

As discussed earlier, the use of constraints is becoming more and more popular, and with good reason—they can be an incredibly powerful tool. While definitions of constraints vary, I'll focus this section on two types: technical and task.

A *technical* constraint is anything physical that restricts or manipulates the athlete's movements, thereby encouraging the correct motor pattern and discouraging deviations. A common example would be the many teaching aids sold to golfers aspiring to fix their slice.

For any change in a motor pattern, the performer must feel what it is they are to do, not just understand it. This is why technical constraints can be so powerful: they force the athlete to *feel* the correct behavior. Especially in the earlier stages of skill development, when awareness is lower, constraints can be a quick way to help an athlete feel the basics of the change. As they acquire the skill and develop more body awareness, they may no longer need the constraint and may benefit from more efficient methods. It should also be noted that some athletes may feel a bit embarrassed or childish being made to look foolish in a constraint. Constraints should only be used in a safe environment where you know the athlete will be receptive.

Task constraints are manipulations of the space, equipment, or rules that encourage a certain behavior or discourage another. A soccer coach might change the size of the goal or the positioning of the defenders; a basketball coach might award more points for certain moves and fewer points for others. As discussed earlier, the environment can help to both push an athlete to change, and reward and encourage them when they do make that change. Task constraints are just another way of shaping the environment.

The Four Phases of Movement

Virtually every motor pattern can be broken into the following four phases:

1. Preparation.
2. Force-producing action.
3. Critical instant.
4. Follow-through.

Consider a tennis forehand. The player loads their legs and coils their upper body (preparation). Then, once everything is prepared, they begin to push off of the ground (force-producing action), the energy from their legs transfers to the hips, and then the torso, the shoulder, the arm, the hand, and finally the racket, which makes contact with the ball (critical instant). As soon as the ball leaves the strings, the racket, along with the rest of the body, begins to slow down (follow-through).

Each stride a runner takes follows the same cycle. The front leg is loaded (preparation), it begins pushing off the ground (force-producing action), the foot lifts off the ground (critical instant), the runner travels through the air (follow-through).

When teaching technique, it's important to recognize that an intervention at one phase can impact the others. The notion that your preparation may impact the rest of your motion might be intuitive, but less so is the fact that the effects can work in the opposite direction.

Sticking with our previous examples, let's imagine that I'd like my tennis player to use their hand and wrist more. I could address the force-producing action by telling them to snap their wrist. I could address the preparation by getting them to prepare with a looser hand and a more flexed wrist. Or I could address the follow-through by challenging them to finish with their wrist flexed. Each of these interventions has a very real chance of changing what happens at the critical instant, which is what matters most.

With my runner, I might want to see more downward force from the front leg. I could address the preparation by changing the angles at their hip and knee, creating more potential for energy. I could address the force-producing action by giving them a cue word or analogy. Or I could address the follow-through by challenging them to take longer strides, or to feel their triple extension. Again, each of these interventions could lead to a change in what happens at the critical instant.

Your choice of what to address will depend on a few factors. If a certain force-producing action is *impossible* without a specific preparation, then it follows that the preparation should be addressed. If, however, the preparation only *encourages* a movement in one of the later phases, then the intervention may not be as effective as addressing the movement itself. The same follows for the relationship between the follow-through and the earlier phases.

In addition, some athletes are more or less fluid and more or less coordinated. Some can do whatever you ask of them, even if its inefficient, in which case you may want to address the motor pattern directly. Others can only do things if the conditions are perfect, in which case you may have to address the earlier phases first. Experiment with intervening at different phases and reflect on what works best for you and your athletes, and think about why.

Tactical Development

Skill development is not just technical—in fact, depending on the sport you coach, tactics may play an even more valuable role than technique. But how do we define tactics? What does it mean to be a "smart" athlete? And can game sense be taught?

Observing Tactics

As with technique, it may be valuable (if you haven't already) to spend some time identifying what makes a "smart" performer in your sport. As an example, I've included the structure I use with tennis players:

Table 9.4. Tactical skills in tennis

Time	Tactics
Pre-match	Can identify the opponent's strengths and weaknesses (if given the chance to scout) and formulate a game plan based on the six main tactics.
During the match	Can make changes to the game plan based on the progress of the match.
	Can recognize momentum and exert influence over it.

Time	Tactics
During a point	Makes appropriate decisions given the game plan and a) their position, b) the opponent's position, c) the ball they're receiving, and d) the ball they just sent.
Post-match	Can identify both the key points and overall tendencies of the match.

I've tried hard to ensure that my tactical rubric includes not only micro "in-action" skills, such as choosing the correct shot at the correct moment, but also bigger-picture "game IQ" skills, such as formulating a game plan and scouting an opponent.

ACTIVITY: Take three minutes to list as many qualities as you can of a "smart" athlete in your sport.

Now, spend a few minutes trying to put those qualities into a clear, defined, structure that will help you develop tactical skill.

Now that you have a structure—a framework through which you can observe your players—consider the following keys to good tactical observations:

1. *Know your limitations*: Tactics can be harder to develop than technique for one simple reason: while technique is about what the player *does*, tactics are concerned with what the player *decides*. Those decisions occur in the athlete's mind—a space only they have access to. As such, it's vitally important that we as coaches remain mindful of our greatest limitation: we cannot always know what our athletes are thinking.

   One of the mistakes I often see coaches make is assigning an incorrect decision to what was, in fact, an execution mistake. Sometimes it is easy to determine with relative certainty a player's intention. A soccer forward who kicks the ball, with force, toward the opposing team's goal was, in all likelihood, attempting a shot. However, depending on their skill level, it may not be clear where they were aiming. Their shot may have gone toward a particular spot, and that could have been exactly their intention. But it's also possible that they were aiming somewhere else and missed.

Suddenly, our job becomes more difficult. As mentioned earlier in the section on questioning, giving feedback based on assumptions risks damaging the coach–athlete relationship or impeding progress. In such cases, some variation on the question "What were you trying to do there?" is a coach's most powerful tool.

2. *Identify the root cause*: If we are certain that a tactical mistake has occurred, then it's important to identify its root cause.

    a. *Tactical error caused by technical limitation*: In these cases, an athlete makes a suboptimal decision simply because the optimal decision would require them to use a technique or skill that they haven't yet acquired. In this case, their decision is actually the optimal one for them, since making the textbook "correct" decision would cause them to perform worse. Identifying these situations is therefore critical, as giving tactical feedback rather than technical intervention can have damaging effects. If the athlete takes the advice, they'll begin using a skill they haven't mastered and are not as comfortable with, resulting in a drop in performance and possibly a loss of confidence or motivation. If the athlete chooses to ignore the advice, the coach may become frustrated, and the athlete will learn that they don't always have to listen to their coach. Trust issues may develop.

    b. *Tactical error caused by mental limitation*: In these cases, an athlete makes a decision because it relieves some of their mental stress, even if it is not the best decision. An athlete who is mentally tired or simply lacks focus may make decisions that require little thought. An angry player may make aggressive, impatient decisions, seeking to run away from the emotion. What's notable about this situation is that, in most cases, the athlete knows that their decision was the wrong one. As such, tactical feedback will not be helpful, and can even be harmful if it leads to resentment or lack of trust. Instead, the coach should seek to address the underlying factors, when the athlete is receptive.

    c. *Tactical error caused by physical limitation*: In these cases, a player makes a decision based on the capacity of their body.

> Someone who is especially tired may choose a play that relieves them of having to engage. Someone who is too slow may choose to take shortcuts or make guesses in order to keep up. Someone who is too weak may choose to play with touch and finesse rather than power. Once again, the underlying issues must be addressed before the tactics can be discussed.

In all of these cases, these issues should be addressed by developing the technical, mental, or physical skills necessary to support the required decision-making. If, however, the tactical error is indeed a purely tactical one—that is to say, caused by a lack of knowledge or an error of perception—then we can begin teaching tactics.

Teaching Tactical Skills

Thankfully, teaching pure tactics is relatively easy, at least compared to teaching technique. In theory, while technical skills require numerous repetitions before they are acquired, tactical skills should only require one. You give the athlete the information, and then they know it.

In reality, this is not quite true. First, human beings forget things, and the only way to store something in long-term memory is to review it regularly (see Chapter 3, Figure 3.3). Second, not all tactical skills are created equal; some are more time-sensitive than others. Formulating a game plan can be done at a leisurely pace the night before the game, while reacting to an opponent's right hook requires slightly more urgency. That's where automaticity comes in.

In open-skill sports, the ability to make decisions quickly is paramount. As such, decisions must be trained to the point of automaticity: the point at which an athlete will, upon perceiving the relevant cues, make a decision before their conscious mind even realizes they are doing it. This type of decision-making happens all the time in our day-to-day lives, from the mundane (taking your keys out of your pocket as you approach the door) to the life-saving (braking to avoid a swerving car). In sports, automatic decisions decrease reaction time and speed up execution. In some cases, this is the difference between winning and losing. In others, it's the difference between performing and freezing up.

Another important distinction: part of tactical intelligence comes purely from a performer's knowledge base, while another part depends on their ability to perceive certain situations. Take, for example, the difference between understanding what type of formation to use against a certain team and recognizing when to make a run for the goal. In one case, the decision is made based on information already acquired (e.g. knowledge of each team's style, knowledge of the players' strengths and weaknesses, knowledge of past games). In the other, the decision is made based on information perceived in the heat of the moment (e.g. the position of the defender, the orientation of the attacker, the speed of the ball).

This distinction is worth mentioning because, while both types of intelligence can be developed through practice and repetition, perception-based decision-making must be developed in situ—that is, in an environment that replicates the relevant perceptual cues. Knowledge-based decision-making, however, can be practiced at home, in the hotel room, or on the bus.

So how do we help our athletes make smart, automatic decisions based not only on their knowledge, but also on their perception? Here are some key ways to do this:

1. *Repetition, repetition, repetition*: Legendary American football coach Bill Belichick is known for his pop quizzes (Championship Performance, 2020). Whether in the hall, at team meetings, or out on the practice field, Belichick can spontaneously turn to a player to ask them, "Hey, we're in the high red zone, it's second-and-six from the 18. What's Indianapolis's favorite blitz?" When he gets an answer, he might turn to another teammate and ask if they agree. There are two important takeaways from this practice. First, the fact that Belichick has developed a reputation for doing this shows that he is constantly challenging his players to answer tactical questions. Second, his technique of asking a teammate to agree or disagree with the original answer forces the whole team to engage, because they don't know if they will be called on to give their opinion. In other words, Belichick is giving lots of repetitions of the tactical skills he's teaching, *to the entire team*.
2. *Progress the time pressure*: When athletes need to be smart *and* quick, it's time to implement some time pressure. This can be artificial (e.g. buzzers, clocks) or more realistic (e.g. speed of

play). Start slowly, giving the performer time to find the correct solution. After all, there's no point being quick if you're not also correct. Give them repetitions until they are consistently correct. Then, gradually decrease the time available to them and repeat the process.

3. *Be systematic with perception-based decision-making*: Depending on your sport, an athlete may be forced to evaluate anywhere from one to a dozen different factors in order to make a decision—factors like opposing players' and teammates' positions, the movement of the ball, and the orientation of their body. For any situation you are looking to train, first list the different decisions an athlete could make (i.e. what options they have), then list all the different cues they would have to perceive in order to make an informed decision. Finally, determine which cues influence which decisions. Here's an example from the sport I know best—tennis:

   Situation: A player receives a ball to the forehand corner.
   Possible decisions: 1) Play the ball crosscourt, 2) play the ball down the line, 3) play a short angle.
   Cues to perceive:

   a. Opponent's positioning: If they're well off the court, play down the line. If they're recovered in the middle, maybe play crosscourt.
   b. Opponent's movement: If they're running toward the other side, play behind them.
   c. Width of ball: If the ball is further out to the side of the court, going down the line is riskier, but hitting the short angle is easier.
   d. Height of ball: On lower balls, it may be harder to go down the line. On higher ones, it may be harder to go for the angle.
   e. Depth of ball: Shorter balls make it easier to go for the angle, whereas deeper ones make it harder.
   f. Speed of ball: If the ball is faster, it is safer to go back crosscourt

   Once you've done this exercise , train players' decision-making by introducing one cue at a time and asking them to make decisions based on relatively simple black-and-white rules: if this, then that. In the case above, I might start by varying the opponent's positioning. "If they're here, hit crosscourt. If they're there, hit down the line." Then, I might test them on the width of the ball. "If it's this wide, go crosscourt. If it's this wide, go down the line." Then, I might combine them. "If the ball is here *and* the opponent is here, do this. If the ball is here *and* the opponent is there, do that." And so on.

Of course, some cues will be easier to pick up than others. Some athletes may already be perceiving some while ignoring others. Most importantly, very few decisions will be black and white, with only one right answer. My point is not that each decision and perceptual cue should be introduced in a textbook fashion, but rather that we must consider which cues need training, and then train them systematically so that athletes always remain in their ZPD.

Chapter 10
Maximizing Performance

So far in Part 3 we've covered fundamental concepts behind leadership and skill development. To be the best coaches we can be, we're left with one piece of the puzzle: maximizing performance. Where Chapter 8 dealt with setting the stage for coaching to occur and Chapter 9 dealt with taking players from point A to point B, this chapter will deal with what happens when practice is over. You've run your drills, you've finished your progressions—now it's time to compete.

In this regard, coaches tend to operate on a spectrum. Some take a more Darwinian approach—investing all their time and energy into practice and then seeing where the cards fall, believing that the better prepared player or team will win. "Every battle is won before it is fought," as Sun Tzu once wrote. Other coaches take a more pragmatic approach, investing more time and energy in the battle itself—mental preparation, equipment, scouting, and so on—than in the practice beforehand, believing that it all comes down to who competes best on the day. Of course, the best coaches prioritize both skill development and performance maximization, understanding that each one plays a role in both short- and long-term success.

Helping athletes get the most out of themselves on game day is a critical part of the player development equation, as it can lead to better results and better performances, which then inspire confidence and further progress. Maximizing performance is about more than just inspirational speeches and ice baths, however. There are numerous elements of performance to consider, as well as strategies for maximizing them. In this chapter, we'll look at optimizing physical, mental, technical, and tactical outcomes, minimizing choking, and other factors that influence athletic performance.

Maximizing Performance

Peaking

In the world of sports, "peaking" refers to an athlete reaching their maximum level at a specific point in time—ideally during competition. Sounds nice, but how is it done? To figure that out, we first need to look at the different ways in which someone can peak.

Planning Load

The first way in which athletes can peak is physical. We want to ensure that an athlete is fit and fresh in time to perform. In other words, we want to make sure they are prepared: they have trained enough, they have made the intended gains, and they are not feeling any negative side effects from that training (e.g. fatigue, soreness).

We want that same combination—fit yet fresh—when it comes to how our athletes feel mentally. Depending on your sport, this may be more or less relevant. Sports with a higher cognitive load will require that an athlete be "switched on" and ready to make decisions in the blink of an eye. Training for this can induce mental fatigue, so it's important that an athlete is mentally rested before competing.

Similarly, athletes may experience periods of emotional fatigue or, conversely, emotional energy. While some aspects of this may be out of our control, the best athletes (and their coaches) aim to put themselves in a position where they will feel emotionally strong during competition.

Each of these elements, while difficult to manage, can be quantified by the concept of load, which is the product of volume and intensity:

$$\text{Load} = \text{Volume} \times \text{Intensity}$$

Whether physical, mental, or emotional, the concepts are the same: volume is the quantity of effort, and intensity is the difficulty of effort. Load is the result of multiplying the two: the total effect on the athlete's brain or body. If an athlete trains for two hours (120 minutes) and rates the difficulty as five out of ten, then their total load is 600 (5 × 120). Numerous studies have shown that if the load in any given week is significantly (e.g. more than 25%) higher than the average load from the previous weeks, the risk of injury increases dramatically.

The solution is to taper: to gradually *reduce* the load as the athlete gets closer to competition. This is usually done by reducing the volume but maintaining (or even increasing) the intensity, such that athletes are more rested but still prepared for the rigors of competition. This usually means reducing training hours but engaging in more game-like practice activities. However, volume can also be decreased by reducing repetitions and increasing rest time, and intensity can be increased by simply demanding more effort, without increasing realism.

Scheduling Skill Development

For sports that are more technical, another important factor to consider is whether an athlete's *skill* will be at its peak at the right moment. Imagine a soccer player who hasn't kicked a ball in a month—they might be physically and mentally fresh, but they'll still feel rusty. Or a snooker player who makes a big change to their cueing technique the day before a match. Chances are, it won't hold up in competition.

These situations are all too common and describe the two concerns regarding peaking: first, ensuring that athletes have had sufficient recent game-like practice, so that they feel ready and warmed up when the time comes, and second, ensuring that the skills they have been working on have not only been acquired but also solidified, made automatic and robust such that they won't break down under pressure.

The first concern (let's call it concern A) is relatively easy to manage: just make sure your athletes get good practice in the lead-up to competition. However, there are a few traps coaches fall into. The first is that, since volume is being decreased, coaches are left with less practice time, and either by accident or on purpose they end up allocating time to the wrong things. As competition nears, the focus should shift to the aspects of the game that are most important to performance. However, given less time on the pitch, coaches will sometimes try to cram everything into a shorter session, giving athletes a few reps on a lot of things, as opposed to a lot of reps on a few things. Of course, balance is everything, and it's up to you to decide which skills are worth prioritizing. The important thing is to make that decision deliberately and evaluate it against your athletes' performances.

The second trap that coaches fall into with concern A is practicing the right things at the wrong intensity. As stated earlier, while volume should decrease when tapering, intensity should remain steady or even increase. As competition nears, practices should become more and more realistic—and that includes their intensity. An athlete who has practiced 500 three-pointers at 50% intensity will be less prepared than the one who has practiced 100 at full intensity.

Concern B, however, is more challenging. As discussed in Chapter 9, the acquisition of any skill goes through four stages, from unconscious incompetence (not knowing you can't do it) to unconscious competence (being able to do it without thinking). The stages in between require the performer to think a lot—first to learn the skill (conscious incompetence), and then to keep doing it right (conscious competence). This thinking puts a lot of pressure on the performer's working memory (the memory we use in the short term to retain new information and process problems). Their working memory will be taxed extensively during competition, where there are cues to perceive, decisions to make, and emotions to manage. As the load on working memory increases, skills that are not automatic break down. That's why skill mastery is so important—so that the skill is encoded into long-term memory and can be performed subconsciously, freeing up the brain to deal with the stresses of competition.

The solution to all this is quite simple: plan your skill development carefully such that all skills will be acquired well before a peak. Do not start working on a skill that you will not be able to solidify in time. Remember that for many technical changes, performance deteriorates before it improves. The goal is to make sure that athletes don't have to compete when they're in that valley.

Of course, some changes can be made almost instantly, while others will require months of work. That timeline is dependent not only on the skill, but on the athlete. It's not always easy to estimate how long it will take; all we can do is plan carefully, reflect deliberately, and learn from each experience.

Aggregating Marginal Gains

In Part 1, I referred briefly to Dave Brailsford, the cycling coach and manager who reinvented British Cycling with his no-stone-unturned approach. By assessing every factor that could possibly contribute to performance, and then aiming to improve each one by only a little bit, he theorized that the cumulative effect would be sizable—and he was right. In the ensuing years, the formerly mediocre British Cycling team won an astounding 18 Olympic gold medals and even more World Championships, popularizing what is known as the "aggregation of marginal gains" (Clear, 2018a). The crux of the philosophy is depicted below:

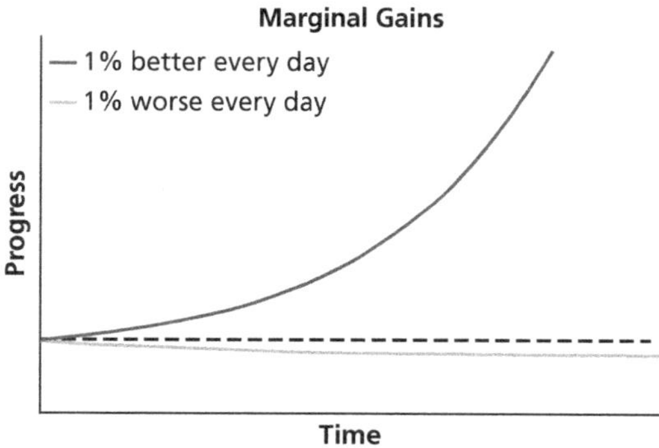

Figure 10.1. The power of tiny gains. (Adapted from Clear, 2018a)

A small 1% improvement compounded every day leads to massive gains in the long term. And this principle doesn't just apply to rates of improvement—it also holds true when it comes to game-day performance.

Perhaps the best example of a marginal gains approach to performance comes from professional motor racing, where hundreds of millions of dollars are at stake and, just like in business, teams fight for the slightest competitive edge. Before each event, race strategists must convene to make a plan: what tires to use, how many pit stops to take and when to take them, what style of race to run, and so on. To an outsider, the sport may seem simple—drive fast and don't crash—but the reality is far from it. As tires are used, they degrade, impacting their performance. Stopping to change tires can take valuable time but lead to greater speeds later on. Air and track temperature will affect the tires' ability to maneuver and grip the surface of the road. The car's weight can be factored into calculations, but not without remembering that it changes as the car burns fuel—the car gets lighter and therefore drives faster. Wind speed and direction, starting position, the length of the pit lane, and the likelihood of a safety car can all come into play when planning a race.

Of course, it's impossible to predict the future—no matter how much data you collect and factor in, there will always be (for the time being) unforeseen circumstances (e.g. crashes, unpredicted rain) that throw a wrench in the works. Nonetheless, with budgets of $135m and a total prize pot of nearly $2.2b, it's in the teams' best interests to try to account for every single marginal gain.

That same approach can be found in the habits of John Wooden, legendary NCAA basketball coach (Davis, 2014). One of the most famous examples is the first thing he taught his team at the start of the year: how to put on their socks. He reasoned that socks that bunch up create friction, and friction can cause blisters. Ensuring that his athletes put their socks on properly is just one detail of many that he aimed to improve by 1%.

If you want another example, here's Phil Mickelson explaining his shot selection process:

> *There's a lot that I process on every shot, and there's a lot of detail. ... One of the things that people will say is, you know, "I hit my wedge 120." Well, you might hit it 120 under certain conditions, but in the morning, the ball's not going to go 120, maybe in the afternoon when it's warmer, and the ball heats up, but it's going to go five to 10 yards shorter in the morning. People don't factor that in. If you get a bit of water between the club face and the ball, people don't know it actually increases spin, causes it to go shorter. The first cut always comes out 6-8 yards dead; if the grain is into you, it's going to launch and hit lower on the face, launch lower and have more spin. If it's down grain, the club slides a little bit quicker, you'll get more out of it. If it's sitting up on zoysia or off of a tee, it always goes five yards farther with each iron, based on the fact that*

> *the center of gravity is underneath the ball and it launches higher, a little bit less spin. All these things I have to factor in when I look at the lie. (Game Like Training, 2019)*

Your sport will no doubt have its own variables and factors, but there are some common ones that, when maximized, can do wonders for performance. In no particular order, sleep, nutrition, equipment, warm-ups, and cool-downs can all have an impact on performance and make the difference between winning and losing.

In discussing these marginal gains, I feel I should make an important point: these things are the 1% for a reason. In other words, don't neglect the 99% to focus on the 1%. Coaches and parents can sometimes get addicted to trying to maximize the 1% for a very simple reason: it feels like coaching but doesn't require as much effort. Disappointing results are attributed to faulty equipment. New energy drinks will fix bad fitness programs. Good warm-ups will make up for flawed technique. But the reality is that high-performance coaching is, at its core, the efficient allocation of resources, and one of our most finite resources is time. Be careful to allocate your time to the things that will make the greatest impact. Sometimes they will be the big-ticket items, whatever that may be for your sport (e.g. explosiveness, concentration, technique). Other times they will be the marginal gains. As discussed in Chapter 9, make sure you're choosing what to work on based on the greatest possible return relative to time spent.

Lastly, a quick note on the psychology of marginal gains and some potential traps to avoid. First, focusing on all the factors that influence performance can easily lead a player to start *thinking* about all the factors that influence performance—including those that are outside of their control. Overemphasizing the maximization of marginal gains can create too much focus on the things an athlete *can't* control, distracting them from what they *can*. Second, even when focusing on things that can be controlled, trying to squeeze every last bit of juice out of the lemon can lead to an unhealthy obsession in some athletes and cause anxiety or counterproductive behaviors.

The solution to both of these issues is the same: the approach to maximizing marginal gains should be led by the coach, not the athlete.

This is not to say that players shouldn't retain any autonomy or decision-making ability, but rather that the process should be guided by the coach. This way, the coach can select which items to focus on and to what extent, mitigating (but not eliminating) the risk of an athlete focusing on the wrong things.

Peak Performance States

So far in this section we've dealt with the preparation *before* competition: planning load, scheduling skill development, and optimizing the tiny details. But what about *during* competition? How is it that certain athletes seem to enter "the zone" when it's time to perform?

This is linked to the study of peak performance states (PPSs): the states of mind and body that allow performers to be at their best. PPSs are comprised of thoughts, emotions, and physiological parameters, and they have been studied for decades in multiple fields. In a 2006 study, Krane and Williams found that, generally speaking, peak performance tends to be linked to the following mind/body state:

- Feelings of high self-confidence and expectations of success.
- Being energized yet relaxed.
- Feeling in control.
- Having total concentration.
- Having a keen focus on the present task.
- Having positive attitudes and thoughts about performance.
- Being strongly determined and committed.

However, every individual athlete is different—both physically and mentally—and different sports, positions, and disciplines place differing demands on athletes. As such, the best coaches adopt an individualized approach to peak performance. In this section, we'll look at the Individual Zones of Optimal Functioning (IZOF) model, as well as two other models of optimal performance: flow and clutch states.

The IZOF Model

To understand the IZOF model, we first have to understand its roots. Initial theories of peak performance were focused primarily on arousal—one's level of activation. You may have seen variants of this graph before:

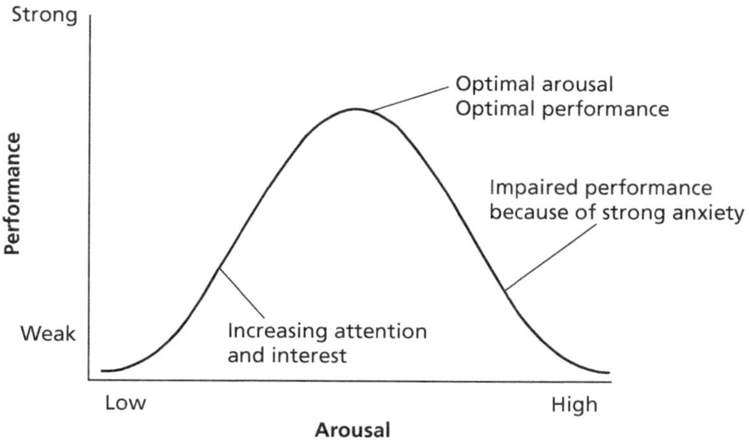

Figure 10.2. The Yerkes–Dodson law, depicting the relationship between stress and task performance.

The theory, known as the Yerkes–Dodson law, is that as a performer's arousal level initially increases, their performance improves, since they are more physically ready for and mentally engaged with the task (Yerkes and Dodson, 1908). However, this effect reduces until performance is at a peak, after which point any further arousal actually impedes performance—heightened arousal causes anxiety, which leads to distraction and impaired coordination and physical performance.[22]

The first breakthrough toward the current IZOF model was the recognition that each performer has their own individual curve. In other words, while everyone's performance follows the Yerkes–Dodson law, each person's peak may lie at a different point along the arousal scale. Some athletes do best at a low level of arousal—those who prefer to be calm, composed, methodical. Others, who thrive on energy and adrenaline, may peak at higher levels of arousal.

22 The Yerkes–Dodson law is relatively well supported by empirical research (Broadhurst, 1957; Duffy, 1957; Anderson et al., 1989). However, the nature of the curve can change depending on the type of task, as well as the degree to which the performer is competent or familiar with it.

Coaches can apply this simplified model by imagining a scale of arousal from 0 (nearly asleep) to 10 (ready to explode). Athletes can recall good and bad performances and reflect on their ideal arousal level. In competition, they can increase their arousal level through intense physical actions, pump-up phrases, high tempo music, and stimulating imagery. Similarly, arousal can be decreased through long, deep breaths, calming phrases, soothing music, and peaceful visualization.

This one-dimensional model of arousal is a bit simplistic, however, which is why some practitioners consider not just the intensity of emotion felt (high or low), but also its quality (positive or negative). For example, some emotions might be categorized as follows:

Table 10.1. Effect vs. intensity

High negative	**High positive**
Anger Rage	Exuberance Excitement
Low negative	**Low positive**
Disappointment Sadness	Satisfaction Contentedness

Again, different athletes will perform at their best in different zones. Some may prefer to be pumped up, others may prefer to stay calm, and still others may reach their peak when they've got a chip on their shoulder, something to prove. Also, different zones may be required for different phases of a game or event.

The most up-to-date IZOF model categorizes emotions not only as positive or negative, but also as helpful or harmful. For example, a bit of nervousness or dissatisfaction, while negative, can be a helpful motivator for a performer. Similarly, strong feelings of satisfaction or joy might lower intensity and focus.

Sports psychologists and coaches will often create an "emotion profile": a profile of the emotions and intensities required for optimal performance. The first step in emotion profiling is identifying the emotions associated with previous best and worst performances. This usually starts with a conversation: "Tell me about your best performances." Listen for action words (e.g. "energized," "fired up," "killed," "destroyed," "calmed") and adjectives (e.g. "sharp," "solid," "smooth," "alert"), and try to throw these same words back at the athlete and see what sticks.

Another useful tool is an emotion wheel:

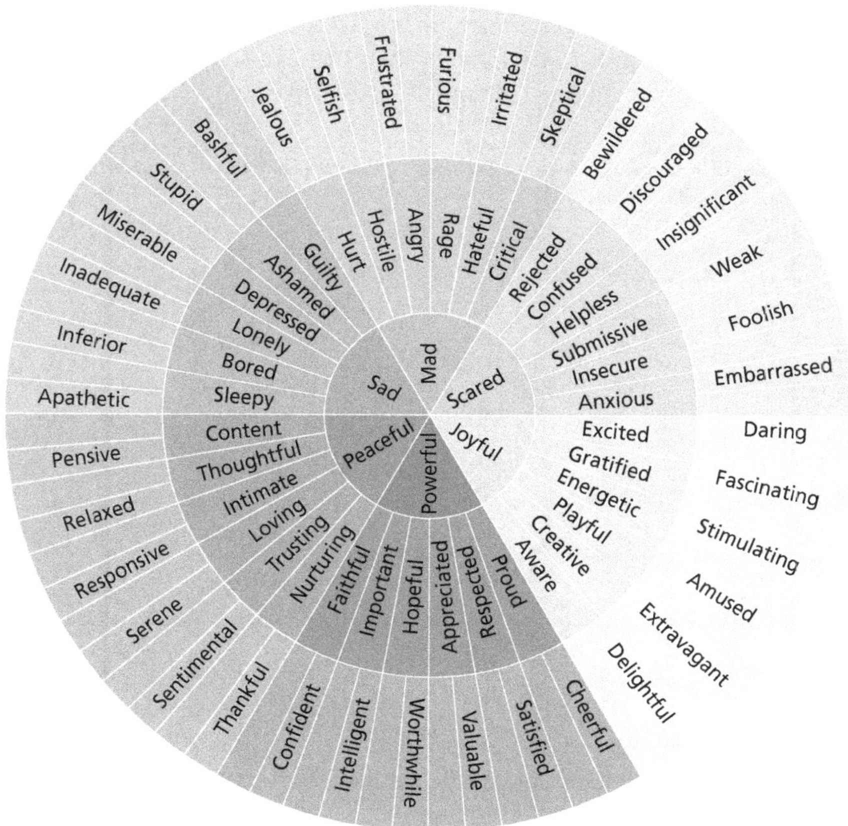

Figure 10.3. Emotion Wheel.

Put simply, we can't understand what we don't have words for. As Doug Lemov (2018) astutely points out in his Field Notes blog, if it is indeed true that Inuit have 50 words for snow, then what they see falling from the sky is drastically different than what we see. Where we just see snow, they see wet snow, dry snow, big snow, small snow, blowing snow, and so on. Their vocabulary shapes what they see and, by consequence, what they can talk about. Giving athletes a dictionary like an emotion wheel can help them put into words what they feel during their best or worst performances and paint a picture of their PPS.

Along with the types of emotions, ask athletes to identify their associated intensities. Do they feel strong dissatisfaction, or just mild? Are they at 10 out of 10 confidence, or more like 7 out of 10? What are the ranges that help them perform at their best? Once you've done this, those ranges can be mapped out onto a graph, like so:

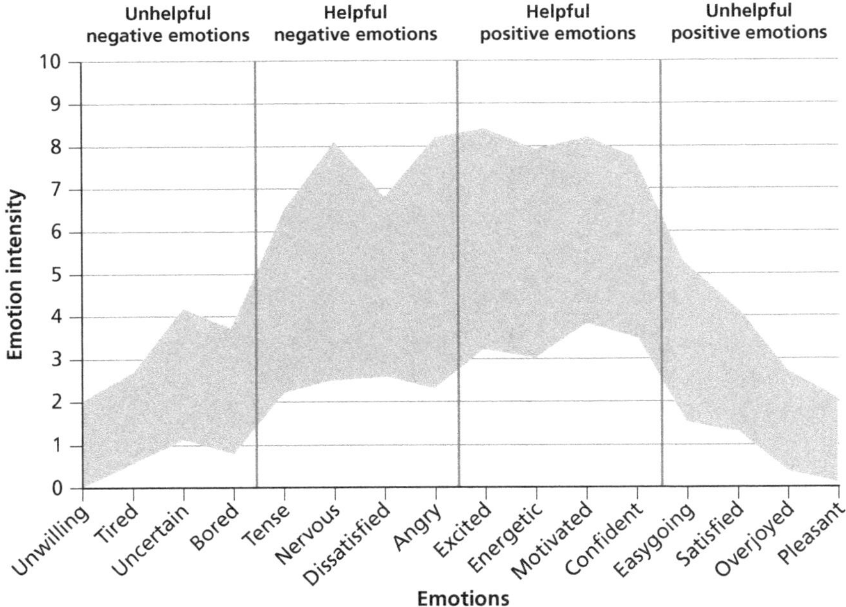

Figure 10.4. Example emotion profile for peak performance. (Adapted from Hanin, 2000)

Once your athlete is aware of their PPS, the next step is to teach them how to get into it. To do that, they will need to make use of a few techniques:

- *Self-talk*: This is especially powerful because it can be used to manipulate both the quality and the intensity of emotions felt. Self-talk generally falls into the following categories:
  - Arousal regulation (calming vs. energizing).

  - Attentional control (refocusing vs. distracting).
  - Emotion regulation (positive vs. negative affirmation).

  Many professional athletes are known to script their self-talk: to plan specific phrases that they find impactful to use in key moments. You may want to observe and record (either through note-taking or videos) your athlete's current self-talk tendencies. Then, after identifying what they need most (arousal regulation, attentional control, or emotion regulation), you may find it beneficial to sit and talk with them to jointly develop useful key phrases.

- *Physical actions*: Body language and facial expressions can be used to induce specific emotions. Since emotions regularly produce physical responses (hence our ability to read people's moods), the brain associates the two—a fact that can be used to our advantage. A well-publicized study from 1988 showed that participants who were asked to hold a pencil between their teeth (forcing them to smile) were more amused by cartoons than those who didn't (Strack et al., 1988). Athletes may want to consider what a confident player looks like, a relaxed player, an eager player, and then mimic that body language when they feel they need to "get into the zone."

  Physical actions can also be used to regulate arousal. Players who want to relax may shake out their arms and legs, stretch certain muscles, or focus on relaxing their jaw. Players who want to get pumped up may jump up and down or perform quick, explosive movements.

- *Breathing*: This too can serve multiple purposes. It can be used to regulate arousal—long, slow breaths calm the body and mind, and shorter, quicker ones activate them. Breathing can also be used as a tool for attentional control, to shift focus away from distractions. Athletes can perform breathing routines (e.g. inhale for four seconds, hold for four seconds, exhale for four seconds) as a way of refocusing during competition.
- *Imagery or visualization*: This can also be used to induce specific emotional or physical responses, and again the options are varied. To relax, an athlete may choose to imagine their "happy

place." To get fired up, they may visualize their team chant, or the opposing team getting in their face. Someone looking for confidence might recreate their best performances in their head. Coaches and athletes generally focus on positive images, for obvious reasons, but I feel it's worth mentioning that sometimes it can be worth picturing moments of adversity. If an athlete is exclusively prepared for scoring goals and playing well, there's a chance they may freeze up or become despondent if things don't go their way. Let's not forget that nearly every game includes at least one or two moments of struggle. For some players, visualizing things not going well *and them overcoming the struggle* can be especially powerful.

- *Music*: It should come as a surprise to no one that music is an emotionally evocative medium and can therefore influence the way we feel prior to (or during) competition. Music can influence not only our mood, but also our physiology—experiments have shown that the tempo of a song can raise or lower our heart rate (Watanabe et al., 2017).
- *Mindfulness*: This can be used to manage the cognitive side of PPSs—the thinking. Mindfulness, at its core, is the practice of raising awareness of one's thoughts. There is considerable support for the link between mindfulness and attentional control, not to mention the fact that mindfulness can effectively reduce feelings of anxiety (Chambers et al., 2008; MacDonald and Olsen, 2020). Mindfulness can be integrated into an athlete's daily or weekly practice routine as a way of developing concentration, and it can also be used in the lead-up to competition as a way of facilitating a PPS.

Flow States

Sometimes athletes don't just perform well—they perform *so* well. They lose track of time and become totally immersed in the game, becoming one with the sport. This is known as being in *flow*. Interestingly enough, anyone can enter a flow state—not just elite athletes—and most of us have probably experienced one, maybe while reading, cooking, gardening, painting, or playing a game. Being in flow is almost always described as effortless and energizing, and it is often accompanied by a sense of achievement and intrinsic reward.

Mihaly Csikszentmihalyi studied flow for over 50 years, in all walks of life. Through his research, he identified seven key features of the state (Nakamura and Csikszentmihalyi, 2009):

1. Action and awareness are merged ("I think and act at the same time, without hesitation or rumination").
2. Centering of attention ("I'm focused solely on the task at hand").
3. Loss of self-consciousness ("I'm not worried about what others think of me").
4. Time distortion (time either slows down or speeds up).
5. Control of action and environment ("I feel that things are in my hands").
6. Demands for action and clear feedback ("I know what I have to do and can see if it's working").
7. Autotelic experience ("I do it for myself; the activity is intrinsically rewarding").

Most importantly, perhaps, Csikszentmihalyi and his colleagues determined that flow occurs when perceived challenges and skills are *both* higher than average.

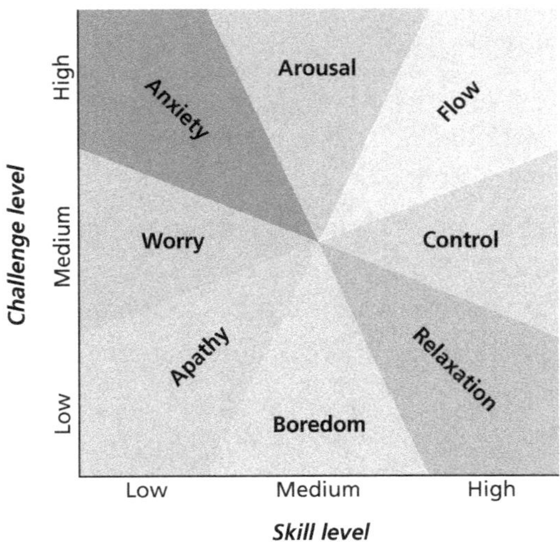

Figure 10.5. Challenge vs skill.

Earlier models theorized that flow was simply about the balance between challenge and skill level—a bit like the theoretical arousal–performance curve. In fact, athlete experiences tell us that flow occurs when challenge and skill are both *high*. When challenge surpasses skill, athletes experience worry or anxiety. When skill surpasses challenge, they experience boredom or relaxation. When the two are matched and low, athletes experience apathy. The state of flow is an energizing one wherein difficult challenges are met with high levels of skill.

It's also interesting to note the step-by-step process through which flow occurs. Swann et al. (2017) interviewed dozens of athletes and identified a common order of events:

1. *Initial positive event*: This kicks off the flow state, oftentimes early in the game. This could be a strong start, for example, or an early goal. For some, flow states occur later in the game but are still initiated by a positive event.
2. *Positive feedback*: From there, the athlete receives positive feedback—usually from themselves—about their physical, mental, or competitive state. They notice that not only has something good happened (e.g. a goal), but they are feeling and playing well.

3. *Gain in confidence*: With this positive feedback in mind, the athlete's confidence increases. In interviews, athletes describe steps 2 and 3 as a sort of back-and-forth cycle: as a result of increased confidence, they play more confidently and better. As a result of improved performance, their confidence increases.
4. *Challenge appraisal*: With an increase in confidence, the athlete feels ready to take on the challenge they're facing. This step is where the athlete decides to "go for it," whatever "it" may be. I'll discuss challenge appraisals in more depth later, when we look at clutch states.
5. *Open goal-setting*: Lastly, the athlete sets open goals—goals that are less specific or objective. These are goals like "try to hit a bit harder" or "see if I can go a bit further." These open goals encourage exploration and a sense of play, while avoiding judgment.

These findings, from Csikszentmihalyi, Swann, and others, provide us with some useful takeaways. The first is to consider what we can do to avoid a mismatch of challenge and skill. Research from Csikszentmihalyi (2014) and Swann et al. (2017) has identified some relevant facilitators of flow:

- *Good preparation (physical, mental, competitive)*: Pre-performance preparation can be broken down into these three categories—coincidentally, very similar to the breakdown I presented earlier in the sections on load, skill development, and marginal gains. For flow to occur, athletes need to feel physically prepared, on the edge between well trained and well rested. They need to be mentally sharp without being burned out, having prepared for the focus that will be required. And they need to be competitively ready—to have mastered the required skills, to be confident in their abilities, and to have a clear game plan. Of course, good preparation doesn't just apply to the weeks or days before competition; it also applies to the moments just prior, which is why we see athletes getting ready by doing specific warm-up activities and listening to music.
- *Optimal environmental and situational conditions*: As stated earlier, flow depends on an even pairing of challenge and skill.

Sometimes this is the result of good weather, the right kind of opponent, or other conditions over which we have no control. But there is a subtle aspect of this that some of us, sometimes, have control over: the selection of competitive opportunities. Depending on your sport, you may well be beholden to a league schedule of some sort; there are games you have to play. But there are often other games or events that we choose ourselves: practice matches, invitational tournaments, individual events, etc. The details will vary depending on your domain, but often some control can be exercised over an athlete's competitive planning. This is where we can be deliberate in choosing events that will have a good chance of evenly matching challenge and skill. The more we create those opportunities for our athletes, the more confident and motivated they will become, and the more likely they will be to experience flow.

- *Starting well*: Since flow is usually initiated by a positive event, it makes sense that most athletes report experiencing flow after a strong start. That's why, in line with the earlier point on preparation, it's important to ensure that athletes are well prepared in all aspects *and* that they have a plan for the first few moments that will increase the chances of them feeling successful.
- *Positive team play and interaction*: Athletes in team sports report flow states blossoming from cohesive interactions with their teammates—when they are all acting as one. Emphasizing and teaching team play, effective communication, and shared values and behaviors can facilitate flow.

The second important insight is that flow occurs when *perceived* challenge and *perceived* skill are high. Flow, needless to say, occurs in the mind. As we saw earlier, while flow can be kicked off by an initial positive event, it is the process of positive feedback, a gain in confidence, challenge appraisal, and open goal-setting that nourishes and supports it. That's why researchers have also identified facilitators that are more connected to an athlete's mental approach to competition (Harmison, 2006; Swann et al., 2012):

- High level of focus.
- High motivation.

- Optimal arousal level.
- Positive thoughts and emotions.
- Confidence.
- Positive feedback (internal and external).

You'll note that each of these topics has been discussed earlier in the book. When looking at the IZOF model, I showed how arousal level, thoughts, and emotions can be manipulated. We discussed motivation and confidence in Chapter 8, and I brought up methods for developing attentional control in Chapter 6, when discussing coach performance, and in Chapter 8, when discussing resilience. It should also be noted that many athletes mention using their focus abilities to take their mind *off* the task at hand—to distract themselves in a positive way, shutting their brain off, allowing their body to take over, and eliminating analytical or critical thoughts. Attentional control is crucial to develop—not just to keep focus, but also to distract oneself when appropriate.

Suffice it to say, each of these facilitators of flow can be influenced by us coaches—by what we do both in practice and in competition. While athletes can't enter a flow state on demand, no matter how well trained they are, our job is to create the conditions for flow to occur, through both the practical (e.g. good preparation and planning) and the psychological (e.g. developing attentional and emotional control skills). By doing so, we increase the chances of our athletes playing at their best when it counts.

Clutch States

Flow is not the only model that describes optimal performance in competition. While flow is described as "*letting* it happen," clutch states are a process of "*making* it happen." Whereas flow is usually described as effortless and energizing, clutch states are described as intense, effortful, and exhausting—periods of heightened concentration and awareness with an almost tunnel vision–like focus on the outcome. While flow usually occurs in exploratory contexts, athletes often enter clutch states at an important stage in the game, often at the end, when they are in contention to win.

While perhaps not as outwardly appealing as flow states, clutch states can be just as (if not more) beneficial, leading to sudden increases in performance when it matters most. According to athletes' retellings of their own experiences, clutch states are triggered through the following process (Swann et al., 2017):

1. *Deciding to embrace the challenge*: In this step, the athlete takes awareness of the demands and possible outcomes of the situation. "What am I faced with? What's going to happen?" They assess the demands and their own capabilities, and then decide to, as one athlete put it, "settle into the arena." This is also known as a "challenge appraisal."
2. *Setting an objective outcome goal*: Whereas flow states deal more with open, exploratory goals (e.g. "Let's see how fast I can run"), clutch states deal with fixed-outcome goals (e.g. "Just win," "Get to the top"). While coaches often emphasize process goals, anecdotal evidence from high-performing athletes suggests that in crunch moments, when the game is on the line and the athlete has decided to embrace the challenge, outcome goals can serve a powerful motivating and focusing purpose.
3. *Deciding to increase effort and intensity*: In response to the embraced challenge and the new outcome goal, the athlete makes a conscious decision to increase their effort and intensity. Athletes emphasize that this isn't a subconscious process, something that happens automatically; it is a conscious decision to "switch gears" or "take action." As one athlete put it: "It's now or never."

There are a number of psychological skills that athletes use, and that we can teach, to make it easier to enter a clutch state (Swann et al., 2017):

- *Maintaining perspective, rationalizing, and positive self-talk*: Athletes describe how maintaining perspective (e.g. "This will be over soon, keep pushing") or rationalizing (e.g. "You've done this before, you know you can do it") help them increase or maintain effort. Positive self-talk is described as a way of maintaining confidence in clutch moments. These are all examples of thought-regulation strategies, which I discussed in more detail in Chapter 8, in the section on resilience.
- *Short-term goals*: Athletes in clutch states also describe setting short-term goals (e.g. "Just make it to the bridge") as a way of maintaining motivation.

- *Self-monitoring*: Being disciplined with their execution is a way of keeping focus and optimizing performance when conditions are difficult.

While flow states cannot be forced, clutch states can arise from a deliberate decision on the part of the performer. As such, they can be discussed and practiced. Coaches can present the process above and talk about the importance of a challenge mindset: embracing adversity and pushing through it. We can introduce specific mental skills (like self-talk and goal-setting) and develop them over time. And we can create demanding yet supportive environments that put our athletes to the test in ways that strengthen them in the build-up to competition.

Minimizing Choking

No discussion of maximum performance—that is, bringing our best selves to the table in a competitive setting—would be complete without mentioning choking, a concept so powerful that it has transcended its sports origins and entered the vocabulary of business, relationships, and everyday life.

Despite (or perhaps due to) its ubiquity, the term "choking" is used somewhat sloppily—applied to everything from missed shots to disappointing losses. Despite our comfort with the idea of choking, it can be quite hard to define. For this chapter, we'll use the following definition: "a considerable decrease in performance when self-expected standards are normally achievable as a result of increased anxiety under perceived pressure" (modified from Mesagno and Hill, 2013).

Let's break this definition down into its key components:

- *A considerable decrease in performance*: Playing "slightly worse" than usual is not enough for a performance to be considered a choke.
- *When self-expected standards are normally achievable*: If performance decreases for identifiable reasons (e.g. fatigue, injury, poor preparation), then it is not choking. Conditions must be such that "normal" performance would be possible.

- *As a result of increased anxiety*: Similarly, the impaired performance must be due to anxiety. Just because someone plays poorly in a pressured situation doesn't mean it was a choke if they played poorly for other reasons. The participant must be feeling some amount of anxiety.
- *Under perceived pressure*: Although there must be some pressure, it's not so much the *real* amount of pressure that matters as the pressure *perceived* by the athlete.

To understand how to minimize choking, we must first understand how choking works. With the above definition in mind, let's look at some of the theory.

How Choking Happens

While it will be years before we fully understand why performers choke, one of the things we are most sure of is that choking is linked to anxiety. Numerous studies in both experimental and real-world conditions have found higher levels of anxiety in participants whose performance level decreases under pressure, and while some have suggested that it is the choking that is causing the anxiety (i.e. the performer chokes under pressure and then begins to feel anxious about this fact), multiple experiments have induced anxiety before performance and found detrimental outcomes (Beilock and Gray, 2007).

But what is it exactly about anxiety that causes choking? In short, anxiety changes the way our brain operates, switching from "top-down processing" (setting a goal and then focusing on the tasks required to accomplish it) to "bottom-up processing" (observing threats and reacting to them). Psychologists also refer to this as "goal-driven processing" vs. "stimulus-driven processing." As anxiety increases, our brains become more on the lookout for threats. This influences three operations in the brain—attention, interpretation, and response—each of which becomes more threat-focused as opposed to goal-focused.

Attention

Under increased anxiety, we pay more attention to perceived threats and less attention to what's relevant to the task at hand. This change manifests itself in a few ways. On the visual level, athletes experiencing anxiety will often "take their eye off the ball," to use the common phrase—in other words, take their gaze off the key focal-point moments before execution. This period of fixation before the critical instant is known as the "quiet eye" period, and multiple studies have found that experts have longer quiet eye periods than novices, that successful executions have longer quiet eye periods than unsuccessful ones, and that, under pressure, quiet eye periods can shorten and lead to choking, since movements are disrupted by the shift in gaze (Vickers, 2007). Not only that, but anxious performers also tend to spend more time looking at perceived threats (e.g. the goalkeeper during a penalty kick), which studies have found can cause movements to deviate in that direction (Wilson et al., 2009).

On the cognitive level, increased attention to perceived threats can take up working memory, leading to missed cues (e.g. not noticing an opponent's movement, or reacting too slowly to a change in balance). It can also lead a performer to consciously monitor and control their movements in order to ensure success. This is called "movement self-consciousness" or "motor reinvestment." Imagine walking up on stage in front of thousands of people and suddenly being aware of how your legs move, or getting ready to hit a tee shot in front of a packed clubhouse and focusing on your stance, your leg drive, your hip rotation, and so on. Even though this sort of focus is on-task, it ultimately interferes with the automatic execution of the movement and negatively affects performance.[23] Numerous experiments have tasked participants with consciously focusing on their movements as they execute them and have found impaired outcomes (Beilock and Carr, 2001; Gray, 2004).

Interpretation

Anxiety doesn't just affect what we look at or what we think about, it also affects how we *interpret* those things. One study showed that participants who were afraid of heights judged them to be higher than others who had no such fear (Teachman et al., 2008). Another experiment conducted in police trainings found that officers experiencing anxiety were more likely to identify an innocent individual as a suspect with a gun compared to when they were not anxious (Nieuwenhuys and Oudejans, 2011). In a sporting context, this could translate into a defender overestimating an attacker's speed, or an

23 This is known as the "self-focus theory of choking."

athlete misinterpreting a teammate's facial expression. These sorts of threat interpretations ultimately affect an athlete's decision-making as well as their execution. Misinterpreting certain cues as more threatening than others can tip the balance toward making the wrong decision, or might simply cause an athlete to pay more attention to these cues, thereby making them miss other relevant ones. At the same time, threat interpretations can cause athletes to panic and jump the gun—to overreact and respond with jerky and poorly calibrated movements.

Response

Lastly, anxiety can affect our movements themselves. Research has shown that, under anxiety, people experience an increase in heart rate, blood pressure, breathing frequency, fatigue, muscle activation, force production, and blood lactate concentration (Nieuwenhuys and Oudejans, 2012). The result? Movements that are stiffer, less fluid, and less efficient—leading to worsened performance. In addition, there are some preliminary findings that suggest that humans may have an inborn tendency to make emotion-congruent responses—put simply, to move away from threatening stimuli and toward positive ones (Krieglmeyer et al., 2011). In high-anxiety situations, the theory is, we revert back to these tendencies. As such, athletes may inadvertently pull away from threats during movement execution.

Choking Prevention Strategies

So how do we go about managing these effects and ensuring that our athletes can still perform well under pressure? There are a number of possible routes we can take, and each targets a different segment of the anxiety–performance relationship. They are as follows:

- *Reduce the amount of anxiety experienced*: Anxiety can be reduced in two ways. First, through the mitigation of situational factors. Creating a challenging yet supportive environment and eliminating unnecessary causes of stress will go a long way toward reducing anxiety. Coaches should strive to challenge their athletes, while promoting a mastery and self-development focus, rather than an ego-oriented one. Coaches should also be wary of external factors that may increase anxiety, such as the influence of peers, parents, or social media.

Second, through the teaching of general anxiety-reduction techniques, such as visualization (picturing the sights, sounds, tastes, feelings, and smells of a calm and relaxing environment), deliberate breathing (focusing on long, deep breaths), and cue words (repeating calming and encouraging phrases).

- *Increase task attention and decrease threat attention*: Athletes can direct more attention to the task at hand through techniques like thought stopping, replacing, or confronting (see the section on resilience in Chapter 8). At the same time, athletes can reduce the attention they direct toward threats through techniques like visualization or pre-performance routines, which distract the mind. In this context, visualization refers more to imagining successful execution and performance.

  Pre-performance routines can vary from athlete to athlete, but what's important is that they are consistent in terms of both the actions performed and the time they take. Pre-performance routines can serve as a distraction from threat-related stimuli and can also serve as a trigger to automatic performance—over time, the body and mind associate the routine with the skill that follows, and under pressure allow the performer to execute automatically.

- *Inhibit motor reinvestment*: As mentioned earlier, anxiety can lead athletes to consciously monitor and control their movements, thus interrupting their automatic execution. This effect can be inhibited in a few ways. First, there is some evidence that squeezing the left hand repeatedly for 10-15 seconds (known as "left-hand contractions" or "left-hand dynamic handgrip") prior to performance can activate certain segments of the brain and stabilize performance under pressure. In five different studies, researchers found that participants who performed left-hand contractions prior to skill execution maintained or improved their performance under pressure, whereas the average performance of the participants in the control group decreased (Beckmann et al., 2013; Gröpel and Beckmann, 2017; Gröpel and Beckmann, 2018). However, it's unclear if these effects carry over into situations of greater pressure and how exactly this works. There are also some challenges to implementing left-hand contractions, since not all sports allow athletes to prepare themselves prior to pressure moments.

Second, it has been shown that athletes who are taught using internal foci of attention (e.g. "Angle your foot this way," "Extend your arm that way") are more prone to motor reinvestment than those taught using *external* foci of attention (e.g. "Try to feel like ...," "Imagine that ...") (Farrow, 2013). Coaches should strive to minimize internal feedback when developing skills, such that athletes are less likely to revert to it under pressure.

Third, athletes can do "dual-tasking" in competition: performing a secondary task to distract their brain from the movements themselves. Examples include singing a song, counting backwards, or saying "Hit" at the moment of impact. It should be noted, however, that dual-tasking only works for skilled performers, since for them execution is normally automatic, and the secondary task distracts the mind enough to allow for normal performance. Novices, on the other hand, perform worse under dual-task conditions, since they have not mastered the skill, and the dual-task simply acts as a distraction, impeding performance. It should also be noted that dual-tasking should only be used in competition settings; in practice settings, when an athlete is trying to develop a skill, it will inhibit learning.

- *Increase fixation periods*: Research has also found that quiet eye training—teaching athletes to prolong their quiet eye period, the length of time that their gaze remains focused on the critical point—can positively impact performance under pressure (Vickers, 2007). Athletes can be trained to keep their eyes on the target for longer, and with practice this can minimize disruptions under pressure, thereby improving movement outcomes.
- *Counter physiological symptoms*: To address the physiological symptoms of anxiety, athletes can use different breathing patterns in order to reduce their heart rate. Progressive muscular relaxation is another popular technique, whereby a performer tenses up their entire body and then gradually relaxes each part. This has been found to reduce feelings of tightness. Some athletes also find that performing a series of high-intensity movements (e.g. sprints or jumps) can increase blood flow and relax muscles. Static stretching is also commonly seen to loosen up muscles.

Generally speaking, what works for one athlete may not necessarily work for another. Of course, some interventions are more suited to certain manifestations of anxiety than others. If an athlete is clearly impacted by strong physical symptoms of anxiety, then beginning with strategies to address those may be logical. But even then, athletes with the exact same experiences will often benefit from different techniques. Everyone responds differently, and so the best approach is often to provide a variety of tools and see what works.

That being said, the research is quite clear on how to go about developing these skills for the best results. It's not enough to simply tell someone, "Visualize yourself hitting a good shot"—a specific process must be followed (Kegelaers and Oudejans, 2024; Fletcher and Sarkar, 2016):

1. *Introduce the skill and the rationale*: A lot of athletes, coaches, and administrators still undervalue mental skills training. Athletes need to buy into the process in order to benefit from it. Explain why you're doing this (e.g. to help them perform under pressure; research shows it works; top athletes do it), what you're going to teach (e.g. thought stopping), and what the steps will be.
2. *Teach the skill*: Ideally, begin in a classroom setting, where athletes will be less distracted or impatient. Explain what the skill is, how it works, and give examples. Have the athletes practice the skill (e.g. "Take two minutes to visualize your match tomorrow" or "Write down what you might say to yourself before a big moment").
3. *Practice it without pressure*: In a training environment, have athletes practice the skill. For example, you might have your team play a scrimmage but ask them to visualize their performance beforehand, or have athletes take penalty kicks and practice their self-talk before each one.
4. *Simulate pressure and practice the skill*: This is the most important step. There is ample research suggesting that "acclimatization" (also known as "pressure training" or "pressure inoculation") can be extremely effective in limiting the effects of pressure on performance (Kegelaers and Oudejans, 2024; Farrow, 2013). Acclimatization consists of exposing athletes to pressured

situations in practice, while teaching them the skills to cope. Pressure can come from various sources:

a. Fatigue (making athletes perform while tired).
b. Competition simulation.
c. Self-consciousness triggers (e.g. performing in front of a video camera or an audience).
d. Consequences (for losing) and rewards (for winning).
e. Rule manipulations (to make a task more difficult or to make it unfair).
f. Stronger competition.
g. Distractions (e.g. sights, sounds, thoughts).
h. Changes of location (e.g. to a venue that can induce pressure).
i. Other novel techniques (e.g. survival camp).

As with everything, the ZPD is key, so there are two key variables to manipulate: the degree of pressure and the level of mastery of the skill. Your goal is to create just the right amount of pressure. Too little and athletes will be overwhelmed come competition time; too much and they'll collapse and lose confidence. At the same time, your players have to have mastered the mental skill enough that they can withstand the pressure with some effort. If that's not the case, return to steps 2 and 3. Under pressure, athletes will likely need to be reminded to use the mental skills you've taught them and will need encouragement to stay focused. Creating the pressured environment is not enough—*the teaching must continue.*

5. *Increase the pressure while maintaining the skill*: As your athletes' mental skills strengthen, you can increase the simulated pressure in practice until they are fully prepared for the stresses of competition.

It's worth noting that there are some popular choking prevention strategies that the research shows are *not* effective (Gröpel and Mesagno, 2019). One example of this is the common piece of advice given to athletes: "Focus on the process." This well-intentioned advice stems from the perspective that an overemphasis on the outcome and its potential ramifications can cause anxiety and pressure, and while that's true, this advice can have detrimental effects if not implemented carefully. In an attempt to "focus on the process," certain athletes will focus on the step-by-step execution of skills that are normally automatic, which, as we've covered, will lead to a drop in performance. We see this in experimental settings: participants who are told to focus on specific elements of a movement perform worse under pressure than those who are told to behave normally (Beilock and Carr, 2001). That being said, focusing on the process can be a good thing, so long as that process is something the athlete normally focuses on in non-pressured situations (e.g. certain cues, tactical intentions).

Goal-setting is another technique that is sometimes touted as a pressure management tool. In reality, numerous studies have found it to be beneficial for motivation (Locke and Latham, 2002), but to have no effect on choking.

Lastly, while more and more research is being conducted into choking, and we are learning more every year, a lot is still unknown. Furthermore, our current knowledge, much of which is summarized above, is almost entirely based on laboratory tests on simulated sporting tasks. This poses two challenges: first, while experimenters have been successful in artificially creating feelings of pressure in performers, there's no guarantee that this sensation is the same in type or intensity as the pressure felt in real competition. Second, the simulated tasks, while of the appropriate difficulty, are often simpler than actual sporting tasks and lack elements of real competition (e.g. fatigue, opposition).

For these reasons, it's still unclear to what extent the findings presented above can transfer into real-world contexts. That's not to say that we should ignore the research, but rather that we should experiment ourselves. Multiple theories of and approaches to preventing choking have been presented above. Some will be more or less applicable to your sport. Of the ones that could work, implement one at a time, assessing both the quality of your intervention and the observable result. Over time, you will find what works best in your context.

Other Factors That Influence Performance

Athlete Beliefs

When it comes to maximizing performance, a player's beliefs can be productive or counterproductive, and usually center around three themes: the purpose of competition, the nature of competition, and the impact of the results.

Table 10.2. Examples of beliefs impacting performance

Theme	Counterproductive example(s)	Productive example(s)
The purpose of competition	Competition is where I need to prove myself.	Competition is fun; this is a game.
The nature of competition	I need X to happen in order to perform well. If Y happens, then I will play poorly.	Whatever happens, I can handle it.
The impact of the results	If I lose, it means I'm bad. If I lose, I'm letting down my parents/coach.	I am more than just an athlete. Being a good person is better than being a good athlete.

An athlete's beliefs manifest themselves through both their speech and their actions. Their self-talk and body language can be revealing, as can their choice of words (do they *have to* compete this weekend, or do they *get to* compete this weekend?). Small things like the first reaction after a loss or the choice of tournaments to participate in can, over time, paint a picture of someone's mindset around competition.

These beliefs are so important to recognize because they can have outsize effects on performance and wellbeing. An athlete who views competition as inherently stressful and unenjoyable is unlikely to perform well and may struggle with their mental health. Someone who believes that every performance is an evaluation of who they are as a person will probably have difficulty entering their PPS.

Thankfully, coaches can influence the beliefs of their athletes. As I outlined in Chapter 8, we can move the needle in the right direction through the feedback we give, the words we use, and the small gestures we make. Feeding back on effort and self-improvement can remind athletes of the true purpose of competition. Using words like "opportunity," "challenge," and "process" can reinforce the nature of the experience. And small gestures, like celebrating all effortful performances (not just wins) and asking about the process rather than the outcome can also send a message.

Coach Behavior

Your ability to immediately impact your athlete's performance depends on your sport. In a sport like basketball or soccer, for example, a coach can do their job throughout the game, limited only by their ability to project their voice. In a sport like downhill skiing, however, one can coach up to the buzzer and after the race, but not during.

No matter the specifics, one thing is certain: as coaches, we play a role in the performances of our athletes. After all, if we didn't, why would we attend their events? Beyond observing and supporting, part of our role is to help our players perform at their best. But is it just a question of showing up and shouting instructions? Giving inspirational locker-room speeches and patting players on the back? If we have the potential to improve their performance, is it possible we could also harm it?

While the athletes themselves always deserve the credit, we shouldn't disregard the potential impacts (both positive and negative) we can have as coaches in competition—not in order to feel good about ourselves, but to remind ourselves to be on the top of our game when it counts. In this section, I'll evaluate the different roles we can take on according to the different stages of competition: before, during, and after. We'll look at our performance through three lenses: our feedback, our tone, and our body language and facial expressions.

Feedback

The most obvious way in which we as coaches can try to influence performance is through what we say. After all, we can't run onto the pitch and play for our athletes, so we must wield our words carefully. The temptation, as many parents can also attest to, is to tell them what to do: "Keep your weight on your front foot! Pass! Don't lose focus!" While this urge is understandable—after all, we know what they should be doing, and they aren't doing it, and it's our job to coach them, so why shouldn't we tell them?—the logic behind it falls apart with one simple question: why aren't they doing it already?

The first possibility is that they don't know how to do it, in which case telling them won't help. The second possibility is that they do know how to do it, but they're focusing on something else. Competition is a stressful environment wherein athletes have to process dozens of sources of information in a split second. In some cases, an athlete will lose focus, and a simple reminder from the sideline is all they need. But in many cases, a coach yelling instructions is just one more distraction to add to the athlete's overload, and what usually happens? The athlete doesn't do what's asked of them, both the coach and athlete get frustrated, and performance deteriorates.

There are two important principles to keep in mind when coaching in competition:

1. *An athlete's ability to focus on multiple things*: Again, my favorite quote: "If you try to catch five rabbits, you'll end up catching none." Put into more academic terms, long-term memory is large, but working memory (the part of our brain we use for processing and retaining new information) is small. Consider all the information you have stored in your long-term memory: names, birthdays, street address, phone numbers, email addresses, passwords, and so on. But if I give you a seven-digit number and ask you to recall it in five minutes, you'll have to repeat it to yourself until prompted. If I give you an 11-digit number, you'll really struggle.
   In competition, athletes use their brains and their bodies in much the same way. Certain skills are retained in long-term memory—skills that have been mastered, that have become automatic, that have been practiced for long enough that they can be done without thinking, just like walking. But working memory is also being used—to adapt game plans, to observe relevant cues, to make conscious, deliberate decisions. And as we've established, working memory is small and can only hold a few items at a time, for a very short time—hence the rabbit analogy. Coaches will sometimes make the mistake of shouting out too many different instructions at once, overloading the athlete's working memory.

In the best of cases, the athlete focuses on one instruction and ignores the others. But more commonly, as the analogy points out, the athlete will become overwhelmed and either follow none of the instructions, or attempt several and fail at each of them.

2. *An athlete's ability to focus on something during the stress of performance/competition*: The working/long-term memory model also helps clarify another common mistake coaches make, which is to give instructions for a skill that has not yet been acquired. Acquired skills are stored in long-term memory, where very little cognitive processing is required. New skills, however, require much more intentional mental effort and therefore are executed in working memory. The challenge is that working memory can be severely taxed in competition, especially in stressful circumstances. Since working memory is already limited, telling a player to do something that they cannot do unconsciously will often overwhelm it.

Both before and during a game, coaches should aim to restrict their guidance to one or two key points, and make sure that they are points the player can execute confidently.

There are two other common mistakes that I'd be remiss not to address. First is the use of negative instruction: "Don't lean back. Don't hit so hard. Don't hesitate." Here's an exercise for you, the reader. Ready? Close your eyes for three minutes and whatever you do, don't think of a pink elephant.

Within a few seconds, maybe more if you're good, you'll be thinking of a pink elephant. This is a common example you may have already come across of "ironic processes theory." Intentionally avoiding a thought, feeling, or behavior can cause people to engage in it even more than usual. An experiment involving tennis serves found that participants told *not* to hit to a particular zone while under pressure ended up hitting there *more* than they did in low-pressure conditions. The theory is that while our brains are consciously trying *not* to think of the thing we are avoiding, they must inevitably think of it, and this overrides our operating processes and causes so-called ironic errors.

Therefore, when giving instructions in competition, it's much more effective to tell players what *to* do instead of what *not* to do.

Table 10.3. Instruction focused on the solution, not the problem

Instead of...	Use...
Don't lean back.	Lean forward.
Stop hitting to her forehand.	Hit to her backhand.
Don't give up.	Keep fighting.

Lastly, we should consider the subtle messages that our instructions or exclamations can send. Before we even get into tone, body language, facial expressions, and gestures, we should consider context—from the Latin meaning "with text." In other words, the information surrounding the text (i.e. our words) is impactful too.

A simple example would be if your partner, who usually says "I love you" before going to work, one day stopped. Or even more innocuous, if someone who usually calls you by your nickname suddenly called you by your full name. While there is nothing wrong with the content of the message per se, and the tone or body language hasn't changed, the *context* suggests that a different message is being sent (whether rightly or wrongly).

In a coaching context, this is most obvious when coaches, as a result of anxiety, start giving more feedback than usual, or at times when they normally wouldn't. Athletes can sense the change, and while some will ignore it, others will lose confidence, get frustrated, or begin to feel anxious themselves. Here's Swedish professional coach Pia Sundhage: "It's absolutely vital that even if you're feeling stressed, your players should absolutely never see it. In fact, as often as possible they should see the opposite" (Woitalla, n.d.).

Tone

Sticking with the topic of the information you convey outside the words you use, let's talk about the most impactful aspect of speech: tone. You may well be aware of what tone is, and hear examples of it from people in your own life, but it can be beneficial to take some time to consider its use (and abuse) in coaching.

Let's begin by making what hopefully isn't a controversial statement: the tone we use affects the message that is received. For example, consider a phrase heard around the world of coaching: "Come on." Here's another exercise: how many different emotions or messages can you convey using the phrase "Come on" simply by changing your tone? I believe I can convey at least five: celebratory, encouraging, pumped up, disappointed, and angry.

But why is this important? Why bother worrying about this stuff when we can simply tell our athletes exactly what's going on? Two reasons: first, in competition, we will often be short on time. The more information we can deliver in fewer words, the better. Second, while our intentions may be clear to us, there's no guarantee that our athletes will understand them the same way. Consider how often the phrase "But I didn't mean it that way!" is uttered in arguments. If we are to use our voice as a tool for effective coaching, then we must take care to deliver as clear a message as possible, and that includes being deliberate with our tone such that no message is misconstrued or misunderstood.

The first step, of course, is to carefully consider which tone you want to use in which situation. This decision can be based on a handful of factors—among them, your athlete's PPS (as discussed earlier) and their personality or communication style.

The next step is to ensure that the message being received is the one you're sending. One way to do this is to ask your players for feedback, using questions like: "What were you focusing on at that moment?" and "Is there anything I could have done differently to help you?" I still remember the day a player I trusted told me in passing that I looked grumpy when I watched her from the stands. My intention was to look calm and focused, but clearly I had failed. How I was feeling on the inside didn't matter—what mattered was what she perceived when she looked over to me for support.

You may find it useful, if a bit unnatural, to practice delivering messages in different tones of voice. Pick some common phrases from your coaching and imagine a few different scenarios: team is down, team is up, team is getting overconfident, player needs encouragement, and so on. Practice saying your phrases out loud, modifying your emphasis and tone for effect. If you really want to step out of your comfort zone, the best way to master using your voice is to record yourself saying the phrases. Listen to how they sound from the outside. Do you really sound calm there? Would you be encouraged if you heard that? Listen, rerecord, and listen again. Another option is to record yourself during a real game. Open the voicenotes app on your phone, set it to record, and then put it in your pocket. You may surprise yourself.

Body Language and Facial Expression

Lastly, the same principles that apply to tone also apply to body language.

Imagine Coach A who is hunched forward, eyes intently focused, hands clapping compared to Coach B with one hand in his pocket, a relaxed posture, his head leaned in toward the player. What messages are these coaches sending? I'd argue that Coach A is conveying energy, enthusiasm, and focus. He doesn't look angry; he looks locked in and energetic, pumping his team up. Coach B is relaxed and calm and seems to be listening to his player. Neither is right or wrong—it's simply a question of when and why they are acting this way. There will be times when you want to drive the energy and times when you want to calm things down, just like there will be moments for making impassioned speeches and moments for making intellectual points. The important thing is to be deliberate about what message you want to send and ensure that you're doing everything possible to make sure it is received.

One of the best ways to be a better sideline coach is to film yourself. You may be surprised by what you see. Just like it can be jarring to hear your own voice ("I didn't know I said that!"), seeing yourself coach can be equally enlightening ("I didn't realize I was fidgeting so much!").

Again, here's Pia Sundhage:

> *I try to use my body language to emphasize what is good. I'm really happy to hear that when you watch the women's team play you think I'm calm, because that's what I want my players to believe - because I have faith in the way we play and in our players. I emphasize the good things. I'm looking for good things, instead of doing the opposite and try constantly to adjust mistakes. (Woitalla, n.d.)*

Pre-Competition

It's important to remember that everything we've just discussed applies not only to the heat of competition, but also to the moments before and after the game or event. Pre-competition, one of our key objectives should be to help our athlete or team get into their PPS. Films like *Any Given Sunday* and *Coach Carter* have given us the impression that pre-game pep talks are all about firing players up—screaming, yelling, and rushing out the door. But it's never that simple. John Wooden was known sometimes to conduct pre-game talks with the lights dimmed low, saying, "I wanted a business-like approach, covering the essentials; not to try to get them all fired up. I wanted them ready when we started play and not to lose their fire warming up or in the dressing room" (Davis, 2014).

While Wooden's approach may not seem conventional, his logic was coherent (and his results speak for themselves). Whether or not this is right for you or your athletes is another story—the important thing is to consider the impact that your pre-game behavior will have on the players.

Another objective of the pre-competition locker-room talk is to go over strategy, to discuss the game plan. This is where our discussion of feedback comes in. A pre-game talk that contains too many objectives, negative instructions, or strategies that athletes don't have the skill to implement will only confuse and impair them. Instead, focus on one or two clear, actionable items.

During Competition

During competition, as long as you can be seen or heard while your athletes are performing, you can have an impact. Beyond what we say, the subtleties of body language, tone, facial expressions, and gestures all communicate mountains of information. In a 2021 study, researchers showed soccer players footage of coaches on the sidelines without displaying the score (Fanny and Furley, 2021). In the first part, one group of study participants was asked to guess whether each coach's team was winning or losing. In that task, they were accurate nearly 70% of the time. In the second part, another group of participants was asked to rate how much confidence they got from the coach's body language, without knowing if the team was winning or losing. Coaches whose teams were winning were consistently rated as more confidence-giving than those whose teams were losing.

This shouldn't come as too much of a surprise. After all, myths around non-verbal communication have been circulating for years. What *is* surprising, however, is how little it's discussed in the world of coaching. If we are always communicating (and we are), then what messages should we be sending? That is somewhat less clear. There are some messages that all athletes want to hear: "I believe in you," "I trust you," "I have confidence you can win," "I am here for you," etc. These can be communicated verbally, and also through our actions and responses. Making eye contact at a key moment, giving a supportive nod of the head. Allowing them to call a play or make a key decision. These messages are sent in the subtlest of interactions, and it may be worth spending some time reflecting on what your behavior around competition is communicating.

Then there are messages that will vary depending on the athlete or team and their PPS. As a general rule of thumb, a coach on the sidelines should behave and communicate in such a way as to keep or get an athlete or team in their PPS. What does that mean? Sometimes, in competition, a player will stray from their ideal level of arousal—this can happen when they're winning or losing. They might have lost a little energy and become lackluster; this could happen due to disappointment or the boredom of an easy game. They might also be too pumped up, too emotional, which could be the result of anger at a missed call or excitement from a good performance. In any case, our job in competition is to direct their energy toward their ideal state, whether that means calming them down or pumping them up.

Post-Competition

The scenes after an event has concluded are often as dramatic as the event itself—tears, laughter, exhaustion, anger, and more. Now that the game is over, what is our duty as a coach?

First, we generally want to mirror our athletes' emotions. After all, high-performance sport is simultaneously emotional and isolating. Players want to feel that you are with them on this emotional journey. If they are excited, you can be excited. If they are disappointed, you can be disappointed. The important thing is for them to feel *seen* and *heard*. You don't have to agree with everything they are feeling, you just have to show them that you empathize with them. If they're frustrated by an opponent who cheated, you can show frustration that this happened to them, while reinforcing good sportsmanship and more controllable aspects of performance. If they're disappointed in themselves, you can show sadness at the fact that they're feeling down without supporting the negative beliefs they may be harboring. Empathize with the emotion, even if you're trying to send a different message.

Another paradigm to consider is that of the stick and the pillow: the stick pushes you to be better, while the pillow encourages you when you are down. Everyone needs both—challenge and support—but at different times. After a game, consider how your athlete or team is feeling and which of the two they might need.

Finally, our job post-competition is to encourage behaviors that will lead to more development and better future performances. Most athletes have a post-game routine (e.g. stretching, debrief, massage). After a win, how do you ensure they stay focused and disciplined? After a loss, how do you ensure they are receptive to feedback? Furthermore, what message do you send about future competition? Does your tone suggest that they are in trouble for losing, that next time they should be fearful? Do you tell them what they *should* have done, implying judgment, instead of what they *could* have done? Ultimately, our goal is to ensure that they feel seen, challenged and supported, and that they learn from this performance and prepare for future ones.

Acknowledgments

While this project began in earnest in 2023, its seeds were planted over the course of more than a decade, while I honed my coaching and formulated my own views of tennis, how it should be taught, and how I should go about getting better. It goes without saying that a great number of people have contributed to both this book and my career, and while I'd like to be brief, it's not often you get the chance to explicitly thank those most important to you. I'd like to do that now.

My *sambo*, Sydney Ross, has stood by me every step of the way – when I was away from home, coaching on the road 25 weeks a year, and when I was home but distracted, getting a master's degree and writing a book at the same time. You listened to every podcast and read every chapter, and your unending, unreserved, and certainly undeserved love and support have kept me going year after year. I am eternally grateful.

My parents, Peter Ohlin and Berkeley Kaite not only provided a wonderful, joyous childhood but continued to love and support me unconditionally when I made the absurd decision to drop out of school to coach full-time. You instilled in me responsibility and ownership; you taught me how to self-reflect and accept the things I can't control. For that, and for much, much more: thank you.

To Po, Pia, Alix, and Jens: thank you for being the older siblings you didn't have to be, both now and when I was younger. To have family like you can't be taken for granted and it means the world to me. To Ellie, Auggie, and Peter: thank you for bringing me so much joy and laughter. I am beyond excited to watch you grow up.

I also want to express my gratitude towards a few friends. Al Millar, you are the epitome of someone who takes their job seriously but not themselves, and I so value that. Thanks for all the phone calls. Michael (Jimmy) Loomer, you've been there for me in tough times and are so good at reminding me that there's more to life than coaching. Thank you. And of course, where would I be without Mansib Rahman, area best friend and mental sparring partner. Beyond just being the inspirational and motivational force behind this book, you have led by example and taught me so much about life, work, and everything in between. Here's to 20 more years.

Professionally, I've been very, very lucky. Simon Laurendeau, you believed in my potential as a coach when even I was unsure I could have a future in the business. Those early years were influential and I will always credit you for them. Martin Laurendeau, you took way more time than you should have to answer my phone calls and record marathon voice notes. I hope I can continue to learn from you. Doug Lemov, over and over again, has found time in his busy schedule to help me, first with my coaching, and then with the book. Thanks, as always, for helping out a small fish in a big pond. Rickard Billing and Magnus Ennerberg, you gave me the opportunity and experience of a lifetime. I am beyond grateful for my years in Sweden and will never forget the role you both played. And how could I not mention John Björksund, Wahab Abidi, and Micke Ryberger, who made working there so fun?

Finally, this book would never have come to be were it not for a few key people at Hachette Learning and Westchester Education. Thank you to Mark Combes and Alex Sharratt for believing in me (or at least the book), and Deborah Noble and Abigail Coppin for helping turn a few hundred pages of messy ideas into something publishable.

References List

Anderson, K.J., William, W. and Lynch, M.J. (1989) 'Caffeine, impulsivity, and memory scanning: A comparison of two explanations for the Yerkes–Dodson Effect', *Motivation and Emotion*, 13: pp. 1-20.

Anderson, K. (2023) 'How Tara VanDerveer and Stanford built and maintain a college basketball juggernaut', *Climate Online*, March 2. Available from: https://climaterwc.com/2023/03/02/how-tara-vanderveer-and-stanford-built-and-maintained-a-college-basketball-juggernaut/

Apple (2014) 'Sue Wagner joins Apple's board of directors', *Apple*, July 17. Available from: www.apple.com/ca/newsroom/2014/07/17Sue-Wagner-Joins-Apple-s-Board-of-Directors/ (Accessed 3 December 2024).

Armstrong, T.R. (1970) *Training for the production of memorized movement patterns*. University of Michigan.

ATP Tour (2025) 'Official Site of Men's Professional Tennis: ATP Tour: Tennis'. Available from: www.atptour.com/ (Accessed 26 January 2025).

Auerbach, N. (2015) 'To the relief of NCAA coaches, the wait is almost over', *USA Today*, March 17. Available from: www.usatoday.com/story/sports/ncaab/2015/03/17/ncaa-tournament-march-madness-coaches-pregame-rituals-holtmann-matta/24898241/

Balyi, I., Way, R. and Higgs, C. (2013) *Long-term athlete development*. Champaign: Human Kinetics.

Bandura, A. (1977) 'Self-efficacy: toward a unifying theory of behavioral change', *Psychological Review*, 84.

Bangalter, T., de Homem-Christo, G.-M. and Birdsong, E. (2001) 'Harder, Better, Faster, Stronger'

Becker, A.J. and Wrisberg, C.A. (2008) 'Effective coaching in action: Observations of legendary collegiate basketball coach Pat Summitt', *The Sport Psychologist*, 22(2): pp. 197-211.

Beckmann, J., Gröpel, P. and Ehrlenspiel, F. (2013) 'Preventing motor skill failure through hemisphere-specific priming: cases from choking under pressure', *Journal of Experimental Psychology: General*, 142(3): p. 679.

Beilock, S.L. and Carr, T.H. (2001) 'On the fragility of skilled performance: What governs choking under pressure?', *Journal of Experimental Psychology: General*, 130(4): p. 701.

Beilock, S.L. and Gray, R. (2007) 'Why do athletes choke under pressure?', In: Tenenbaum, G. and Eklund, R.C. (eds.) *Handbook of sport psychology* (3rd ed., chapter 19, pp. 425-444). John Wiley & Sons, Inc. doi.org/10.1002/9781118270011

Benoit, A. (2017) '24 hours with Rams coach Sean McVay', *Sports Illustrated*, June 8. Available from: www.si.com/nfl/2017/06/08/sean-mcvay-los-angeles-rams-24-hours-nfl

Blanchette, Sarrasin, Jérémie, Riopel, M. and Masson, S. (2019) 'Neuromyths and their origin among teachers in Quebec', *Mind, Brain, and Education*, 13(2): pp. 100-109.

Bobrownicki, R., Carson, H.J., MacPherson, A.C. and Collins, D. (2023) 'Constraints of the constraints-led approach in American Football and comments on Yearby et al. (2022)', *Sports Coaching Review:* pp. 1-13. doi.org/10.1080/21640629.2022.2158579

Broadhurst, P.L. (1957) 'Emotionality and the Yerkes–Dodson law', *Journal of Experimental Psychology*, 54(5): p. 345.

Carroll, P., Roth, Y. and Garin, K.A. (2011) *Win forever: Live, work, and play like a champion*. Penguin.

Chambers, R., Barbara Chuen Yee Lo, and Allen, N.B. (2008) 'The impact of intensive mindfulness training on attentional control, cognitive style, and affect', *Cognitive Therapy and Research*, 32: pp. 303-322.

Champion, L., Middleton, K. and MacMahon, C. (2023) 'Many pieces to the puzzle: A new holistic workload approach to designing practice in sports', *Sports Medicine – Open*, 9(1) : p. 38. doi.org/10.1186/s40798-023-00575-7

Championship Performance (2020) 'The Bill Belichick quiz method to prepare athletes'. Available from: https://championshipperform.com/the-bill-belichick-quiz-method-to-prepare-athletes/

Chawla, M. (2023) 'Jeff Bezos secrets for a productive meeting', September 2. Available from: www.linkedin.com/pulse/jeff-bezos-secrets-productive-meeting-manoj-chawla/ (Accessed 8 December 2024).

Chua, L-K., Jimenez-Diaz, J., Lewthwaite, R., Kim, T. and Wulf, G. (2021) 'Superiority of external attentional focus for motor performance and learning: Systematic reviews and meta-analyses', *Psychological Bulletin*, 147(6): pp. 618.

Cialdini, R.B. (2007) *Influence: The psychology of persuasion*. New York, NY: Collins.

Clark, M.E., McEwan, K. and Christie, C.J. (2019) 'The effectiveness of constraints-led training on skill development in interceptive sports: A systematic review', *International Journal of Sports Science & Coaching*, 14(2): pp. 229-240.

Clear, J. (2018a) 'This coach improved every tiny thing by 1 percent and here's what happened'. Excerpt from Clear's *Atomic Habits* (Avery Publishing). Available from: https://jamesclear.com/marginal-gains

Clear, J. (2018b) *Atomic habits: An easy & proven way to build good habits & break bad ones*. Penguin.

Coleman, J. (2018) 'The Johnson treatment: pushing and persuading like LBJ'. Available from: www.forbes.com/sites/johncoleman/2018/07/30/the-johnson-treatment-pushing-and-persuading-like-lbj/

Collins, J.C. (2001) *Good to great: Why some companies make the lap ... and others don't*. United Kingdom: Random House Business.

Crafton, A. (2021) 'What made Sir Alex Ferguson so successful?', *The Athletic*. Available from: https://theathletic.com/3033467/2021/12/26/manchester-united-what-made-sir-alex-ferguson-so-successful/

Csikszentmihalyi, M. (2014) *Flow and the foundations of positive psychology: The collected works of Mihaly Csikszentmihalyi*. Dordrecht: Springer Netherlands. doi.org/10.1007/978-94-017-9088-8

Czyż, S.H. and Coker, C.A. (2023) 'An applied model for using variability in practice', *International Journal of Sports Science & Coaching*, 18(5): pp. 1692-1701.

Danziger, S., Levav, J. and Avnaim-Pesso, L. (2011) 'Extraneous factors in judicial decisions', *Proceedings of the National Academy of Sciences*, 108(17): pp. 6889-6892.

Davis, S. (2014) *Wooden: A coach's life*. United States: Henry Holt and Company.

Deci, E.L. and Ryan, R.M. (1985) *Intrinsic motivation and self-determination in human behavior*. New York: Plenum Press.

Dekker, S., Lee, N.C., Howard-Jones, P. and Jolles, J. (2012) 'Neuromyths in education: Prevalence and predictors of misconceptions among teachers', *Frontiers in Psychology*, 3: p. 33784.

Diamond D.M., Campbell, A., Park, C., Halonen, J. and Zoladz, P. (2007) 'The temporal dynamics model of emotional memory processing: A synthesis on the neurobiological basis of stress-induced amnesia, flashbulb and traumatic memories, and the Yerkes–Dodson Law', *Neural Plasticity*: p. 33. doi:10.1155/2007/60803

Din, C., Paskevich, D., Gabriele, T. and Werthner, P. (2015) 'Olympic medal-winning leadership', *International Journal of Sports Science & Coaching*, 10(4): pp. 589-604. doi.org/10.1260/1747-9541.10.4.589

Duffy, E. (1957) 'The psychological significance of the concept of "arousal" or "activation"', *Psychological Review*, 64(5): p. 265.

Ebbinghaus, H. (1913) *Memory: A contribution to experimental psychology*. Teachers College, Columbia University: New York.

EconTalk (2013) 'Doug Lemov on teaching'. Available from: www.econtalk.org/doug-lemov-on-teaching/

Ericsson, A. and Pool, R. (2016) 'Malcolm Gladwell got us wrong', *Salon*. Excerpt from Ericsson and Pool's *Peak: Secrets from the New Science of Expertise* (Houghton Mifflin Harcourt). Available from: www.salon.com/2016/04/10/malcolm_gladwell_got_us_wrong_our_research_was_key_to_the_10000_hour_rule_but_heres_what_got_oversimplified/

Ericsson, A.K., Prietula, M.J. and Cokely, E.T. (2007) 'The making of an expert', *Harvard Business Review*, July-August. Available from: https://hbr.org/2007/07/the-making-of-an-expert

Fadde, P.J. and Klein, G.A. (2010) 'Deliberate performance: Accelerating expertise in natural settings', *Performance Improvement*, 49(9): pp. 5-14.

Fanny, T. and Furley, P. (2021) 'Nonverbal expressions of soccer coaches during the game and their potential effects on observers', *International Journal of Sports Science & Coaching*, 16(5): pp. 1063-73.

Farrow, D. (ed.) (2013) *Developing sport expertise: researchers and coaches put theory into practice*. 2nd ed. London; New York: Routledge.

Fay, A.L. and Mayer, R.E. (1994) 'Benefits of teaching design skills before teaching logo computer programming: Evidence for syntax-independent learning', *Journal of Educational Computing Research*, 11(3): pp. 187-210.

Fletcher, D. and Sarkar, M. (2016) 'Mental fortitude training: An evidence-based approach to developing psychological resilience for sustained success', *Journal of Sport Psychology in Action*, 7(3): pp. 135-57. doi.org/10.1080/21520704.2016.1255496

Friedman, M.C. (2014) 'Notes on note-taking: Review of research and insights for students and instructors', *Harvard Initiative for Learning and Teaching*: pp. 1-34.

Gallimore, R. and Tharp, R. (2004) 'What a coach can teach a teacher, 1975–2004: Reflections and reanalysis of John Wooden's teaching practices', *The Sport Psychologist*, 18(2): pp. 119-37. doi.org/10.1123/tsp.18.2.119

Gambetta, V. (2007) 'Defining supercompensation training', in *Athletic Development*, by Vern Gambetta, 299. United States: Human Kinetics. Available from: https://us.humankinetics.com/blogs/excerpt/defining-supercompensation-training

Game Like Training (2019) 'Phil Mickelson – a great example of the chunking process, Golf's Mental Game'. Available from: www.youtube.com/watch?v=nAeHaOIIx6Y

Gawande, A. (2011) 'Personal Best', *The New Yorker*, September 26. Available from: www.newyorker.com/magazine/2011/10/03/personal-best

Gibson, E.L. and Green, M.W. (2002) 'Nutritional influences on cognitive function: mechanisms of susceptibility', *Nutrition Research Reviews*, 15(1): pp. 169-206.

Gladwell, M. (2007) *Blink: the power of thinking without thinking*. United States: Little, Brown and Company.

Gladwell, M. (2008) *Outliers: The story of success*. Little, Brown and Company.

Gray, R. (2004) 'Attending to the execution of a complex sensorimotor skill: expertise differences, choking, and slumps', *Journal of Experimental Psychology: Applied*, 10(1): p. 42.

Gröpel, P. and Beckmann, J. (2017) 'A pre-performance routine to optimize competition performance in artistic gymnastics', *The Sport Psychologist*, 31(2): pp. 199-207.

Gröpel, P. and Beckmann, J. (2018) 'Personality systems interactions in skilled motor performance: Implications for sport psychology'

Gröpel, P. and Mesagno, C. (2019) 'Choking interventions in sports: A systematic review', *International Review of Sport and Exercise Psychology*, 12(1): pp. 176-201. doi.org/10.1080/1750984X.2017.1408134

Halberstam, D. (2005) *The education of a coach*. New York: Hyperion.

Hanin, Y.L. (2000). Emotions in sport. Champaign, IL: Human Kinetics.

Harmison, R.J. (2006) 'Peak performance in sport: Identifying ideal performance states and developing athletes' psychological skills', *Professional Psychology: Research and Practice*, 37(3): pp. 233-43.

Harmon, Glennice L. 1948. "They Ask Me Why I Teach." *NEA Journal*, September: 375. https://archive.org/details/sim_todays-education_1948-09_37_6/page/374/mode/2up?view=theater.

Harrell, E. (2015) 'How 1% performance improvements led to Olympic Gold', October 30. Available from: https://hbr.org/2015/10/how-1-

performance-improvements-led-to-olympic-gold (Accessed 1 December 2024).

Heylin, C. (2019) 'The story behind the music: The recording of Bob Dylan's *Blood on the Track*'. Route Publishing Blog. Excerpt from Heylin's *No One Else Could Play That Tune* (Route Publishing). Available from: https://routepublishing.wordpress.com/2018/09/21/the-story-behind-the-music-the-recording-of-bob-dylans-blood-on-the-tracks/

Hodgson, L., Butt, J. and Maynard, I. (2017) 'Exploring the psychological attributes underpinning elite sports coaching', *International Journal of Sports Science & Coaching*, 12(4): pp. 439-51.

Howe, J. (2023) 'Why coach Sean McVay has kept pondering retirement, and why the Rams admire him for it', *The Athletic*, September 6. Available from: https://theathletic.com/4835664/2023/09/06/sean-mcvay-rams-retirement/

Inside Tennis (2014) 'Wimbledon: The sacred trust—an interview with Genie Bouchard's longtime coach Nick Saviano'. Available from: www.insidetennis.com/2014/06/wimbledon-the-sacred-trust-an-interview-with-genie-bouchards-longtime-coach-nick-saviano/

Jenks, J. and Sando, M. (2024) 'The secrets of Andy Reid's success: Attention to detail, humor and Haagen-Dazs', *The Athletic*, February 13. Available from: https://theathletic.com/5259559/2024/02/13/andy-reid-oral-history/

Jennings, C. (2024) 'Tara VanDerveer's secret to becoming the winningest college coach? Never stop learning', *The Athletic*, January 19. Available from: https://theathletic.com/5212269/2024/01/19/tara-vanderveer-legacy-stanford-record/

Kegelaers, J. and Oudejans, R.R.D. (2024) 'Pressure makes diamonds? A narrative review on the application of pressure training in high-performance sports', *International Journal of Sport and Exercise Psychology*, 22(1): pp. 141-59. doi.org/10.1080/1612197X.2022.2134436

Killgore, W.D.S. (2010) 'Effects of sleep deprivation on cognition,' *Progress in Brain Research*, 185: pp. 105-29. doi:10.1016/B978-0-444-53702-7.00007-5

Kirk, K. (2007) 'Self-efficacy: helping students believe in themselves'. Available from: https://serc.carleton.edu/NAGTWorkshops/affective/efficacy.html

Kleck, R.E. and Strenta, A. (1980) 'Perceptions of the impact of negatively valued physical characteristics on social interaction', *Journal of Personality and Social Psychology*, 39(5): p. 861.

Knapp, B. (1963) *Skill in sport: The attainment of proficiency*. Routledge and K. Paul.

Knudson, D.V. and Kluka, D. (1997) 'The impact of vision and vision training on sport performance', *Journal of Physical Education, Recreation & Dance*, 68(4): pp. 17-24. Available at: www.tandfonline.com/doi/abs/10.1080/07303084.1997.10604922

Kouzes, J.M. and Posner, B.Z. (2017) *The leadership challenge: How to make extraordinary things happen in organizations*. 6th ed. Hoboken, New Jersey: The Leadership Challenge, a Wiley Brand.

Kovacs, M. and Ellenbecker, T. (2011) 'An 8-stage model for evaluating the tennis serve', *Sports Health*, 3(6): pp. 504-13. Available from: https://journals.sagepub.com/doi/10.1177/1941738111414175

Kraft, M.A. and Blazar, D. (2018) 'Taking teacher coaching to scale: Can personalized training become standard practice?', *Education Next*, 18(4).

Krane, V. and Williams, J. (2006) 'Psychological Characteristics of Peak Performance', In J.M. Williams (ed.), *Applied sport psychology: Personal growth to peak performance*. New York: McGraw-Hill.

Krieglmeyer, R., De Houwer, J. and Deutsch, R. (2011) 'How farsighted are behavioral tendencies of approach and avoidance? The effect of stimulus valence on immediate vs. ultimate distance change', *Journal of Experimental Social Psychology*, 47(3): pp. 622-27.

Krzyzewski, M. (2018) 'Coach K Standards vs. Rules', video, April 8. Available from: www.youtube.com/watch?v=L_EJnyQgzXE

Kushalnagar, P. (n.d.) 'Field of view for sighted people', *ResearchGate.net*. Available from: www.researchgate.net/figure/Field-of-View-for-Sighted-People-We-propose-a-multiple-view-approach-that-utilizes-mobile_fig1_241623481

Kushalnagar, R. S., Ludie, S. A., and Kushalnagar, P. (2011) "Multi-view platform: an accessible live classroom viewing approach for low vision students." In *Proceedings of Conference on Computers and Accessibility (ASSETS)*, 267-268.

Lara-Bercial, S. and Mallett, C.J. (2016) 'The practices and developmental pathways of professional and Olympic serial winning coaches', *International Sport Coaching Journal*, 3(3): pp. 221-39. doi.org/10.1123/iscj.2016-0083

Lavery, J.J. (1962) 'Retention of simple motor skills as a function of type of knowledge of results', *Canadian Journal of Psychology/Revue canadienne de psychologie*, 16(4): p. 300.

Lee, M.O.C. and Thompson, A. (1997) 'Guided instruction in LOGO programming and the development of cognitive monitoring strategies among college students', *Journal of Educational Computing Research*, 16(2): pp. 125-44.

Lee, S. (2016) 'The tragic and triumphant story of Manel Estiarte, Pep Guardiola's secretive right-hand man', November 15. Available from: www.goal.com/en/news/the-tragic-and-triumphant-story-of-manel-estiarte-pep-guardiolas-/blte08ef625fe3b2e82 (Accessed 3 December 2024).

Lemov, D. (2018) 'James Beeston's model shared vocab list + why vocabulary is critical to your athletes' success', Web log. *Doug Lemov's Field Notes* (blog), October 14, 2018. Available from: https://teachlikeachampion.org/blog/james-beestons-model-shared-vocab-list-vocabulary-critical-athletes-success/

Lemov, D. (2020) *The coach's guide to teaching*. John Catt.

Lemov, D., Woolway, E. and Yezzi, K. (2012) *Practice perfect: 42 rules for getting better at getting better*. John Wiley & Sons.

Levav, J., Heitmann, M. and Iyengar, S.S. (2008) 'Order in product customization decisions', In: *The Proceedings of the Society for Consumer Psychology*, Winter Conference, p. 168.

Locke, E.A. and Latham, G.P. (2002) 'Building a practically useful theory of goal setting and task motivation: A 35-year odyssey', *American Psychologist*, 57(9): p. 705.

MacDonald, H.Z. and Olsen, A. (2020) 'The role of attentional control in the relationship between mindfulness and anxiety', *Psychological Reports*, 123(3): pp. 759-80.

Mageau, G.A, and Vallerand, R.J. (2003) 'The coach–athlete relationship: A motivational model', *Journal of Sports Sciences*, 21(11): pp. 883-904. doi.org/10.1080/0264041031000140374

Mallett, C. and Lara-Bercial, S. (2023) *Learning from serial winning coaches: Caring determination.* 1st ed. New York: Routledge. doi.org/10.4324/9781003427292

Mallett, Clifford J., and Sergio Lara-Bercial. (2016) "Serial winning coaches: People, vision, and environment." In Sport and exercise psychology research, pp. 289-322. Academic Press.

Marca.com. (n.d.) 'Video of Curry scoring five full-court shots in a row is not real, but it might as well be'. Available from: www.marca.com/en/basketball/nba/golden-state-warriors/2022/12/05/638d6e02e2704e55a58b45a6.html

Markland, R. and Martinek, T.J. (1988) 'Descriptive analysis of coach augmented feedback given to high school varsity female volleyball players', *Journal of Teaching in Physical Education*, 7(4): pp. 289-301.

Márquez, B. (2023) 'Never too late', *Coaches' Voice.* Available from: https://learning.coachesvoice.com/cv/tintin-marquez-qatar-espanyol/

Mayer, R.E. (2004) 'Should there be a three-strikes rule against pure discovery learning?', *American Psychologist*, 59(1): p. 14.

McCroskey, J.C. and Teven, J.J. (1999) 'Goodwill: A reexamination of the construct and its measurement', *Communication Monographs*, 66(1): pp. 90-103. doi.org/10.1080/03637759909376464

McNicholas, J., Lawrence, A. and Ornstein, D. (2019) 'Freddie Ljungberg: the making of a model coach', *The Athletic*, November 29. Available from: https://theathletic.com/1289739/2019/11/29/freddie-ljungberg-the-making-of-a-model-coach/

Mencinger, T. (n.d.) '7 steps to correct serve technique', FeelTennis. Available from: www.feeltennis.net/wp-content/uploads/2015/11/Tennis_Serve_Checklist.pdf

Mesagno, C. and Hill, D. (2013) 'Definition of choking in sport: Re-conceptualization and debate', International Journal of Sport Psychology, 44: p. 267.

Moreira, B.F.T., Pinto, T.S.S., Starling, D.S.V. and Jaeger, A. (2019) 'Retrieval practice in classroom settings: A review of applied research', In: Frontiers in Education, 4: p. 5. Frontiers Media SA.

Müller, S. and Rosalie, S.M. (2019) 'Transfer of expert visual-perceptual-motor skill in sport', In: *Anticipation and Decision Making in Sport*, pp. 375-93. Routledge.

Muth, A-K. and Park, S.Q. (2021) 'The impact of dietary macronutrient intake on cognitive function and the brain', *Clinical Nutrition*, 40(6): pp. 3999-4010.

Nakamura, J. and Csikszentmihalyi, M. (2009) 'Flow theory and research', *Handbook of Positive Psychology*, 195: p. 206.

New England Patriots (2022) 'Transcript: Bill Belichick press conference 12/6', December 6. Available from: www.patriots.com/news/transcript-bill-belichick-press-conference-12-6 (Accessed 8 December 2024).

Newton, P.M. and Salvi, A. (2020) 'How common is belief in the learning styles neuromyth, and does it matter? A pragmatic systematic review', In: *Frontiers in Education*, 5: p. 602451. Frontiers.

Newport, C. (2016) *Deep work: Rules for focused success in a distracted world*. Hachette UK.

Nieuwenhuys, A. and Oudejans, R.R.D. (2011) 'Training with anxiety: short-and long-term effects on police officers' shooting behavior under pressure', *Cognitive Processing*, 12: pp. 277-88.

Nieuwenhuys, A. and Oudejans, R.R D. (2012) 'Anxiety and perceptual-motor performance: Toward an integrated model of concepts, mechanisms, and processes', *Psychological Research*, 76(6): pp. 747-59. doi.org/10.1007/s00426-011-0384-x

Norlander, M. (2023) 'Citing burnout from NIL, transfer portal and non-stop recruiting, college basketball coaches make big changes', *CBS Sports*, July 27. Available from: www.cbssports.com/college-basketball/

news/citing-burnout-from-nil-transfer-portal-and-non-stop-recruiting-college-basketball-coaches-make-big-changes/

Ohlin, Z. (2020) 'On the use of questions when coaching'. Available from: www.zackohlin.com/post/on-the-use-of-questions-when-coaching

Online Casino Canada (n.d.) *'Analysis of the most common personality traits shared by NFL coaches'*. Available from: www.casino.ca/nfl-coach-personality-analysis/ (Accessed 4 December 2024).

Olusoga, P., Bentzen, M. and Kentta, G. (2019) 'Coach burnout: A scoping review', *International Sport Coaching Journal*, 6(1): pp. 42-62.

Perarnau, M. (2014) *Pep confidential: The inside story of Pep Guardiola's first season at Bayern Munich*. Birlinn, 2014.

Pérez-Olmos, I. and Ibáñez-Pinilla, M. (2014) 'Night shifts, sleep deprivation, and attention performance in medical students,' *International Journal of Medical Education*, 5: p. 56.

Petit, F. (2016) 'Vincent T. Lombardi: Three key lessons for today's executive that go beyond football', *The Sport Journal*, August 11. Available from: https://thesportjournal.org/article/vincent-t-lombardi-three-key-lessons-for-todays-executive-that-goes-beyond-football/

Pilcher, J.J. and Huffcutt, A.I. (1996) 'Effects of sleep deprivation on performance: a meta-analysis', *Sleep*, 19(4): pp. 318-26.

Rivera, G. (2024) 'Ex-patriots exec reveals origin of Bill Belichick's 'Do Your Job' mantra' *NESN*, October 15. Available from: https://nesn.com/2024/10/ex-patriots-exec-reveals-origin-of-bill-belichicks-do-your-job-mantra/

Royle, C. (2023) *Second set of eyes: How great coaches become champions*. United States.

Salao, R.P. (2021) 'Warriors news: Steve Kerr emotional ode to Gregg Popovich over success', December 21. Available from: https://clutchpoints.com/warriors-news-steve-kerrs-emotional-ode-to-gregg-popovich-over-success-in-golden-state (Accessed 3 December 2024).

Schmidt, E., Rosenberg, J. and Eagle, A. (2019) *Trillion dollar coach*. Ryan Dingler Publishing.

Schmidt, R.A., Lange, C. and Young, D.E. (1990) 'Optimizing summary knowledge of results for skill learning', *Human Movement Science*, 9(3-5): pp. 325-48.

Schmidt, R.A., and Lee, T.D. (2014) *Motor learning and performance: From principles to application*. 5th ed. Champaign, Ill., Windsor, On, Stanningley, Leeds: Human Kinetics.

Schmidt, E. and Rosenberg, J. (2014) *How Google works*. Grand Central Publishing.

Schön, D.A. (1983) *The reflective practitioner*. United States: Basic Books.

Schulman, B.J. (2018) 'Lyndon Johnson left office as a deeply unpopular president. So why is he so admired today?', *The Washington Post*, March 30. Available from: www.washingtonpost.com/news/made-by-history/wp/2018/03/30/lyndon-johnson-left-office-as-a-deeply-unpopular-president-so-why-is-he-so-admired-today/

Scot Shot Basketball (2018) 'False shooting advice even Steph Currey gives (no palm)'. Available from: www.youtube.com/watch?v=C4_nZM3N948 (Accessed 1 December 2024).

Seattle Seahawks (2017) 'Practice is everything: Learning how the Seahawks practice'. Produced by Seattle Seahawks. Available from: www.youtube.com/watch?v=NMLa6fM10KA

Seifert, L., Wattebled, L., Orth, D., L'hermette, M., Boulanger. J. and Davids, K. (2016) 'Skill transfer specificity shapes perception and action under varying environmental constraints', *Human Movement Science*, 48: pp. 132-41.

Semple, R.J. (2010) 'Does mindfulness meditation enhance attention? A randomized controlled trial', *Mindfulness*, 1: pp. 121-30.

Shabir, O. (2020) 'Levels of hydration and cognitive function', *News-medical.net*. Available from: www.news-medical.net/health/levels-of-hydration-and-cognitive-function.aspx

Skowronek, J., Seifert, A. and Lindberg, S. (2023) 'The mere presence of a smartphone reduces basal attentional performance', *Scientific Reports*, 13(1): p. 9363.

Smith, M. (2001) 'Ivory league coach / VanDerveer takes up piano', *SFGATE*, October 29. Available from: www.sfgate.com/bayarea/article/ivory-league-coach-vanderveer-takes-up-piano-2863058.php

Smolen, P., Zhang, Y. and Byrne, J.H. (2016) 'The right time to learn: mechanisms and optimization of spaced learning', *Nature Reviews Neuroscience*, 17: pp. 77-88. doi.org/10.1038/nrn.2015.18

Staley, D. (2018) 'Challenge accepted', *coachspeak.net*. Available from: www.coachspeak.net/challenge-accepted-by-dawn-staley/

Sternberg, R.J. and Horvath, J.A. (1995) 'A prototype view of expert teaching', *Educational Researcher*, 24(6): pp. 9-17.

Strack, F., Martin, L.L. and Stepper, S. (1988) 'Inhibiting and facilitating conditions of the human smile: a nonobtrusive test of the facial feedback hypothesis', *Journal of Personality and Social Psychology*, 54(5): p. 768.

Summitt, P. and Jenkins, S. (2013) *Sum it up: A thousand and ninety-eight victories, a couple of irrelevant losses, and a life in perspective*. United States: Crown.

Swann, C., Crust, L., Jackman, P., Vella, S.A., Allen, M.S. and Keegan, R. (2017) 'Psychological states underlying excellent performance in sport: Toward an integrated model of flow and clutch states', *Journal of Applied Sport Psychology*, 29(4): pp. 375-401. doi.org/10.1080/10413200.2016.1272650

Swann, C., Keegan, R.J., Piggott, D. and Crust, L. (2012) 'A systematic review of the experience, occurrence, and controllability of flow states in elite sport', *Psychology of Sport and Exercise*, 13(6): pp. 807-19. doi.org/10.1016/j.psychsport.2012.05.006

Swinnen, S.P., Schmidt, R.A., Nicholson, D.E. and Shapiro, D.C. (1990) 'Information feedback for skill acquisition: Instantaneous knowledge of results degrades learning', *Journal of Experimental Psychology: Learning, Memory, and Cognition*, 16(4): pp. 706.

Tandon, A. (2023) '"I'm Not the Coach; I'm the Dad" – 41-year-old Roger Federer reveals petty problems of being a father as he gives a sneak peek into his life post retirement'. Available from: www.essentiallysports.com/atp-tennis-news-im-not-the-coach-im-the-dad-forty-one-year-old-roger-federer-reveals-petty-problems-of-being-a-father-as-he-gives-a-sneak-peek-into-his-life-post-retirement/

Teachman, B.A., Stefanucci, J.K., Clerkin, E.M., Cody, M.W. and Proffitt, D.R. (2008) 'A new mode of fear expression: perceptual bias in height fear', *Emotion*, 8(2): p. 296.

The Daily Coach (2024) 'Tara VanDerveer's 8 rules for leading a team', January 23. Available from: www.thedaily.coach/p/tara-vanderveers-8-rules-leading-team

Thompson, E.R. (2008) 'Development and validation of an international English big-five mini-markers', *Personality and Individual Differences*, 45(6): pp. 542-48.

Thompson, K. (2023) 'To help your team grow, give them space to struggle', *Harvard Business Review*. Available from: https://hbr.org/2023/07/to-help-your-team-grow-give-them-space-to-struggle

Tzu, S. (2012) *The art of war*. United States: Chartwell Books.

Vickers, J.N. (2007) *Perception, cognition, and decision training: The quiet eye in action*. Human Kinetics.

Vygotsky, L.S. (1978) *Mind in society: The development of higher psychological processes*. Cambridge, MA: Harvard University Press.

Wallace, M. (2015) 'Heat's Dwayne Wade relishes final clashes with Kobe Bryant', *Truehoop*, November 9. Available from: www.espn.com/blog/truehoop/miamiheat/post/_/id/21385/heats-dwyane-wade-relishes-final-clashes-with-kobe

Walsh, B., Jamison, S. and Walsh, C. (2009) *The score takes care of itself: My philosophy of leadership*. Penguin.

Watanabe, K., Ooishi, Y. and Kashino, M. (2017) 'Heart rate responses induced by acoustic tempo and its interaction with basal heart rate', *Scientific Reports*, 7(1): p. 43856.

Weinshall-Margel, K., and Shapard, J. (2011) "Overlooked factors in the analysis of parole decisions." *Proceedings of the National Academy of Sciences* 108, no. 42: E833-E833.

Werthner, P. and Trudel, P. (2009) 'Investigating the idiosyncratic learning paths of elite Canadian coaches', *International Journal of Sports Science & Coaching*, 4(3): pp. 433-49. doi.org/10.1260/174795409789623946

Wilson, M.R., Wood, G. and Vine, S.J. (2009) 'Anxiety, attentional control, and performance impairment in penalty kicks', *Journal of Sport and Exercise Psychology*, 31(6): pp. 761-75.

Winstein, C.J. and Schmidt, R.A. (1990) 'Reduced frequency of knowledge of results enhances motor skill learning', *Journal of Experimental Psychology: Learning, Memory, and Cognition*, 16(4): p. 677.

Wooden, J. and Jamison, S. (2009) *Coach Wooden's leadership game plan for success: 12 lessons for extraordinary performance and personal excellence*. McGraw Hill Professional.

Woitalla, M. (n.d). '*The role model coach: Pia Sundhage*', Michigan Youth Soccer League. Available at: https://michigansoccer.com/the-role-model-coach-pia-sundhage/

WTA Tennis (n.d.) 'Jessica Pegula'. Available at: www.wtatennis.com/players/316956/jessica-pegula

Yerkes, R.M. and Dodson, J.D. (1908) 'The relation of strength of stimulus to rapidity of habit-formation', *Journal of Comparative Neurology and Psychology*, 18(5): pp. 459-82.